EDUCATING ALICE

The Essential 4-Step Guide to Training the Perfect Puppy

J J Fitzpatrick

MCGI, MCFBA, MBIPDT

ISBN: 978-0-9954901-0-9

First published in 2016

CONTENTS

INTRODUCING THE AUTHOR

John Fitzpatrick (Fitz) has been training dogs professionally since 1980. His Service career spanning 36 years began at the age of 16 in the Royal Navy as an aircraft mechanic, before transferring to the Royal Air Force Police at the age of 18 to become a dog handler. During his Royal Air Force career he served at home and abroad, including service in Northern Ireland, The Falkland Islands, Iraq and Afghanistan, before retiring from the Service in 2013 as the Senior Instructor, Joint Service Dog School, at the world-renowned Defence Animal Centre, in the rank of Warrant Officer.

During the period 2010-2013 he played a major role in the concept, design and implementation of the Young Military Working Dog Development Programme, which involved the sourcing, selection, development and training of specially bred puppies from whelping to licensing as qualified Military Working Dogs and Service Police Dogs.

He established Cosford Dog Training in 2001 to conduct training and behaviour modification with private clients.

Since retiring from the RAF Police in 2013 he has continued to work full time as a professional dog trainer and behaviourist. He is a member of the British Institute of Professional Dog Trainers, a Full Canine Practitioner with the Canine and Feline Behaviour Association, a council member of the Pet Education Training and Behaviour Council, Vice Chairman of the British Police and Services Canine Association and Editor of Service Dog Magazine.

He competes in working trials with his Welsh Sheepdog, Tilly (Star at Concenn, WD Ex) and his Malinois, Jimmy (Threenines Ace of Clubs, WD Ex). Jimmy is the 2015 British Police and Services Canine Association Working Dog of the Year and 2015 Victor Ludorum, having been Reserve Champion in 2013 and 2014.

He holds a Foundation Degree in Canine Behaviour and Training awarded in 2007 by Hull University and a Certificate in Education (Post Compulsory Education) awarded in 2009 by Wolverhampton University.

He now shares his knowledge and experience, accrued and refined during 35 years training and developing Military Working Dogs and thousands of family pets with you, to ensure your new puppy becomes a happy, balanced, valued and much loved-member of your family.

INTRODUCTION

Let me say from the outset that I absolutely love dogs. Not in a soppy, snoggy sort of way, but in a way that is based upon a deep respect for them. I love working with them, and my dogs work with me, not for me. There is an important difference.

In 1983, along with my RAF Police dog, Air Dog Khaled, we became RAF Police UK Working Trials Champions. Khaled was the youngest dog ever to be crowned champion, being 1 day short of his second birthday. The day we won the title, I made a promise to myself. From that day on, every single day I would either train a dog, watch a dog being trained, or read a book on dogs. In short, every single day I would learn something more about my favourite work mate. I have never broken that promise.

Since retiring from the Royal Air Force my dog training workload is highly varied. Whilst some of it is devoted to the development and training of detection dogs and high level security and protection dogs, the most enjoyable aspect of my work is working with pet dogs and their owners. I began working with pet dogs in 1983 and have continued ever since.

This work with pet dogs is divided into three different elements:

Part one involves training newly acquired puppies aged from 8 weeks to 8 months, which are generally a clean slate. The younger the puppy, the cleaner the slate.

Part two involves working with older puppies, adolescent and adult dogs, which generally possess sound temperaments, but lack training or social skills.

Part three involves behavioural modification work with dogs that have, through various means, acquired serious problem behaviours. The vast majority of this work involves dog to dog aggression and to a lesser extent dog to human aggression. Other problem behaviours make up a small percentage of consultations. Whether this is because the other problem behaviours are less common, or dog owners are more prepared to live with them, is unclear.

What I do know is that if the owners of this third category of dog had read this book, my workload with such dogs would be greatly reduced and this is my main motivation for writing the book. No matter how good I am at my job and no matter how hard the owner tries, we can't always repair problems that may have been bred into the dog, or which have developed over many years and which are adversely affecting the quality of its life and the dog/human relationship.

In this book I focus on training from puppyhood. Most years I personally deal with the initial training of well over 250 puppies and owners. Whilst on occasion I may mention training older dogs in the book, it is less confusing for you if I deal solely with training your puppy from eight weeks to one year of age.

I have based the content upon the training and development of the puppies under my control in the Young Military Working Dog Project, and the training and education of my last six dogs, focusing on the training and development of my youngest Malinois; Alice. Hence the title of the book.

The book explains, often in great detail, the methods which I have used successfully with my own dogs, and hundreds of others, to develop enthusiastic puppies into well-balanced and well-trained dogs.

You will note that the book concentrates on what you should do, rather than what you should not do, in order to make sure you achieve this goal. This is how it should be.

The problem with telling you what you should **not** do, is that it doesn't tell you what you should do, leaving you to make further mistakes. As I have always tried to do with baby Alice, and all my other pups, civilian and military, I teach a puppy to do the few simple things that I want her to do and make success rewarding, rather than trying to stop her doing the dozen or so things I don't want her to do. If she is busy doing the simple actions that I like, she can't be doing any of the bad stuff, which I don't like. It's the same with you lot!

There are many books regarding puppy training on the market. Almost without exception they take up the story far too late. The essential aspect of any relationship is compatibility and the starting point for this book is to ensure that you and your puppy are a good fit, right from the outset.

If we get this first step right, and follow the advice in the subsequent sections, it will ensure that you get the right puppy for your family and that you develop a happy, respectful and fulfilling relationship with your dog. If the book sells well I might be able to take a couple of days off each week as there will be fewer problems to deal with!

I have tried to set out the book in a logical sequence, always remembering that the training for life and training for control will often take place in parallel.

You will learn as you train your puppy that you seldom progress in a straight line. Occasionally you will have to revisit earlier stages and go over them again. I promise you that your puppy won't object if you have to do the same when reading this book.

It is important that by the end of this book you have a good understanding of how your puppy learns and the techniques to help her do so. You should also have a good understanding of how much well-directed work is involved.

This book is not a theoretical "How to do it" book, based upon some abstract idea of a composite, imaginary puppy. It is a "How I did it" book, based upon the training and development of a real puppy. In this case Alice, my young Malinois. The cover picture is the actual baby Alice, when she really was a baby.

I am a dog trainer and instructor. I train dogs every single day. I write as I speak, although I have left out a few of my more colourful phrases. This is my method. Copy it, if you wish, or better still; adapt it to your own needs.

I have tried to avoid using scientific terms that will send you scuttling for the behavioural text books and I have tried to avoid treating you like a dimwit, as most of the population falls somewhere between Professor Stephen Hawkins and the blokes from Dumb and Dumber. I hope I have got the balance right.

At the time of writing, Alice is 16 months old. She is friendly towards people, confident, polite around dogs, other species of animal and is responsive to commands.

She walks nicely on a lead and she always comes back when called, no matter how strong the distraction. I can take her to the shops and to the pub.

These are all the things most dog owners want from their dog.

She can also search a two-acre field to locate the head of a farrier's nail. She can follow an hour-old track over about ¾ of a mile. She can pursue and apprehend a running "Criminal", or defend me against attack by someone firing a gun. These are the things most of you will hopefully never need your dog to do.

She is a challenging and extremely "enthusiastic" girl, but she is developing into a young lady with a fantastic temperament, bags of character and into a highly proficient working dog. She is a lovely dog to be around. I wouldn't change her for the world.

I have trained her using only the equipment and methods specified in this book.

FOREWORD

I thought about writing this chapter myself and giving it a different title. I reckon I could do a decent job of it, because I know quite a bit about dogs. But I don't know as much about dogs as my little dog does; so over to baby Alice.

"Thanks, Dad. Thank you for choosing me. I am very happy to be here, even though it was a long journey. As you were in the Royal Air Force for so long, I think I should give you a bit of a briefing about how you should treat me and how you should train me. (See below). I am sure you will understand the points I raise and we will get along just fine. I am a good puppy; help me become a great dog.

Point 1

I am a dog, not a robot. I have feelings. I like to learn things, but sometimes I struggle to understand what you are trying to teach me. I don't speak human and you don't speak dog, so we have to establish a good way to communicate.

Point 2

I do not come pre-programmed. I have knowledge and abilities that nature has given me, but I need your help. For instance, I know how to eat, but not what to eat. I know how to chew, but not what to chew. I know how to bite, but not what or who to bite. I know how to piddle and poo, but not where to piddle and poo. These are just some of the things you will have to help me learn.

Point 3

As I said in Point 2, I just love to chew stuff up. I have great little needle-sharp teeth and I need to build the strength of my jaws and sometimes I need to relieve a sore mouth. Although I am very good at chewing stuff up, I don't know what I am allowed to chew. I need you to help me learn these things.

Point 4

I like it when I feel nice. Some things make me feel nice and I enjoy doing them. If I enjoy doing things I want to do them again and again, until I am really good at them. If you teach me to do things that make me feel nice, I will want to do them for you.

Point 5

I don't like it when I don't feel nice. If you make me do things I don't like it makes me sad and I don't want to do them again. Sometimes you can help me learn how to do things I don't like, by making them nice for me, so I am happy to do them for you. Eventually, I will forget that I didn't used to like doing them, as they are now so much fun to do and make me feel nice.

Point 6

I won't like it if you become angry with me. This will make me sad. If I didn't know why you were angry with me that would be even worse, because I wouldn't know what to do to make you happy again and make me feel nice again. (This is a very important point Dad, so pay attention.)

Point 7

I am not disposable. I am yours for my whole life and you are mine for my whole life. Care for me and train me like you love me, because I love you."

Baby Alice xx

Acknowledgements and Thanks

I would like to express my thanks to Fiona, Mary, Denise and Julia, for their invaluable help preparing the manuscript.

My appreciation goes out to Alex, Iona, Charlotte and Emily who feature in many of the photos with my dogs or their own dogs, and for those people who permitted me to use their photographs in the book.

Thanks to Shaun; for the many lengthy discussions we have on an almost daily basis...about dogs.

To Mark and Janet; for the care devoted to producing Jimmy and Alice, and to Gail, for doing likewise with Daisy May and finding Tilly for us.

To Carol; for putting up with me. (And for picking up 11 tons of Alpaca poo whilst I have been otherwise engaged.)

To George Pace; who encouraged me to **think** when I was working my RAF Police dogs.

And to all my dogs, past and present, just for being my dogs.

Alice Colette Fitzpatrick
25 May 1940 to 25 November 2015.

Our Mam was the light in our lives. She was only a little light, but when you are in the dark, a little light is all you ever need.

When she left us, she left a hole in all our lives that will never be filled and a million wonderful, funny, happy memories that will never be erased. How you made us all laugh!

P.S. Little Molly still looks for you, every day.

PART 1

Planning and Preparation

Introduction

Taking on a puppy is a big step and not one that should be taken lightly. It is expensive and time consuming. It is a commitment that may last for up to 15 years, if you are lucky.

If entered into lightly it always ends badly, particularly for the unfortunate puppy. Not wanting to own a puppy or dog is normal. Lots of people like dogs, but do not want the responsibility. They are not bad people. In fact they are fantastic people, because they have made the best decision possible for some unknown puppy.

Entering into puppy ownership lightly and without sufficient thought and preparation can be a frustrating and miserable experience for the family and disastrous for the unfortunate, soon to be discarded puppy.

Entered into responsibly it is one of the most life-enhancing experiences imaginable, for both human and dog.

===

Dog Ownership: a Cost/Benefit Analysis

Introduction

I firmly believe that dog ownership is a privilege, not a right. The relationship between dog and human should be balanced and mutually beneficial. Sadly, the UK has a population of many thousands of dogs in rescue centres on any given day of the year. Virtually every one of these dogs previously had a home.

In some cases a tragic event led to the family concerned being compelled to place their dog in a rescue centre, but this represents a tiny percentage of cases and in 99% of cases this is not so, and the dog is a victim of people who, in the majority of cases, were well meaning and who took on the puppy that grew into the dog, without adequately considering or being prepared for the responsibility of dog ownership. There is no excuse for this.

But the fault isn't all with the dog owner. What about the breeder who is knocking out pups every time their bitch is in season and who takes the money without a thought for what lies in store for the puppy a few months down the line? Breeders who are happy to sell to the first person who walks through the door with the requisite sum of cash.

I am not just talking about a dog owner casually breeding pups in their back room, or from their shed. There are plenty of supposedly reputable breeders who don't do any checks on the suitability of a potential owner, or who persuade the potential owner to take on an extra pup as it's the last one in the litter, often using a bit of emotional blackmail to ensure the additional pup is offloaded without a care for the additional problems that often occur when taking on siblings.

It is always good to set things out clearly, so here goes.

Finance

A good place to start when considering taking on a puppy or older dog is the monetary expense involved in having a dog. A person who has not previously owned a dog is likely to have seriously underestimated this, whilst the family who have owned a dog several years before might not realise just how much costs, especially veterinary costs, have risen in recent times.

I am sure that most potential dog owners realise that "free to a good home" puppies and dogs are few and far between and will have budgeted for a considerable initial outlay for their puppy. Very few pedigree dogs can be purchased for under £500 and most breeds, and "designer" cross breeds are considerably more.

Consideration must be given to the amount of money it takes to keep a dog in good health. There have been many studies that estimate the cost of keeping a dog, but off the top of my head, I reckon you are looking at £1 per day for feeding a medium-sized dog. Annual inoculations, worming and flea treatments mean you are unlikely to see any change from £500 each year.

Throw in pet insurance at £30 a month and a single, fairly minor illness requiring veterinary care, and you are looking at another £400 - £500. The running total is now closer to £1,000 per year, at today's prices.

In the first year you should budget for dog lead, collar/harness, bed, dog toys and training, which will add up to another £200, giving a fairly conservative estimate of £1,200 in the first year. In fact that is not a conservative estimate. That is the bare minimum.

Don't even think about a family holiday unless you budget a couple of hundred quid for kennelling, which amounts to the price of taking an extra child on holiday with you.

Time

What about time? I remember watching Tomorrow's World as a kid and I have to tell you I feel really let down by not existing on a diet of 3 pills a day and travelling by flying car. I am also a bit hacked off at not having to work for just 12 minutes a day whilst my pet robot does all the work. Most of you will have noticed that modern technology has increased, not decreased the human workload. Most people have less leisure time than ever before. Do you have enough time for a dog?

Will there be an adult at home with the dog the majority of the time? Does everyone in the family work, or attend school/college?

Puppies are time-consuming. Dogs are social animals that thrive on contact with humans. Solitude is not their natural state. Have you considered a cat instead? They don't care about humans! That was a joke, by the way, but cats are far more solitary in nature and are generally happy within a working family.

House training your puppy is a time-consuming business. Chucking her into the garden and hoping that she has had a poo by the time you bring her back in is the ultimate game of Russian Roulette, or in this case Poolette.

Daily walks as a puppy, and I include time spent standing in the garden to watch her piddle and poo, will easily amount to an hour a day.

A few short training sessions each day in accordance with your trainer's instructions; an additional 15 minutes. Several short play sessions cover another 30 minutes. A visit to the training school for an hour, which invariably takes 2 hours when travelling time is taken into account, and you are easily looking at about 10 - 12 hours, the equivalent of an additional day at work, with overtime thrown in, every week.

Are you prepared for that? Because if you are not, you are going to become tired and resentful and your puppy will be the one who pays for your lack of preparedness.

Family Considerations

Who is the driving force behind the idea of dog ownership? Is the whole family committed to the idea of having a dog? At the very least the adults in the family should be.

That isn't to say you should discount the wishes of your children to take on a family dog, but be in no doubt that it is the adults who will be looking after her for the next 15 years! If the adults are not totally committed, pursue the idea of dog ownership no further. Thank you for buying my book, but you can stop reading now. If the adults are committed, then read on.

How will dog ownership affect the children in your household? Are the children old enough to deal with a puppy tearing around and swinging off their feet and trousers? How are you going to cope with that?

If you don't have children yet, are you planning a family? If so, how will you deal with this? Many of the dogs in rescue centres were perfectly well behaved dogs who were callously dumped when the family discovered that a human baby was due. Suddenly, the family dog is viewed as a potential problem rather than a valued family member.

Do you have a back-up plan, in the case of a family emergency? Someone who will step in at short notice and take care of your puppy?

Another consideration is how the arrival of a new puppy will impact on your other animals. No one ever asks the 14-year-old cocker spaniel, who spends most of her time sleeping peacefully, or the timid (or not) family cat, if they think getting an 8-week-old Border Collie is a great idea. Often bringing a new puppy in gives an older dog a new lease of life, or so the humans think, but just as often it is unsettling for the established animals. Please give them careful consideration.

Your Home

Is your home suitable for a dog? Small dogs don't take up a lot of room in the house, especially if given their own bed, but space may be a factor with a dog the size of a German Shepherd.

What about your garden? Not only does it have to be a reasonable size, but it must be secure, unless you wish to come into conflict with the law. Dog proofing is likely to be quite expensive. Please add the expense of installing a secure fence, or the upgrade of an existing fence to the running total.

Are you prepared for the potential loss of your prized garden? Puppies can be hazardous to the continued aesthetic effect of a well-manicured lawn and herbaceous border.

Do you have any hazardous plants in your garden? If so you will need to have them removed before puppy arrives, as she will certainly remove them once she gets her paws under the table.

Transport

Will you need to buy a different model of car? Your Nissan Micra is probably a smashing little runner, but it's going to struggle with a Great Dane on the back seat. Potentially more expense.

Health

Are you fit enough for dog ownership and fit enough to fulfil the exercise needs for the particular breed of puppy you have chosen? Walking an active puppy several times a day is going to have a serious impact on your dodgy knee, although it is not a show stopper. My Mam managed perfectly well walking her puppy, Molly, to the park each day on her burgundy, turbo charged, wheeled, walking frame. As Molly got older, Mam would sit on her wheels and use her ball chucker to ensure that Molly received the correct amount of vigorous exercise each day, come hail, rain or shine. (Mostly hail and rain, in fairness!)

One thing is for certain, if you become a responsible dog owner it will improve your level of physical fitness and you can always offset the additional expenditure of dog ownership against the gym membership and Weight Watchers fees you will no longer require.

===

The Benefits of Dog Ownership

What can you offer a dog? What can a dog offer you?

Everyone is aware of the companionship that a dog can offer, but the relationship between human and dog should always be a two-way street. It never ceases to surprise me that humans often think that the dog is there to provide them with companionship, but then think nothing of locking her away, or shoving her out in the garden for hours on end when it suits their purpose.

Health and Wellbeing

There are a number of scientific studies that highlight the positive health benefits of pet ownership. The calming effect of handling and stroking a dog or a cat is well established.

Where the dog ownership scores over cat ownership is the health benefit of dog walking. As your puppy reaches adulthood most breeds of dog will comfortably enjoy a couple of brisk half-hour walks with their owner each day. Now even with my basic GCSE maths I can work that out to be 365 hours of exercise per year, and in a leap year the health benefits are even greater, as you get an extra hour.

How many people do you know that spend that many hours exercising? Not many, and if you excluded dog owners from that list you would be left with marathon runners and those blokes who shave their chests and spend far too much time looking at their reflection in the gymnasium mirrors!

When we think of the companionship that dog ownership provides we all think of the relationship between human and dog, but what about the relationship between fellow dog owners?

Social

When I retired from the RAF I spent at least 90 minutes every day walking my dogs. Most days I would meet up with the same people and spend that time discussing important, world-shaping events like football, and er, football. But the point is I got to know people who I would never have met, or with whom I would have exchanged no more than a nod and a "Good Morning".

Dog walking has brought me into contact with many people from different age groups, different social classes and different interests. Dog ownership caused friendships to be formed and a state of common purpose and identity developed. Most people enjoy belonging to a group of like-minded people and walking a group of dogs together promotes this in a really relaxed manner. And let's not forget that whilst the humans enjoy forming friendships, in most instances, so do the dogs. It has even led to me developing a liking for civilians, although I still struggle to understand some of them. Who would have thunk it?

Several years ago, when the local fields contained only stubble, there were 8 or 9 dog owners and their dogs, over 25 of them, enjoying a long walk around the village. There were dogs of all shapes and sizes, ages and breeds including a blind Field Spaniel, who had no problem keeping up with his companions.

We did have to fetch him on one occasion when one of the dog owners threw a tennis ball. All the dogs chased it, including the little blind fella. He went off with his mates, hell for leather, following the sound of the stampeding pack. Unfortunately, as he was on the outrun, the fastest dog fetched the ball and returned at full speed to his owner, followed by the rest of the gang, except the poor little fella who was still on the way out and was now on his own listening in vain for his mates, who were by now 200 yards in the opposite direction.

Even when meeting with non-dog owners my dogs have proven to be a fantastic ice-breaker for a conversation. I could not even begin to estimate the number of hours I have spent in conversation with complete strangers after they had asked a question about my dogs. These are conversations I would never have had. Once again, in more than a few instances lasting friendships have been formed.

New Interests

You may even get bitten by the training bug and decide to develop your dog ownership into a hobby. Whilst there are not a great number of dog training clubs, or working trials societies out there, they **are** out there if you look for them. Although in the UK they tend to be just for training, whereas on the continent they have a real social aspect to them. In the town of Lorrach, Germany, close to the Swiss border, where my sister lived for almost 10 years, there are three working dog training clubs on a 3-mile stretch of river. At those clubs, along with the dog training, there was a great deal of human "socialising" going on!

In the UK there are a growing number of groups where enthusiasts of a particular breed meet up every few weeks to take their dogs on long walks together. These clubs give the dogs a chance to be exercised, and both dogs and humans to establish friendships, whilst owners may increase their knowledge of the breed.

Providing that these groups are not merely an excuse for the dogs to run wild, they are an enjoyable way to spend a Saturday morning for both human and dog. If considering joining such a group bear in mind that these walks are often quite long, so puppies should be on a lead for much of the walk and you should not attempt to walk a distance that is too far for their stage of development.

===

Which Type of Dog Fits My family?

The start point for this question is to decide whether you wish to take on a puppy, or adopt an older dog?

Puppy or Adult Dog?

The answer to this question may depend upon a number of factors, but will most probably be strongly influenced by your family circumstances. Whilst I am not suggesting that there is a dog for any family circumstance, clearly there is not, selecting the puppy, or dog, after thinking things through and doing thorough research can ensure that your dog does not become a square peg in a round hole; a perfectly good dog in imperfect circumstances, because in such instances there is inevitably only one loser; the dog.

Think carefully and for a long time. This dog will be part of your life for up to 15 years. Making the right choice can ensure that they are 15 great years for human and dog alike.

There are advantages to taking on a puppy and there are definite advantages to taking on an older dog.

A puppy is generally a clean slate. If you select a pup from a reputable and knowledgeable breeder you should acquire a healthy puppy with a good stable temperament. If you have selected a pedigree puppy you will have a good idea how big he is going to grow and what he will look like. If you have selected a crossbreed or Heinz 57 you will not be so sure. But this uncertainty can be a thoroughly enjoyable experience watching him grow and develop into a beautiful adult dog. Mind you, I don't think I have ever considered any dog I met as being anything other than a beautiful dog.

Puppies are time-consuming. They must be nurtured and developed in much the same way as a human baby. It takes care and it takes patience.

Your puppy needs to be socialised and habituated to everything and everyone he is going to meet throughout his life. You need to build a tidy sum in his piggy bank of experiences.

In the case of an older dog, you may know his previous owners and know how he has been raised, but the chances are you will not.

You know what he looks like. He is unlikely to change. By taking time to get to know him before adopting him, you can get a good idea of his temperament, whether he is sociable with people, dogs and children.

If he has issues in any of these areas, your circumstances may be such that they are not a problem. But beware, your circumstances may change. If they do, how will you cope with his issues then? Perhaps you have the time and knowledge or the resources to help him overcome these issues and become a happier dog.

You might even be considering a senior dog. Such dogs are often overlooked because of their advanced years, but they are often absolutely fantastic, loving, undemanding companions. Content with small amounts of regular exercise and content to spend much of their time resting and just being good company.

So you have now decided between a puppy, adult or senior dog. As you are reading this book I am assuming you have chosen to go down the puppy route. Perhaps in a few years, having enjoyed several years of dog ownership, you will make a different choice next time.

Choosing a Breed or Type

What about breed, or in the case of a cross breed, type? I strongly urge you to base this decision on your current lifestyle, not the one you aspire to. If your idea of vigorous exercise is ripping the wrapper off a well-known brand of Cornish Pasty, then obtaining a Border Collie or a German Shepherd is not going to turn out well. I don't like to be judgemental, but I will make an exception in this case.

If you believe you really do have the determination to change your lifestyle and take up fell-running, then do it first and having established your new lifestyle, choose your dog accordingly.

Likewise, if the whole family likes nothing better than shinning up the peaks of Snowdonia, a Neapolitan Mastiff should not appear anywhere near the top of your chosen breeds.

Research the Breed

Knowing the origins of the breeds you like will help you make an informed decision. Consider the history of the breed and what it was bred for. Don't buy a breed which has a highly developed guarding instinct and then expect it not to bark when a visitor knocks on your front door.

Don't buy a Border Collie from a local farm and then complain that she is a bit lively! Of course she is, she's a sheepdog. As a puppy, if she is not being lively, it is probably because she is sleeping, or dead!

Male or Female?

Often this decision is influenced by a childhood companion dog. Because you had a male or a female as a child, or when you were growing up, you wish to do the same with your own companion dog. There is nothing wrong with using previous experience as the basis for your decision on gender, but there are other factors that may influence your decision.

Dogs tend to be a little more headstrong and may be more difficult to manage, particularly as they reach adolescence. Bitches tend to mature earlier and may be easier to housetrain. This is a sweeping generalisation, and there are marked differences depending upon breed. In the majority of breeds there are minor, but noticeable differences, but in others, these differences can be quite significant. Research your breed, discuss it with knowledgeable breed specialists and make a well-considered decision.

Base your decision on knowledge and your family circumstances.

Companion, Show, or Working Dog?

If you want a dog as a companion, seek out a suitable puppy. Get away from the idea of buying a companion puppy in order to show her at Cruft's. I often see the advert, although in fairness they are not so common these days, "Irish Setter pups for sale. Show or pet." This is generally nonsense. Pet puppies are for pets. If you want a show puppy, because that is what you wish to do with your puppy in the future, buy a show puppy.

If you do want a puppy with a view to showing her in the future you may need to "earn your spurs". Breeders who produce puppies for show generally earn their reputation by the success in the show ring of the puppies they sell. They are highly unlikely to sell a top puppy to a novice owner.

What they may do is sell you an entry-level puppy, to allow you an introduction to the world of dog showing, and this might be a good option. As with all dog-related competition, most dog owners aren't interested. Some will have a dabble, then continue with their lives, whilst some will get hooked. It doesn't matter which category you are in. Just enjoy your dog.

Similarly, don't be tempted to take on a dog that has been bred from what a breeder may describe as "Working Stock". If at this point I need to go into a detailed explanation of what that term means, then you should steer well clear. If you understand the term, then you will have a good idea of whether you want to take on such a puppy and all it entails.

===

Selecting a Breeder

By the time you have reached this point you will have decided that a puppy is right for you and your family. You have researched and selected a breed and decided upon the gender of your chosen puppy.

Before you get to see any prospective puppies you need to select the right breeder. This may not be a single breeder, but a shortlist of 3 or 4 depending upon the popularity of your chosen breed. In some breeds there are hundreds of breeders, in some very few.

Whilst breeders obviously want to sell their puppies, a good breeder is much more concerned in finding the right home for their pups. Just as you are looking for the right puppy, the breeder is looking for the right family or working home for their puppies.

If I could give one single piece of advice about selecting a family puppy it would be this; try and select a puppy that has been bred in circumstances as close to your family circumstances as possible. Many of the most professional and caring breeders do not have a "commercial" or "professional" set-up. Fancy equipment does not equate to good puppies. Anyone who has served in the armed forces will understand the following observation often made; "All the gear and no idea!"

Shiny kit might be impressive to look at, but it is knowledge and care that you want from your breeder. To breed a good-quality litter requires very little "Gucci" kit; a whelping box, a good supply of newspaper to line the box, a quiet, draught-free room, a heat lamp and not much more. But it does depend upon good breeding stock, a depth of knowledge of their chosen breed and the process of breeding, whelping and puppy development through the first 8 weeks of life.

A good trainer can help you to make the right selection. I am often engaged at the point a family is considering taking a dog into the family. I spend time speaking with them and talk about all the things we have discussed in the earlier part of this book. Whether dog ownership is right for the family, whether they should look for a puppy, consider an older dog, or a rescue dog.

I admit that my initial approach is to play devil's advocate, trying to point out the disadvantages of dog ownership. Most are quite shocked when I point out that to kennel a dog whilst the family takes a holiday is usually about the same price as taking another person on holiday with them.

I then guide them through the process of deciding upon breed, age, male or female etc. before helping them draw up a shortlist of potential breeders and provide them with a list of questions to ask during the first telephone conversation.

I don't give them a list of answers to give to the breeder, who will no doubt have quite a few questions to ask them. Just as a prospective owner should expect honest, personal answers from the breeder, the opposite also applies.

As a prospective owner, you must be honest with the breeder. All the best relationships are built on honesty and trust and this relationship will be very important for you, the breeder and, most of all, your chosen puppy, because she is the most important one here.

Personal recommendation from a person you trust is the best method of finding a good, knowledgeable, honest breeder.

Select a breeder who has a verifiable history of producing good-quality and healthy puppies, and who breeds the type of puppy that is right for your family. If you want a pet German Shepherd Dog, do not select a breeder who uses strong working lines producing potential police or sport dogs. Select a breeder who breeds for the pet market. Similarly if you are selecting a dog for work, or sport, then select a breeder who breeds them.

Speak at length with several suitable breeders and ask them when they will have puppies available. Most will have a waiting list of prospective owners.

If they haven't yet bred the planned litter, or Mum is in the early stages of pregnancy, ask to visit. Go and see them and their set-up. Look at the facilities. Speak with them at length. Ask yourself if they are a person you can trust.

Look at the details of previous litters. A friend of mine, who breeds German Shepherds for the police, security and sport has a massive scrapbook, with cuttings and letters from various handlers about how his dogs have performed. Everyone thinks they breed great dogs, but written evidence from those who have taken puppies from them in the past carries an awful lot of weight, in my opinion.

Another breeder from whom I have bought 2 pups over the years, sends out a twice-yearly newsletter to all those who have previously bought pups from her. She asks for regular updates on her pups in order to pass information to the other owners. Our Daisy May is now 10 years old, but she always gets a birthday card from Gail and she is always included in the newsletter.

This may be a bit over the top you might think, but a good breeder cares, and that care doesn't end when you waltz out of the door with a puppy under your arm.

Puppy Farms and Imports

Avoid puppies from puppy farms, both in the UK and overseas. They are poorly bred and are a bad investment. That is not my opinion, it is a fact.

There is an abundance of evidence for shutting down such places and it is shameful that they still exist. Some sell directly to the public and prospective owners visit and buy their pup from the premises. At least in this circumstance the buyer sees the premises, but many end up buying a puppy just to get the poor little mite away from the place. Sadly, this just ensures the scumbag running the establishment will be encouraged to breed again.

As most people try to avoid such places, such establishments are quite devious and are not averse to shipping their pups to a "family home" to be advertised as home-bred puppies.

Always be careful that the home-bred litter that you visit is actually a home-bred litter and that it hasn't been dropped off at the seller's home from a puppy farm in the UK, or hasn't just been delivered along with the rest of the litter out of the back of a transit van from the far side of Europe.

Beware the seller of a slightly older puppy, say 14 weeks or so, who claims to be selling a puppy on behalf of their Mum, Dad, or Auntie Ethel, who has suddenly developed an allergy, and needs to sell their beloved puppy on.

Baby Alice and siblings with Mum; Miss Red (M&J McFadyen)

Unless Mum, Dad or Auntie Ethel has supplied a doctor's note, or is wheezing on the sofa, the person in front of you is probably lying. If you have been duped in to viewing the puppy, walk away. Don't get sucked in.

So how can you tell? Selecting the breeder carefully as described earlier is the best way, but there are other tell-tale signs.

If you are buying a pedigree puppy, the breeder should have prepared the pedigree, or be able to show Mum and Dad's papers, in preparation for drawing up the puppy's pedigree. Check carefully. Don't accept any old flannel. You wouldn't buy a car without checking the documentation; don't do it with a puppy.

Observe the puppies and their Mum together and satisfy yourself that they are clearly Mum and pup. How do they interact? Does she look like she has recently had a litter of pups? Is Mum still producing milk? No Mum present? Any doubts? Walk away.

Ask to see the puppy food that the breeder has been using to feed the litter over the previous few weeks. They should have a good supply on hand. If they haven't, ask yourself why?

Always ask to see some photographs of the pups shortly after they were born. Unless the breeder is knocking out pups on a production line, they always take some photos of Mum and puppies soon after birth. It's human nature. If they don't have any it would arouse my suspicions.

If the breeder for some strange reason doesn't have any Mum and puppy pics, ask to see some of Mum when she was younger, in family-type pictures. I don't know anyone who doesn't have a series of photos of their dogs in family circumstances. If they haven't, get your Reeboks on and do a runner.

Buying From T'interweb

If you are buying from an advertisement on the internet, and I will be honest, I never would, be extra cautious. Consider all the above points and do an additional bit of research.

Do a Google search on the exact wording of the advertisement, but insert different breed names, or leave them blank. You would be surprised at how many breeders have the same advert running for several different breeds of puppies. If this is the case, get your barge pole out, and whatever you do, don't touch them with it!

Imports

There are a growing number of puppies being transported across the EU from Eastern Europe bound for buyers in the UK. Imported puppies are a very bad idea, unless you are the one importing a single puppy and you have been through the process outlined above. In the event you do enter into an agreement to purchase a puppy from overseas, I strongly recommend that you collect and transport the puppy yourself. That way you can do the checks outlined above, in person, and ensure the welfare of your puppy during the transportation.

In the event you are pondering the purchase of an imported pup, please consider the following points:

Do you think that an 800-mile journey in a poorly ventilated transit van is a beneficial experience for your puppy? I don't.

Do you think the reason that so many pups are transported to the UK is for the good and benefit of the breed as a whole, or the puppy being transported? I don't.

Do you think that a breeder who transports puppies in this way is likely to have given them and their Mum the best care? I don't.

Do you think there will be any redress should you buy a puppy from this breeder and it subsequently develops a serious illness? I don't.

If there is anything you are unhappy about please, please, please, walk away. There are lots of excellent breeders of quality puppies out there, you just have to do your homework and be patient. A good pup is worth waiting for and a good breeder will have a waiting list. Many don't actually breed unless they have potential families for their puppies.

As I said, look for good personal recommendations and a verifiable history of producing good puppies. A good breeder has a sound reputation and guards it fiercely.

And finally, if you are concerned about the welfare of any pup that you view, under any circumstances, call the RSPCA or SSPCA. If you are concerned about the breeder's reaction, get in touch with me and if I share your concerns I will happily do it for you.

===

Selecting Your Puppy

Before going to view the litter, you will have done your research and you will have decided upon a dog or a bitch. Do not be swayed. Stick with your decision.

If you want a bitch and none that you see appeal to you, do not change your mind just to get a pup from that litter. Wait until the next litter is bred, or find another breeder.

If there is anything that you are unhappy about, the size of the puppies, their demeanour, the way they move, the condition of the bitch, cleanliness of the pups and puppy area, just make your excuses and politely walk away.

Sprogs and Dogs

Don't take children to attend the viewing of the litter as an objective selection cannot be made. Kids love every puppy. Puppy selection is the responsibility of the adults in the family. There is no requirement for the children to see the litter, they will love whichever puppy you select, and if you decide not to select one, you avoid bedlam.

The opposite rule applies when just adults are involved in the decision to take on a puppy. Never buy a puppy as a surprise. Please don't, please don't, please don't. It is not a good idea. In fact it is probably the worst idea since a bloke named Adolf decided to send his boys off on a sightseeing tour to

Russia, and we all know how badly that turned out.

Dog ownership should be thoroughly discussed and the selection of the pup should be a joint decision. It must be the right decision and right choice for all involved.

Viewing the Litter

In an ideal world you should be able to view and interact with Mum and Dad. Bearing in mind a responsible breeder probably won't let you view the puppies until they are old enough to be removed from Mum, or Mum given time away from the puppies, this interaction should not be a problem.

You want to be able to gauge the Mum's temperament and Dad's temperament too. But I always believe that Mum's is the most important because as well as providing 50% of the genes for each pup, she also has 8 weeks to nurture them and for them to be influenced by her character. She has an input in regard to both nature and nurture, whereas Dad is purely down to nature. He does his stuff and then makes himself scarce, a bit like on the Jeremy Kyle Show.

A puppy that has spent the first 8 weeks of her life around a stressed, nervous Mum is going to be influenced by that negative experience, just as a pup that has been raised by a calm, relaxed Mum will be influenced by that positive influence.

If for some reason you can't see Dad, then do some detective work. Many dogs have profiles on t'interweb and you can research him and his strengths and weaknesses. You may also be able to research how his previous litters have fared and developed.

When I bred German Shepherds I would not let a prospective owner see the puppies until they had spent about 15 minutes in the company of Mum and Dad. I wanted them to see the size, strength and character of the parents, as it was highly likely this was how their pup would develop.

It also gave me the opportunity to see that they were confident around large, bold dogs. Because that's what they would be living with a few months in the future. On more than one occasion I had to tell the family that they probably weren't the right fit for one of my pups. Whilst this was obviously disappointing for the family, my priority was the future welfare of my puppies.

Be prepared to take the advice of the breeder, who, by the age when you are able to view, should be able to discuss the different characteristics of each individual puppy.

If I was selecting a puppy purely as a pet, having decided in advance to take a female puppy, once I had seen all the pups together and was happy with their health and vigour, I would ask to see just the female pups.

I would ask to see the female pups in a different area of the house or in the garden.

At this point I would want to watch them interact with each other. Whether they responded to me clapping my hands by running towards me, or away from me. How they responded to my hands. If they were happy to be picked up, or fearful, or very bitey.

I would then try to grade them, from the most outgoing and lively to the most reserved. I would probably discount the liveliest one and the fat one that was duffing up her litter mates. I would also discount the nervous little one waiting at the back of the group and avoiding me.

Having done this I may be left with 2 or 3 from the middle order. I would ask to see those pups as a little group, and then finally each puppy individually before making my choice.

There are a number of Puppy Temperament Testing guides available on t'interweb and you should read through a few of these in order to give you an idea of the qualities you might wish to consider when choosing the new family member. But, the final choice is yours. Choose wisely and carefully.

This may appear to be a lot of effort and trouble to go to, but you will have many years to regret a poor decision and the same amount of time to enjoy all the benefits of a good one. It is a sound investment of your time and effort.

Congratulations, you have selected your puppy.

Arrange Collection

Having made all the correct decisions and having selected the right puppy, make the arrangements for taking your puppy home. Your puppy should be at least 8 weeks old when she leaves her Mum for her new family.

You are the person who transports your puppy to her new home.

On one occasion when I accompanied a family to select their puppy the whole process had gone well until the point when the breeder tried to convince the prospective owners to take a puppy before it was 6 weeks old, because they were going on holiday and needed to move the litter on.

At that moment the breeder displayed such a lack of knowledge of the litter's needs and concern for the puppy's welfare at the point of sale, that in my view they were unlikely to have raised the litter with the right level of diligence and care up to that point. I advised the owners to decline the puppy and walk away. A few weeks later an excellent puppy was obtained from another breeder.

===

Selecting Alice

When selecting my own puppy, I went through the whole process outlined above. My preparation had gone well.

I visited Scotland, took a B&B for the night so I could spend a long time picking my puppy. Having discussed my choice of puppy with the breeder; Mark, I knew I was only considering female puppies on this visit.

I had previously established a good relationship with Mark and Janet. I already owned one of their pups and knew the working qualities and characteristics of at least half a dozen others.

My 3-year-old Malinois, Jimmy, had been the British Police and Services Canine Association Reserve Champion in 2013 and 2014. He was to become the Champion in 2015, just before his 4th birthday. The chosen puppy would be his niece, from his older, full sister; Miss Red.

After a great deal of deliberation I selected a confident, strong, attractive, focused little female Malinois. She was the one in a black collar; Miss Black. When the choice was made, both Mark and Janet told me that she was the puppy they had predicted I would select. I named her "Alice" after our Mam; hence the title of this book.

===

Preparing for Alice

I was lucky that one of Alice's brothers was being delivered to Holland, so I did not have to make a return journey to collect her, as Mark was passing about 15 miles from my home and agreed to deliver her to me. She would be 8 ½ weeks old when delivered.

I had about 3 weeks to prepare for her arrival. If you have followed my advice you should have about the same amount of time, or if even wiser than me, you will have started the puppy proofing preparation as soon as you planned to take on a puppy.

The first decision I had to make was where in the house Alice would live and sleep. I recommend deciding upon a few locations. A bedtime location where your pup can bed down for the long night ahead, and somewhere she can rest for shorter periods during the day.

In Alice's case I planned to have her crate in the kitchen as it is warm and draught-free and it is an area that is visited regularly during the day by all the members of the family, but is quiet and peaceful at night. It also has space for a small puppy pen, which can be set up and folded down quite quickly when I need to put her somewhere out of harm's way and away from any potential mischief when I am working and can't keep an eye on her.

I took the time to dig out a couple of old child gates from the shed. These will be used to prevent her getting into anywhere that I don't want her to have access to and also to prevent her following an inch behind my heels when I go from one room to the other. They will be very useful until her toilet training routine has been established and she has learned what she can and cannot chew.

Child gates are a great piece of kit when you are settling in and toilet training and chew training your puppy. They are relatively cheap, and even cheaper from your local charity shop.

I prepared 2 beds for her. The main bed is put into her crate and this is where she will spend her nights. I considered a plastic dog bed with a padded bed inside it, but all my other dogs have been more than happy to lie on a thick piece of vet bed, which I cut to size, but with enough left over and cut at the corners, to make little 6-inch high sides and back, just as an extra precaution against draughts.

I bought a second little plastic bed for her in case I want her to sleep in my office with me from time to time. As it turned out she didn't like this bed and so would pull her vet bed out and just lie on top of that, so if anyone wants to buy a barely used plastic puppy bed please call 07966 73…, well perhaps not. It might do for my next puppy.

So now it is time to prepare your home. I don't have kids, well I do, but they have long since gone on to develop their own breeding programmes, so I don't have to worry about my puppy chewing up the kids' toys, but if you do have human little 'uns then this is going to be high up on your preparation list.

Try and confine toys to a single room, to which your puppy will be denied access during the early days. This means the sprogs can leave their toys around without your puppy chewing them up.

Or if you are clever you can use the impending arrival of a little fur ball to encourage your nippers into putting their toys away after use, or risk losing them to a marauding toy-eating machine.

In all seriousness, explain the risks of your puppy choking on small toys and encourage tidiness. An open-topped toy box is no obstacle to an inquisitive puppy, so any toy box should have a lid, which will at least present her with a challenge. But never forget, you are the adult, so ultimately it is your responsibility.

Mats and rugs present an irresistible challenge to a puppy who has a desperate need to soothe teething pains and also develop her jaws. You favourite rug is an ideal soother in her mind. So in the short term, take any loose rugs or mats up if they are in the rooms your puppy will be able to access.

Being an expert dog trainer I did this and I had no incidents of trashed mats in my house. Who's a clever boy then? Well not that clever really. Because although I puppy-proofed my own home, I neglected to take baby Alice's crate with me on a visit to my Mam's house. I decided that rather than go to bed and have her follow me into the bedroom I would sleep on the large, comfy sofa, with baby Alice next to me on her vet bed, which was atop my Mam's best, brand new, thick red rug.

Alice slept peacefully all through the night, as did I, although in her case it was probably helped by her sucking a large hole, smack bang in the centre of the rug. I did offer to replace the rug, but the hole is now covered by a coffee table. Although the coffee table always moves a couple of feet when I visit so I can be reminded of my error of judgement! Thanks.

There are 3 points that you should consider here, which I failed to consider. Firstly, the chewing phase can last a lot longer than you think. Secondly, a new place presents your puppy, or in this case my puppy, with new, exciting opportunities to chew unfamiliar stuff, and thirdly, crates are portable. Taking your puppy's secure bedroom with you is an extremely good idea when you go visiting.

Remove, or conceal and protect electrical wiring from your puppy. You will be astounded by how fast your puppy can dart behind your television to get at the mains cable and connections to your Sky box. (Other satellite and cable TV providers are available. Sorry, Mr Branson.)

It is a good idea to tuck these away as far as possible and then protect anything left exposed. A good solution is one of those plastic things that you wrap around the bottom of newly planted trees that you can buy in garden centres. Whilst this provides only a little additional protection, it is very noisy when grabbed by a puppy, alerting you to what she is up to. Alternately you can buy cable covers that will provide a greater level of protection, but never underestimate the speed of your puppy's sprint for an exposed cable, nor the sharpness of her teeth.

Secure your Garden

No ifs, no buts, no maybes. Secure your garden to ensure your new bundle of joy cannot escape. You would be astounded at the smallest of gaps that a puppy can wriggle though and the smaller the pup, the smaller the gap needed.

Do not do a bodge job. Do it properly. It might prove to be expensive, but not nearly as expensive or painful as seeing your puppy squashed flat like a little hedgehog on the road, or the bill for damages if she causes an accident after escaping.

Also consider having a floodlight installed, as it makes it far easier to see when she has performed her toilet routine, or if she is up to no good. Many dogs do not particularly like the dark, so lighting the area may also help to encourage her out for her last poo before bedtime.

Prepare Her Toilet Area

A little prior preparation here can promote good toilet habits. At the very least I would recommend blocking off part of your garden to encourage her to toilet in a smaller area.

Most pups prefer to toilet on a porous surface so grass is ideal, but it is harder to keep clean and hygienic. If you have children at home, even though you will clean up after your puppy I recommend having a separate area for children to play and puppy to poo.

At my previous house I built a small toilet area using railway sleepers and inside filled it with bark chippings from the local garden centre. This gave my dogs a deep, porous area in which to poo and piddle. And thanks to the bark chips being easy to pick up it meant I could remove any "dog eggs" with ease and bag them up.

Periodically I would remove the remaining bark chippings and replace with new ones. It probably cost me about a fiver a month and was much cheaper than re-laying a piddle-damaged lawn.

Prepare Her Bed

I recommend you look no further than a suitable crate as her first bed for reasons that will be revisited time and time again in this book. It is not a cage, nor a punishment cell. It is a comfortable bed. Line it with a large sheet of vet bed. This will keep her comfortable and warm. It is also a lot less attractive to destroy than a quilt stuffed with filler, which will soon become a quilt that **used to be** stuffed with filler after your puppy has disembowelled it. This is messy and can also be dangerous to your puppy, if swallowed.

The crate can also be moved with relative ease, if you need to keep an eye on her when you are in a different room. Or, if you prefer, buy a plastic dog bed, which can be lined with vet bed.

Top Tip: When buying a crate you will find they are always cheaper to buy on t'interweb, a minimum saving of about 40%, more than enough to cover your outlay on this book.

Food Utensils

Stainless steel bowls are hygienic, easy to clean, hard-wearing and cheap. If your puppy is a larger breed such as a Great Dane, consider buying a stand, which elevates the bowls to make eating more comfortable and safer.

Puppy Food

A reputable breeder should provide you with a few days' supply of her regular puppy food when you collect your puppy. But some brands are not as common as others and may have to be ordered in by your pet shop, or t'interweb supplier.

Buy it well in advance to be sure of an uninterrupted supply. Your puppy will have enough strange things to deal with when she arrives, a strange diet should never be one of them.

Arrange Veterinary Care

Have you arranged a vet, and one that will continue with the course of inoculations that your puppy has been given so far? Changing the type of vaccination because the vet you chose doesn't stock the one used leads to additional, avoidable expense, but more importantly takes up a very large part of her development period, which you can ill afford to lose.

Remember that you may be moving your puppy quite some distance to bring her home with you. The risk of certain strains of disease may vary and therefore the vaccine used might also vary.

Microchipping should be done at the time of your puppy's inoculations. If it has not been done by the breeder you must ensure that you have it done. It is a legal requirement.

===

Selecting Your Puppy Trainer and Training School

The more perceptive amongst you will have noted that this subject heading refers to **your** trainer, not a trainer, not your dog's trainer, but **your** trainer. Your puppy trainer will train you. You will train your puppy. This is a very important distinction in my view. I am sure some in the dog world would disagree, but they are wrong, and as this is my book, I am happy to disregard their opinion.

So what should you look for in your trainer? I suppose it all depends upon what you want from your puppy. The vast majority of people just want her to grow into a happy, well-behaved dog, who becomes a full and valued member of the family.

A good dog doesn't need to do very much. If your dog:

1. Walks on the lead without pulling you on your face;
2. Has a reliable, quick, recall;
3. Will sit quietly whilst you talk with a neighbour you meet in the street;
4. Will disregard, or politely greet humans and dogs when you meet them;
5. Will travel happily in the car;
6. Has good reliable toilet habits;
7. Can be left for short periods without becoming distressed;

Then she is a great dog.

Engaging Your Trainer

Having read the first few chapters of this book a few months ago, you have decided that you should take a puppy into your family. You have researched the breed and chosen a type of dog that fits in with your lifestyle and circumstances. You have identified the right breeder, or rehoming service. (Some rehoming charities do rehome puppies.) You have prepared your home, picked your puppy and brought her home, so now it's time to carry out some interviews and select your trainer, right?

Wrong!

You should have begun interviewing potential trainers some time ago. A good, knowledgeable trainer can help you through the whole process and help you with all those things. Even if you do not want the trainer's assistance with most of these matters, the time to engage your trainer is long before your puppy comes home.

You should select your trainer after an interview process. Don't pick the first one you speak to, unless it is me, of course. Seriously though, do your research and, having drawn up a shortlist, be prepared to speak with a few.

Have a list of questions you wish to ask written down. If you don't write them down, you will forget them. You can be steered away from the questions by a trainer who doesn't want to answer them, a bit like a good politician. You can also get side-tracked by an enthusiastic trainer and again forget the important stuff.

Don't be scared to ask probing questions and don't be afraid to ask for certificates, professional qualifications etc. Don't be blinded by something that sounds impressive, do some research. An online marketing company is currently offering a Diploma in Canine Behaviour for £27. I'll bet it looks smashing on the office wall, but all it is good for is covering a squashed fly stain on the wallpaper, or picking up a stray puppy poo.

Remember, this little bundle of puppy-shaped fun will be part of your family for many years to come. You owe it to her and yourselves to provide her with the best. Not the cheapest, nor the most expensive, but the best. As with all other issues regarding the care of your puppy, the key is to be prepared.

Be Prepared

Be prepared to **wait**. Good trainers are often booked up for many weeks in advance, which is another reason to start the selection process as early as you can.

Be prepared to **travel**. Good trainers do not occupy every street corner. Although you will always encounter an expert trainer in every pub, it is well worth the investment to travel to the right person.

Be prepared to **interview** and ask probing questions, but don't be surprised if you get asked a few in return.

Be prepared to **check up** on qualifications and references.

Be prepared to **walk away**. If the person you are speaking to doesn't fill you with confidence, or just isn't the right fit for you and your puppy, then simply thank them for their time and go elsewhere.

Be prepared to **put the effort in**. Training your dog can be rewarding and frustrating in equal measure. If you have selected the right puppy, the right breed for you, the right trainer, the right learning environment, frustration should be minimal and the whole process should be an enjoyable and rewarding time for both of you.

Communication

Communication is a two-way street. A good dog trainer also needs to be a good teacher, able to communicate ideas to you when helping you to train your puppy. There are many trainers who can train a puppy extremely well, but are hopeless at conveying their message to you and your pup. This can be extremely frustrating for you, but never forget that communication is a two-way process and you should be able to express your views and, on occasion, concerns, or inability to understand the trainer's instructions.

Many years ago I was criticised by the husband of a lady who was training her dog in one of my group classes. It transpired that the lady had impaired hearing and had missed much of what I was saying to the group, especially when I wasn't facing her directly. I asked her husband why she hadn't told me and was informed that she was embarrassed to mention it. I was quite hacked off with the lady and particularly with her husband for not telling me. Then I realised that I had never asked, and by not taking the time and trouble to do so I had probably made a significant contribution to her reluctance to tell me.

I made sure that from then on I would always give people the opportunity to let me know about anything that might hamper their learning experience and anything I can do to help them overcome any potential barriers to learning.

I also make sure that when I speak to people, before sending out course paperwork I ask if they can read normal-sized font, or if they require bigger font. I also give them the opportunity to ask me for a verbal explanation, rather than a training note.

Once again, at the top of this subject I refer to "helping you to train your puppy," not train her for you. If your trainer is good enough, they will be able to teach you the theory underpinning the principles of dog training and how dogs learn, whilst also understanding human learning theory and how humans learn.

This is one of the reasons why I did a two-year course in Post Compulsory Education, in order to gain a fuller understanding of this subject. It enables me to deliver a better service to those people who entrust me with the responsibility of helping them forge a lifelong relationship with their puppy.

Please don't be shy about asking for anything to help you and your dog get the maximum benefit from your training. You are paying the trainer's wages. Please make sure you get value for money. You and your puppy are a team. You and your dog trainer should also be a team.

Qualifications and Credentials

You must understand that in the UK there is no body that states what qualifications your dog trainer must have, and in the vast majority of cases they have none. That does not always mean that they are a bad trainer. They may be extremely good, but if they were, surely it would be a relatively simple matter to gain some professional recognition. If they haven't, ask them why they haven't, but remember; it's up to you to establish the true reason for this.

Please ensure you verify the credentials of anyone you employ. In 2015 a number of dog trainers displaying the logo and claiming membership of the British Police and Services Canine Association were doing so fraudulently and were instructed in no uncertain terms to remove the logo. I am sure other organisations have similar problems. Just because there is a badge on the website doesn't mean the trainer has earned the right to wear it.

Having established a trainer's credentials please ensure they are credible i.e. worth the paper they are written on and true. Would you believe some people exaggerate the value of their qualifications and depth of experience? Claiming to be a dog trainer is very easy, being one certainly isn't.

Group Training or 1 to 1 Training?

You should consider whether group training classes or 1 to 1 training is best for you and your puppy. If opting for 1 to 1, will you be attending the training school? Or will the trainer be visiting your home?

Will you be engaging a single trainer? Will you book in with the training school and be allocated a specific trainer at a later point? Or, do you just get whoever is available?

In my opinion you should be trained by a specific trainer. That might be the head trainer, or one of his staff, but if you are being allocated another trainer, please ensure that you are getting a qualified trainer, not an assistant trainer, who should be acting under supervision.

Training a person's puppy is a serious responsibility and it is one I always take seriously. You are placing your trust in your trainer. A good one will enhance your relationship with your puppy, a poor one can seriously damage it.

I don't let other trainers train my clients. When you book with me, you get me. I run the classes. I deliver the theory, I demonstrate the practical aspects of the training. I do use assistants and they are there to support you, but they do so under my direction.

I have built my training school with a reputation for quality tuition and results. It is a reputation hard won, and it is one I guard fiercely. Any good trainer will do likewise.

Class sizes are another important factor. Small class numbers, say between 4 and 8 pups in a class, is a good size, depending upon the ability of the trainer.

The maximum number I permit in any of my classes is 8 owners and their dogs. A few years ago, as part of my Cert Ed studies I ran an experiment of increasing the class size to 10 and looked at retention rates.

There was a small, but significant drop in the retention rate, which I was unhappy with. A "drop-out" represented an unsatisfied customer, or a customer who wasn't getting, for whatever reason, what they wanted from the course.

Those lost clients would either not continue training their puppy, leading to potential problems in later life, or maybe they would go to another trainer who was less competent, or used harsh methods, thereby doing the puppy harm.

Both reasons were unacceptable. Reducing the class size back to 8 improved retention rates once again. They have remained at this size for the past 6 years.

Training Environment

Training environment is also extremely important. Environment is one of the barriers to both human learning and canine learning. When considering a training establishment you should consider what facilities are on offer.

For instance a nice warm church hall or community centre provides a warm, quiet learning environment with very few distractions. It also has chairs and gives a greater degree of comfort. But does it provide fewer distractions?

In such a venue a single barking dog can prevent everyone in the class, both dog and human, from learning. Often the solution is to put the offending dog outside the hall with their owner, which then prevents any further learning by that team.

Equine centres are another venue that is becoming more popular and can be a good learning environment. Such venues generally provide shelter from the rain and the worst of the elements, providing a reasonable learning environment. But the surface in such an environment can be a problem. Many are coarse sand, some are sawdust and others are all-weather hardwearing rubber shavings.

The sand is generally good, but the other 2 surfaces retain an awful lot of scent from other dogs, treats used in training that have been dropped and of course the waste products of the horses that have access to it for the rest of the week.

With the rubber surface I have major concerns about the risk of this being ingested when a dog is rooting for a treat and takes in the rubber alongside the small piece of Pilgrim's Choice. (Other brands of mature cheddar are available.)

Outside venues provide plenty of space, and when on well-drained grass provide a good surface to work on. You have room to move about and the barking dog becomes less of a distraction so the team does not need to be excluded, and can still learn under the observation of the trainer.

A major disadvantage is exposure to the elements. In hot weather you must ensure that dogs don't get too hot and in cold weather you have to ensure that teams are not so uncomfortable that the environment creates another barrier to learning. Wind noise can make hearing the instructor difficult.

All venues require some sort of compromise and the best option for you and your puppy can only be determined by you, after considering the above points carefully.

There is no ideal environment unless you have a church hall, a grass field and a large indoor venue all available, which the training classes can alternate between at will. If you find such a place, let me know and I will buy it.

===

Now for a really boring bit, but one that could prove costly if you are unaware of it, or disregard it.

The Law and Your Puppy

Before you acquire your new puppy you should take a bit of time to check up in current UK legislation to ensure that you will be able to comply with the law. If, for any reason, you are unable to comply, don't get a puppy.

Even simple things like walking your dog, on or off lead, are covered by statute and local by-laws. As a responsible dog owner you also have a duty to promote responsible dog ownership. There are enough groups and individuals who are anti-dog and sadly much of the ammunition used to attack the dog-owning population is served up on a plate by inconsiderate or unprepared dog owners.

In reality, there are not many places in the UK where local by-laws are so prohibitive as to make dog ownership impractical, but you may need to take your puppy a bit further afield than your local park to find access to areas where she can be exercised safely and lawfully, whilst off lead.

The law will not take your personal circumstances into consideration. Breaking it may have serious financial implications for you and it could have much more serious consequences for your dog, who through no fault of her own, could end up paying for a crime with her life.

Remember too that there are still regional and national differences in legislation within the UK. In Wales microchipping has been compulsory for several years, but it was only made compulsory in England in April 2016.

I sincerely hope that anyone reading this book is never intending to use an electric collar on their puppy, either now, or when she grows into an adult dog, but, whilst these devices are legal in England and Scotland as of June 2016, Wales outlawed the use of electric collars for training dogs a few years ago. Scotland is currently consulting with the possibility of doing likewise and will in all likelihood introduce a similar ban in the future.

A Very Brief Overview

There are a number of items of legislation governing you and your puppy. This list is not exhaustive and in some instances they may be subject to national and regional variations. All legislation is subject to regular amendment.

The Animal Welfare Act 2006 applies to dogs and many other species. It provides a legal framework for the prevention of harm to animals and to promote their welfare.

The Dogs Act 1953 says it's an offence for dogs to roam free without a lead, or be otherwise closely controlled, in any field or enclosure where there are sheep. In this instance take my advice; closely controlled means on a lead or a short line, under 2 metres is specified in guidance on Open Access Land, so it makes sense to use this length as a good benchmark in all instances.

The Natural England website gives current information relating to the **Countryside and Rights of Way Act 2000**, which covers most recreational activities carried out on foot, including walking, sightseeing, bird watching, climbing and running, but there are some common-sense restrictions in place that limit where people can walk, or take a dog.

The Open Access Land Regulations say dogs must be kept on a short lead, under 2 metres, on Open Access Land between 1st March and 31st July, to protect ground-nesting birds.

The Wildlife and Countryside Act 1981 makes it a criminal offence to intentionally or recklessly destroy, damage or disturb any of the flora or fauna that make the land of special scientific interest. If your puppy does any of these things, you will be liable, not her.

Most people don't like dog poo. But if your dog poos, and they all do, it's yours. There are many clever devices to make the task of picking up poo less unpleasant. Buy one.

Having picked up your puppy's poo please make sure you dispose of it in the proper place. And, just to make sure you get it, Her Majesty Queen Elizabeth 2, God bless her, has kindly signed a piece of paper called **The Environmental Protection Act 1990**, which says it's an offence to throw away "anything that could cause, or contribute to or tend to lead to the defacement of a public place."

If it's good enough for HM Queen and her corgis, it's good enough for you and me. And if you follow the advice contained in this book about toilet training, you shouldn't have to do this too often when on your routine exercise sessions with your puppy.

The Control of Dogs Order 1992 means all dogs must wear a collar with the owner's name and address displayed any time they're on a public highway or in a public place. If you don't, you are guilty of an offence under **Animal Health Act 1981**.

The Dangerous Dogs Act 1991 prohibits ownership of 4 types of dogs originally bred for fighting and imposes restrictions in relation to other types of dog that present a serious danger to the public. Avoid breaching any provision of this act unless you have extremely deep pockets and a team of highly paid barristers on 24-hour standby.

Anti-Social Behaviour Crime and Policing Act 2014 amends certain provisions of the **Dangerous Dogs Act 1991** particularly in regard to keeping a dog under proper control and whether a dog is a danger to public safety.

Some public areas in England and Wales are covered by **Public Spaces Protection Orders**. These were previously called Dog Control Orders and provide for additional control measures when you are in these areas with your dog.

For more information and to keep abreast of changes in legislation, the following websites are helpful:

https://www.gov.uk/control-dog-public/overview

http://www.nfuonline.com/back-british-farming/love-your-countryside/latest-you-your-dog-and-the-countryside/or other countries consult online legislation

http://www.legislation.gov.uk/ukpga/1991/65/contents

=====

PART 2

Training for Life

Introduction

Training for Life is arguably far more important than Training for Control, but good control training will contribute greatly to successful life training. Mind you, without a good grounding in life training, all the tricks and control in the world won't make your puppy a pleasure to live with. Both parts of her education are inextricably linked and can't be achieved in isolation.

Your puppy's first few months are a massive learning curve, during which you are going to habituate her to things you want her to disregard in the future and sensitize her to all the stuff you want her to respond to.

Most importantly you are going to start to build resilience. You are going to prepare her for a rainy day, by putting something by for her. A sort of savings plan for life.

Most of you have been encouraged to save for a rainy day, so when the need arises and you have to dip into the piggy bank, you have enough put by to ensure you get through it. You have developed resilience to financial hard times.

We are looking at a savings plan for your pup's life experiences; her positive experience piggy bank, in order to make her resilient to the unexpected things that life will throw at her. By having a decent balance in the piggy bank we are enabling her to put the occasional unpleasant experience into context and bounce back.

Whilst I have tried to sequence Part 2 in a logical order, most of the life skills discussed will be running simultaneously and, as many are linked, progress in one area will have a beneficial effect on others.

I have placed the emphasis on giving your puppy clear direction and plenty of opportunities to practise desirable behaviour, for which she will be rewarded. I also stress the importance of denying her the opportunity to practise undesirable behaviour, which she may find intrinsically rewarding.

Yes, training for life should definitely come first. Anyway, let's crack on. It's time for a piddle!

===

Toilet Training Your Puppy

Little Molly - Day 1

Introduction

When looking at toilet training there is a difference between training a puppy and training a slightly older dog. With a puppy at, say, 8 weeks you are beginning with a clean slate and you can start her off the right way, rather than having to unlearn bad habits, before good habits can be encouraged.

The same principle underpins both situations. Take the time to create the right environment to develop good toileting habits. Minimise the opportunity to make mistakes and then patiently rehearse the good habits with your pup, reinforcing those habits with verbal praise, stroking and small treats.

Forward Planning

Before you get your puppy, plan ahead. Where will your puppy be trained to go to the toilet? It's worth having a look at the type of toilet area that the breeder has. If the breeder hasn't already started preparing puppy in this regard I would be asking myself why not? And what else they have neglected to start? If they haven't the time or knowledge to start puppy off the right way in this regard they probably haven't started it the right way in other respects.

Look at the breeder's toilet area. If your chosen puppy has already learned to toilet on grass then you might consider creating a small grass toilet area at home in your garden.

If you do not want your dog to toilet on grass then you will need to break this habit when you get your puppy home, but you should do so gradually. She has undergone a lot of other changes. Keep a bit of familiarity in regard to toileting.

For example, if you want your puppy to toilet on concrete you might wish to fence off the grassed area so she cannot access it and develop a habit you do not wish her to continue. Confine your puppy to the area you want her to use. If possible get some soil or surface material from the breeder's toilet area. Put this in your chosen toilet area. If the puppy smells familiar toilet material, it is more likely to use the one at your home.

If there is no pre training by the breeder then you are starting with a clean slate. You should prepare a small, fenced-off area of concrete, paving, grass, or even bark chippings as explained in Part 1, to ensure you train your pup on the surface of your choice.

Should I Teach Puppy to Poo When I Walk Her?

When you get a puppy you can elect to train her to toilet when on a walk, or in your garden toilet area before you take her for her walk. In my opinion the second option is best, as it helps a great deal with other areas of her training.

By teaching toileting in the garden it means that you are not reliant on taking your puppy for a walk in order to have her perform. You are also less likely to have your puppy poo when out walking and have to carry a bag of poo with you for a long time between poo bins. You will of course still need to carry poo bags, but these should be for emergency use only, not regular use.

Teaching toileting in the garden is also beneficial to training loose-lead walking, as you are not in a rush to get your puppy to walk for a poo, because she has already done it before you left home. This means you can strictly stick to your loose-lead walking routine. If you are dependent upon walking your puppy to her toilet area, how do you deal with lead pulling? With a garden-trained puppy, if you are training loose-lead walking and she is trying to pull, you can be resolute and refuse to go on until she walks nicely. With a puppy who needs a walk to perform you may face the choice of a puppy who pulls on the lead, or a puppy who poos in the house. Garden train your puppy and you should avoid both of these issues.

The only downside is that if the puppy has rigidly been toilet trained at home, she might be reluctant to toilet elsewhere, but this is a rare occurrence and can be remedied a lot more easily than correcting poor toilet habits at home.

Setting a Good Poo Routine

In order to create a good routine there are certain things that you need to understand. Your pup's metabolism will process her food at a certain rate. Your puppy will poo when this process has taken place. By noting the time that you feed your puppy and noting when she poos, you will be better able to schedule her pooing routine.

Puppies are not robots, but you will be amazed how quickly you can set a pattern. You will note I said **you** set the pattern. Your puppy needs help with this, so resolve to help her and she will learn quickly. Of course you can choose to ignore this advice and not bother, or cut corners, and you will be cleaning up her poo for many months, or even years to come. It's your choice, but if you don't have the time to help your puppy learn this important routine, then you don't have time for a puppy. Get a stuffed toy instead.

Food In, Poo Out

Puppies will tend to empty after they fill up. Food in, poo out. Get into the habit of putting your puppy's food down at the regular time and giving her no more than 10 minutes to eat it. If she hasn't eaten it in 10 minutes she is not hungry, or you are feeding too much.

When she has eaten, take her out to your chosen toilet area and spend time there with her. Ensure that this area is large enough for her to move around and settle for the toilet, but not so big that she can spend 15 minutes patrolling it.

Don't talk to her, it will distract her. If she does a wee, the second she has finished gently praise her with a nice voice, but not too much, then allow her to carry on to do a poo. Again, be there, but allow her the time and space to toilet. Don't speak, command her or anything else that will divert her from the job in hand. This might take time, but please be patient. If it is raining, wear a waterproof, if cold, wrap up warm. If you are uncomfortable you will rush your puppy and put her off. Don't do this!

When she squats down to poo, let her. Don't distract or interrupt her. When she has finished, reinforce her action firmly in her mind with verbal praise, a gentle fuss, and a little treat.

If it is raining when she has performed you may take her straight inside and this is a further reinforcement. She probably doesn't want to be out in the rain. If, however, it is nice weather and she wishes to explore, let her. You do not want to teach her that as soon as she goes to the toilet, the fun ends. That will encourage her to hold on!

Alternate Routines

Some pups prefer to poo before eating and I would recommend giving the pup access to her designated toilet area for a few minutes before feeding. Depending upon what she has been doing prior to feeding it is likely that she will need to have a wee, so this is a good practice that you can reinforce. This may be something I accidentally reinforced with baby Alice, but it worked really well for her.

Leaving Puppy Alone to Toilet

It is not good practice to leave your puppy unattended in the toilet area during training. How can you know if she has performed? If you have not seen her do it, you should assume that she has not done it. If you bring her in without seeing her perform and she comes inside and does it in the house, then it is your fault, not your puppy's fault. Training involves the rehearsal of behaviour. Every time you make this mistake you allow her to rehearse undesirable behaviour, making the whole toilet-training process much longer.

When Accidents Happen

Try to limit puppy's access to areas where she has mistakenly toileted, as we don't want a pattern to be set. Clean the areas affected with a weak solution of bicarbonate of soda (Baking Powder). This will leave no residual scent, unlike the use of bleach or disinfectant, which will only attract your puppy back to that spot, to toilet there again.

If you are still living in the dark ages and decide to punish puppy for her mistakes, on the advice of a bloke down the pub, you will make matters even worse and in all honesty you should consider whether dog ownership is for you. (You should also consider stopping putting your children to work sweeping chimneys before Social Services get wind.)

Even with the best routine, mistakes can happen. A puppy is not a robot. Dogs are inherently clean animals. It is your job to provide the environment and sufficient opportunities to develop and practise clean habits whilst she is young, and best able to learn.

Leaving the Door Open

In good weather it might seem a good idea to leave the door open so puppy can come in and out and go to the toilet whenever she wants to. This can create both good and bad patterns. Puppy learns to use an outside toilet area, but does not learn to hold herself.

When the bad weather comes and the door is closed, owners think toilet training has been achieved, but she has never learned to wait and hold herself. Suddenly puppy needs to go and the door is closed, so she does it in the house, much to the frustration of the owners and the distress of the puppy. This is more commonly associated with piddling rather than pooing, as pooing tends to be quickly synchronised with the feeding routine. She can only feed when you put food down for her, so you should always be there to take her to her toilet area as soon as she finishes eating.

If you have already gone down the open-door route, the matter can be overcome by a bit of reverse engineering. Puppy knows to go outside and use her specified area. We now need to teach her short periods of control.

Spend time closing the door for 15 minutes then opening it and taking her out for a piddle and praising her. Then extend the period of time the door is closed in a gradual process, until it is closed for an hour or more at a time, always remembering to go out with your puppy to reinforce good toileting, as soon as you open the door again.

Setting the Piddle Pattern

Whilst your puppy will usually do 3 to 5 poos per day, she will go for a piddle far more frequently.

The toilet area has been selected and you need to encourage puppy to use it as often as possible. In the early days I would be taking my puppy to the chosen toilet area every 30 minutes, when she is awake. As she learns to expect regular visits to the toilet area these intervals may be gradually extended from 30 to 40 minutes and so on up to a couple of hours. On days when you can't carry out this routine with her, for whatever reason, confine her to her crate to prevent accidents, but be realistic about what she can do as a puppy. Fortunately she will spend a lot of time sleeping, so ensure she is not disturbed too much, particularly by children. An unscheduled awaking is likely to lead to an unscheduled piddle.

There is a strong link between feeding, sleeping and toileting and setting a good pattern in any of these elements has a knock-on effect on the others. Set good patterns in all these areas and you will be setting good behaviour and training patterns for life.

Waking Up

Your puppy will piddle when she wakes up, so it is good to ensure that puppy is sleeping where you can keep an eye on her. This can be helped if you have decided to crate train your puppy, because you will hear her stirring and moving before she has the time to get out of bed and have a piddle. She is highly unlikely to piddle in her bed, and as she cannot leave the crate, it will give you some vital time to go to her, open the crate and carry her outside to her toilet area. You then remain there, with her, until she piddles and then reinforce it as before.

When she first wakes up, don't let her walk outside. She might want to stop for a quick one on the way out and you won't be quick enough to get down and scoop her up when she starts, so carry her. Create the routine early and be disciplined with yourself.

After Playing

When puppy has been playing she is completely focused on the game in hand. After a period of play it is almost inevitable that puppy will suddenly remember that she needs a piddle and will do it wherever she happens to be.

When the play has taken place in the house most people remember to take puppy outside to perform, but often, when the play has taken place outside, you will assume she is empty because she has been outside and so you will take her in. That's when she suddenly remembers she hasn't been. As before, if you haven't seen her piddle, you must assume she hasn't done so.

After playing, allow the excitement to subside and for her to calm down. If children are present, send them into the house as they are a distraction, take her to her toilet area, and let her perform. Then reinforce her desirable behaviour with verbal praise, stroking and possibly a little treat for being such a good girl.

After Feeding

Your puppy will invariably want to go after eating her meal. Be ready as soon as she has finished eating to take her to her toilet area and go through the toilet routine. For some reason baby Alice would always go for a poo before she had her meal, as soon as she heard me preparing her food she would stand at the child gate asking to go out. After eating, she was still taken out again, but would only do a little piddle after dining. As long as you know her routine, you can accommodate your puppy and ensure there are no little mishaps.

Bedtime Routine

At night your puppy should be able to have a secure, undisturbed night's sleep. Setting a good bedtime routine, coupled with a structured feeding and walking pattern, will help puppy get through the night clean and dry. Be realistic. If you need 12 hours of sleep every night, your puppy will not be able to hold on for that long. Six or 7 hours would be the absolute maximum, so during training you might need to have a few late nights and a few early starts. As your puppy gets older and the toilet training is going well I would recommend slowly increasing the length of her sleep by say 20 minutes per week, until you get back to your regular night-time routine.

I have already explained the importance of setting feed times and noting how long your puppy takes to process her food. I would suggest feeding a light cereal meal such as a Weetabix about 30 minutes before lights out.

Allow your puppy to eat her supper and then take her outside for her last piddle and poo as explained above, reinforcing good behaviour accordingly. Having finished toileting, take puppy to her crate or secure sleeping area and bed her down, with the lights out. Then go to bed yourself and do not disturb your puppy by mooching around and unsettling her.

I recommend an early morning start, say 6am. Get up and go straight down. If puppy is already awake quickly remove her from her bed and carry her outside to perform her morning toilet routine, reinforcing good behaviour as explained. If she is still sleeping allow her to wake, whilst you observe her, then carry her outside.

If she has had an accident during the night remove soiled bedding and wash in a neutral detergent and rinse well. Ensure you also clean the sleeping area thoroughly with weak bicarbonate of soda solution.

In Conclusion

Your puppy is an inherently clean animal, but she is little more than a baby. Take the time to establish a regular and easy-to-achieve routine and reinforce her desirable behaviour by rewarding her. When things go wrong remain calm and do not punish your puppy. That will only make her afraid of you and may also make her afraid to toilet, especially when you are near, for fear of being punished.

Clean up accidents quickly and use a solution of bicarbonate of soda that leaves no residual scent; this may prevent her being attracted back to that spot by the smell of disinfectant.

===

Crate Training Your Puppy

Crate training is an excellent way of managing your puppy by keeping her out of harm's way, and preventing her getting into mischief in the first few weeks. The crate provides her with a safe haven. Everything in the crate belongs to her, and she can do with it as she wishes. Therefore everything in the crate should be strong and chewable without presenting a hazard to puppy's health. Her crate is her bed and her rest area. It should never be used as a punishment. She should never be placed in it harshly, or in anger.

On those occasions when she is getting over-excited, it may be used as a place in which she can be placed to calm down. Whenever you use it for this purpose, go outside in the garden and give yourself a slap. You should have taken steps to calm your puppy before it got to that stage!

Crate training helps to prevent several of the most common and frustrating issues associated with a new puppy. Some of these are listed:

Toilet Training

Using the crate as an aid to toilet training and in conjunction with a correctly designed toilet-training programme is an effective and gentle way of encouraging your puppy to refrain from piddling and pooing until you take her for her regular toilet-training break.

Damage Prevention

All puppies have natural desire and need to chew. Everything in the crate belongs to her. By carefully mixing toys of different textures you can satisfy her need to chew in a safe way. Safe for two reasons. Firstly, you have ensured everything in there is designed for puppies to chew on, so she cannot injure herself by chewing something dangerous, and secondly, because everything there belongs to her, so she cannot be told off for chewing anything that is in there.

By identifying her favourite chew toys, you can ensure that she is trained to chew those, rather than your favourite shoes. Because you won't be putting those in her crate, nor leaving her with access to them anytime soon. Will you?

Bedtime Routine

The crate can help establish a good bedtime routine as it is also her bed. It is a nice, safe place to be. It is somewhere she can relax, away from other pets and children. At night she should have a bedtime routine, a little walk, a period outside to perform toilet-training routine and so to bed. Pop her a little treat. A trainer I know always gives her dogs a gingernut biscuit at bedtime. As it is the last thing she always does, it helps establish a calm, relaxing bedtime routine.

Relaxing in Isolation

Almost as problematic as leaving your puppy alone too much is not leaving her alone enough. Your puppy should learn that she does not always need to be on your heels all the time. Training her for short periods of separation from you is always a good idea. Pop her in the crate, for a few moments, whilst you nip upstairs, leave the room to make a phone call, or even go to make a cup of tea. Child gates and puppy pens are also useful for this purpose.

Preparation for Travel Training

Crate training forms a solid base for training your puppy for travel. By getting your pup content and secure in her crate, the crate can be used as a transportation kennel when she is travelling in the car. I suppose in theory a dog that dislikes travel may come to dislike her crate, but in 30-odd years of working with dogs I have never known this occur.

It's Your Decision

The decision to crate train is yours alone, but some form of confinement is necessary, unless of course you are content to allow your puppy to chew anything she finds, because that is what she will do, unless you buy her a Kindle or an IPad, so she can entertain herself.

You can manage her chewing and build short periods of separation into her daily routine by using a secure, dog-proofed room, or you could invest in a puppy pen. (Similar to a child's play pen, but puppy proof.) Due to the size of most rooms and most pens, there is sufficient room for the puppy to piddle and poo to her heart's content, well away from her bed, so this does not have the same toilet-training advantages as the crate.

How to Crate Train Your Puppy

You have prepared your crate and positioned it in a comfortably warm, draught-proof location in your home before your puppy arrives home for the first time.

The crate should be made welcoming, with a nice comfortable bed and ideally a small blanket that has the scent of her Mum and litter mates on it. The crate should be positioned in a location such as the kitchen that has plenty of passing traffic from the family, but which can be closed when puppy is sleeping or is bedded down for the night.

Prior to her arrival and for the first few days, the crate should be regularly baited with treats so your puppy enjoys exploring and sniffing them out. This way she will be happy to go in and out of her crate of her own accord, learning that it is a pleasant place to be through positive experience.

The crate should be furnished with a selection of toys of different materials and textures. These toys should be tied into the crate with string so she can't just go in and take the toys to a different location in the house. A stuffed or frozen Kong is an ideal treat/toy to put in the crate and this will keep her entertained and comforted for lengthy periods, although I am not suggesting that she should be confined for anything other than short periods, except overnight.

The stuffed Kong should be tied into the crate in a low position, so that she has to lie down to chew on it and cannot just take it and do a runner. It must become associated with her crate, making it a nice place to spend time.

An example routine might go something like this:

Your puppy has been toileted in your garden and then brought back into the house. Leave a few minutes to elapse so that she does not make a connection between coming in from the garden and being crated, then your puppy should be gently placed into the crate and as soon as she is in it, she should be introduced to the stuffed/frozen Kong.

When she is in there, close the door of the crate, leave the room and allow her to settle. It is likely that she will not even notice you have left her, because she will be too busy snuffling at the frozen Kong, but if she cries, ignore her. When she is quiet for a few minutes, return, let her out of the crate and take her out into the garden to stretch her legs, play a little game and have a piddle.

If, as is likely, she has fallen asleep in the crate, wait until she wakes and then take her out into the garden to toilet. Slowly build her daytime quiet sessions in the crate in small, regular increments over the next week or so.

As you extend the time ensure your puppy is not hungry, has been toileted and maybe given a walk, the duration of which should be appropriate to her age, before placing her in the crate. Gradually acclimatise your puppy to increasingly longer periods before you have to leave her for real.

Playing In and Out

After a couple of days at home, with regular daytime periods in the crate, and with her going in and out to check for treats, you can start her going into the open crate by letting her see you throw a few really tasty treats into it and allowing her to go in to eat them. At first offer no words of encouragement and certainly no commands, just let her follow the treats.

When her response has become reliable you can throw the treat in as before and after she has entered say, “Go to bed.” You are adding the phrase to the action she has already performed; attaching a label to the action, if you like.

As she becomes more proficient you will give the “Go to bed” instruction at the same time as you throw in the treats and let her follow them in.

Finally, and this may take three days or three weeks to achieve, make a throwing action, whilst giving the "Go to bed" command, but do not release the treat. When she goes in, only then throw in the treat, or better still give her the treat from your hand.

You can practise this several times; she goes in and is rewarded with a treat. After eating the treat, call her out and, if necessary, lure her out, but don't treat her. Then repeat the cycle. Make a throwing action whilst saying "Go to bed," and when she does so reward her with a treat. You can repeat this 5 or 6 times in a minute or two. Repeating it several times, so the routine becomes slick and fun, helps your puppy to learn the lesson. Finish the training session whilst she still wants to work.

As with all training; you can have quick, or you can have good. **Good is better!**

===

Travel Training

Introduction

Travel training covers all types of vehicle that your puppy will travel in during her lifetime. These will commonly be the family car, the bus and the train.

It makes sense to start with the car, which is likely to be her most common form of transport. The process is almost the same for habituating her to bus and train travel, so you will be able to adapt the method to these forms of transport without any major problems. When there are extra considerations to take into account on different types of transport, I have given additional advice.

Car Travel

The first time your puppy was in a car was probably before you got her. It was most likely when she was taken to the veterinary surgery for an examination and her initial inoculations. The second time was when you collected her from the breeder and drove her for 90 minutes to a strange place, without her litter mates and her Mum. Her next journey will be to your veterinary surgery where once again she will be jabbed. We are establishing a bit of a pattern here, aren't we?

Have you ever heard the joke, "What would you do if you broke your arm in three places?"

"I wouldn't go to those three places again!" (Tommy Cooper, master magician and comedy legend.)

Well, your little girl has just had the canine equivalent, all related to car travel, so she is hardly likely to be asking for a Top Gear Box Set in the near future, whilst dreaming of her next car journey. What you need to do is redress the balance and normalise car travel for her.

If your breeder is a good one, your puppy may have already experienced the car in a positive way. With any litter I ever bred the pups were going in the car 3 or 4 times a week from the age of about 4-5 weeks.

Mum was often desperate for a break, so they would all be loaded into the back of the car and driven a few hundred yards to a mate's house, which had a clean, secure garden. Mum and pups were offloaded and given 10 minutes to mooch about in the new venue, before going back home.

By the time they reached 7 to 8 weeks old they were up to 15-minute journeys, initially with Mum and then without. At 8 weeks or so, when they were collected by their new owners, a couple of them were so comfortable in the car they had applied for a provisional licence. All right, that's not true, but they were extremely relaxed in the car.

It is something I have always done as soon as I took possession of a new puppy of my own. Most days a short car journey was undertaken, even if only to go and buy a newspaper. If for some reason it was not possible I would at least put her in the car and run the engine for 10 minutes or so. The effect of this in most cases was to rock the little one to sleep.

When the first vet visit was undertaken, there were so many good experience pennies in the piggy bank that in the unlikely event that her visit was less than pleasant for some reason, taking a couple of pennies out had minimal effect. She had already begun to develop resilience, especially as trips to the vet were also something we were already regularly training for.

As you probably didn't breed your puppy and in all likelihood your breeder never did any vehicle training with the litter, other than that first vet trip, it is up to you to carry out this training.

Keep it Short and Simple

It is easily done and doesn't take a long time in the car. In fact it should initially take a very short time in the car, but with preparation each training session will take about 20 to 30 minutes. As with all things when training your puppy, remember the 6 Ps; Prior Planning Prevents Poor Puppy Performance.

Keep it simple and start making short, daily trips to different locations, which include, but are definitely not limited to, the veterinary surgery. Remember what you are training for. On these trips you are training to familiarise and acclimatise puppy to car travel, so you should have at least half a dozen different destinations planned. When you arrive at some, you will allow puppy out and about, if safe to do so. At others you will simply return home.

Most puppy owners realise the importance of making sure that journeys don't always end in an experience that might be unpleasant, so it is tempting to ensure that every car trip ends with some wonderful, fun experience. In theory this is a good idea, but it can create unforeseen problems.

If each car journey ends in an unpleasant experience then a bad association may be formed. If on the other hand the trip always ends in a thoroughly enjoyable experience then this can lead to over-excitement in the car. I try as much as possible to create a neutral experience, which is linked to neither extreme.

I am often told by people attending my puppy training courses that their puppy loves coming to training and gets really excited in the car when approaching the training school, as they know that they are going to have an enjoyable experience. Owners are often a bit disappointed when I tell them that they should whack their puppy with a stick to redress the balance. No, I don't really say that, I was just checking that you are reading carefully!

But I do try to explain the importance of travel training that has as many neutral outcomes as possible and illustrate how, many years ago, I inadvertently trained a particular response to vehicle travel in my dog, Sophie, which whilst quite endearing could have become problematic.

Sophie was a beautiful German Shepherd. When she was a puppy I was serving in the RAF in Norfolk and I would travel to visit my Mam, Sophie's Nana, in Liverpool, a 200-mile trek.

Sophie would quickly settle in the car and sleep most of the way. Whenever we left a major road and come into a town or village, Sophie would pop up and have a look around, before settling down to sleep again. When we approached Liverpool we had just over a mile from the M57 motorway until we arrived at the house. After leaving the motorway, within about 400 yards Sophie would be up and looking around. As we approached the house she would become progressively more excited at the prospect of seeing her Nana, and would soon be squealing like a pig.

The main clue for Sophie was the presence of speed bumps. The only place she had ever encountered them was in Liverpool, they didn't have them in Norfolk because they upset the horse and carts, so they were the perfect signal to Sophie that she was soon to arrive at Sleepingonthesofaland and she should prepare for an extended period of tummy tickling.

I then ask the puppy owner how often they take their puppy out in the car each week, other than to come to training. If the answer is never, or not very often, I encourage them to make daily, short journeys to new locations, or even just a 10-minute drive before going back home. The idea is to habituate the dog to routine journeys.

If they take their puppy out regularly, I ask if they get excited in the car all the time, or just when they come to training. I encourage them to drive to the training school and then go straight past, thereby dashing puppy's hopes of an hour's worth of fun and a meet-up with her mates. The idea is to repeat this frequently, so that in time puppy's excitement levels due to anticipation are reduced.

I even go as far as telling them to drive into the training area. Get puppy out of the car and take her for a walk down the drive and out onto the lane outside. She can have a walk and a piddle and poo, clean up, then back into the car and home.

I also encourage owners to regularly drive their puppy to different locations for some of their daily walks. The main benefit is to prevent patterns being established that can lead to over-excitement, distress or apprehension when travelling in the car. Neutral experiences of car travel are good, frightening or exciting ones are not.

Travel on public transport and buses is slightly different, but is helped by good car training.

Travelling on a Bus

There are a number of additional things to take into account when travelling by bus.

The first is the proximity of traffic passing the bus stop. If you live in a small rural village, this may not be a great issue, but if you live in an inner-city area on a busy bus route, you should not undertake bus travel until you have habituated your puppy to the traffic on the roads near the bus stop.

In an inner-city area heavy traffic may create a few additional problems. Alternately, the constant presence of such traffic may have ensured that your puppy is already habituated to traffic noise, whereas the arrival of a one-day-a-week bus in a quiet village may be highly unsettling for the rural pup.

Having carried out your preparatory work to acclimatise your puppy to traffic noise and having achieved a nice relaxed attitude in the car, it is time to begin training for bus travel.

You are not yet ready for your first bus journey. First, you will habituate your puppy to the bus stop for a few days.

Ensure puppy has had a piddle and a poo prior to leaving home. Make sure she has not eaten for a couple of hours, reducing the chance of her being sick.

Take some nice, small treats and conduct a short training session at the bus stop, and do this when no bus is expected. Spend 5 minutes training there, before returning home.

Repeat this process for a few days and then perform it when a bus is expected. Ensure you are not too close to the bus stop so the noise of the air brakes is not too loud. Repeat this routine over the next couple of days, gradually getting closer to the arriving bus.

When she is comfortable, repeat the process, but on this day, you will take her onto the bus, either lifting her on if she is small and carrying her whilst on the bus, or letting her get on herself if she is a bit bigger. If she is getting on and off herself please make sure she is big enough, so she does not have to jump and can get on and off without risk of injury.

When on the bus, if she is comfortable let her sit or stand on the floor, on a short lead. If she requires reassurance, you may give it to her quietly and gently, by stroking her or giving her a little cuddle. Make sure it is gentle reassurance, don't go over the top and reinforce her behaviour.

Travel for just a single stop and get off. Remember the noise of the air brakes and the noise of the doors opening may startle your puppy, so give her space and keep her attention on you as you prepare to get off.

When you get off the bus, remember that when a bus pulls away from the stop it is quite noisy, so move away slightly to reduce the amount of noise your puppy hears. Ask the bus driver to give you a few seconds to get clear.

Once the bus has gone on its way, walk home. If the distance between the stops is too great for your puppy then arrange to be picked up by car when you get off. (Do this when you are planning your journey, not when you are in the middle of nowhere, without a mobile phone signal. (Prior Planning etc.)

Another difference when travelling by bus is the number of people you and your puppy will meet at the bus stop and whilst on the bus. If you are regularly carrying out calm, short periods of puppy-to-human socialisation training, this should not present any problems and is likely to be beneficial as it may distract your puppy from the noises and smells of the bus. But be careful not to let her get over-excited.

By the time you begin public transport training, your puppy should be quite comfortable meeting other people, which is discussed later in this section. You may even have begun to train the controlled greeting, which is also covered later in the book. If you haven't yet introduced your puppy to other people, you should do so before taking her on public transport.

Travel by Train

The method for bus travel is almost identical to the method for trains. There are a few additional considerations to take into account.

Train stations tend to be a lot busier and noisier than most bus stops, so this should be taken into account and trained for. You often have passengers running for trains and this is something that may concern a puppy if you haven't carried out much puppy-to-people training.

Beware of luggage trolleys and suitcases on wheels, all of which are likely to be novel experiences for your puppy. A train station isn't just a place to get your puppy acclimatised to train travel, there are lots of other new experiences there for her.

If you are on a more secluded station with smaller trains, please remember that whilst the train you are waiting for will come to a slow halt at the station, the intercity train that doesn't stop at the platform may go hurtling through at 100mph in order to make up for lost time when running late. Unless you are a puppy walker for the British Transport Police, it is unlikely you will need to habituate her to this amount of noise.

Please ensure that you mind the gap when getting her on and off trains, and when she is small I would recommend lifting her on and off in case of mishaps. A bus driver can see you and your puppy clearly, a train driver can't.

Following the advice in these pages should ensure that your puppy is gradually habituated to all forms of transport she may have to deal with during her lifetime, and with EasyJet offering cheap flights it is probably more cost-effective to take your puppy for a quick flight to Iceland than a train journey to Blackpool. (Other short-haul airlines are available, but it is probably best to avoid the one that is likely to levy additional charges for each leg your puppy has!)

Enjoy your travels together.

===

Veterinary Training

When selecting a vet most people simply book their puppy in with the closest veterinary surgery to their home.

I think this is a big mistake. Your puppy's vet is going to be one of the most important people in her life, so you need to ensure that you are happy with what the vet and the surgery have to offer.

Do not be blinded by science and shiny objects. Meet the vet and speak with her, or him. Meet the reception staff and the veterinary nurses. These are the people who will be caring for your puppy during this formative period of her life and hopefully for many years to come.

Most veterinary surgeons and their staff are more than happy to help with acclimatising your puppy to the sights and smells of the veterinary surgery; if the surgery you visit first isn't happy to help with this, then go elsewhere.

One of the biggest problems that pet owners encounter is that many independent veterinary surgeons are now being drawn together into larger veterinary groups. In this way they have more resources.

In my experience more resources mean higher overheads. Higher overheads mean higher charges. So ask about fees. The amount that practices charge, even in the same area, varies widely and whilst cost should not be a primary factor - quality of care should, but unless you have recently won the lottery, the cost of treatment is something most of us have to take into account.

With a large group practice, which vet will care for your puppy? Will you be able to choose? Or will you have to deal with whoever is on duty? In a practice with just a couple of vets, you can get to know the individual veterinary surgeons and your dog can build a relationship with them.

Does this matter? I think it does. You want to establish a long-term relationship between you, your puppy, the veterinary surgeon(s) and surgery staff. At some point you may have to put your puppy's life in the hands of these people and if you are anything like me, you don't want to entrust that responsibility to any Tom, Dick or Ethel.

Puppy's First Visit

Having chosen your veterinary surgery, make arrangements to visit. Make this first visit when your puppy is not receiving treatment. If you are bringing home an 8-week-old puppy she will have received her first inoculations before you collect her. Depending upon the vaccine used you may have a couple of weeks to wait before she can have the second set.

Don't waste this precious time. It is a golden period in her development and it is an ideal opportunity to habituate your puppy to the veterinary surgery. On the first occasion I would recommend arranging the visit just before the surgery opens to the general public. Maybe 10 minutes before the practice opens. Of course your puppy will have to be carried as she can't walk on the ground.

Why should you go before it opens, rather than after it closes?

Well, after the surgery closes, the place has been visited by dogs that have been, in all likelihood, in a state of stress. Dogs in fear produce all sorts of smells. Some may have been sick, some may have piddled through fear. They might have even pooed.

Whilst the staff will undoubtedly have cleared any mess as quickly as possible, the smells will linger and your puppy will detect these smells and it will affect her. If a dog is sensitive enough to detect cancer, or the onset of an epileptic fit, they can certainly detect when a premises has been occupied by animals under stress.

How would you feel, if whilst waiting for your first trip to the dentist, you heard screams coming from within, followed by patients exiting in tears? Full of confidence? I think not!

Now, later on when you visit the vet you may encounter other animals in distress, but by that time you will have ensured your puppy's resilience and have lots of pennies in the piggy bank.

The Importance of Early Vaccination

The best period to habituate and socialise your puppy is very short, sometimes estimated to be as short as the 16th week of her life. If you collect puppy at 8 weeks, only 8 weeks remain. If the vet you select uses a different type of vaccine and you have to start the course again this could eat up another 4 weeks of this precious time, and that is time you can ill afford to squander.

Check that the vaccine which your puppy has been started with is effective in your area. If it is, select a vet that uses this vaccine, even if you only use that practice for the inoculations and your chosen vet for the rest of her care.

I had to do this with baby Alice. All it meant was that I had to do a little pre-treatment vet training at two different surgeries, but as I was habituating her to as much stuff as possible during this period, it didn't present a great problem. In fact it presented many additional opportunities, meeting more people, visiting different locations and making short journeys travelling in the car. Neither veterinary surgeon had an issue with my decision and baby Alice was perfectly happy visiting the vet - and still is.

===

Separation Training

Home Alone

One of the most important lessons you can teach your puppy is to spend time alone. Having collected your new puppy you will want to settle her in to her new life and with her new family as quickly as possible.

Have you taken time off work to settle the little lady in? You have? Surprisingly this might be a problem.

I strongly recommend getting your puppy into her new routine as soon as possible. Bear in mind that if you are at work for eight hours a day then you should not have a puppy; the length of time when your puppy is left alone should certainly be no more than 4 hours a day.

In the early stages even four hours is too long, so you should have arranged a neighbour, relative, or puppy walker to come in after a couple of hours and take puppy out for a piddle and a poo, a short walk (if allowed out), or a period of play and companionship, before settling her down again and leaving her to await your return. Always remember that anyone helping out should be following your comprehensive written instructions to ensure continuity in all aspects of her care and education.

One of the most distressing issues that can affect owner and dog alike is distress experienced by your puppy during periods of separation and this often begins shortly after bringing your puppy home. One of the best ways to avoid the problem developing is to start training puppy to be "Home Alone" right from the outset.

This must be done even if one member of the household is usually going to be at home every day. Unless you plan taking your puppy with you everywhere you go, including trips to the bathroom, then this is the time to teach your puppy it is OK to be alone sometimes.

In the section where I advise on crate training the siting of the crate is important, i.e. a high-traffic area. This enables puppy to see comings and goings right from the start of her time with you.

Another good idea is to invest in a puppy pen, similar to a child's play pen, only more robust, or a couple of child gates. Child gates can usually be purchased second-hand from a local charity shop and puppy pens off t'interweb.

Making use of the crate is great for toilet training when you can't have your beady eyes on your puppy, the other two items are great for ensuring that whilst your puppy can see you moving around the house, she cannot be under your feet all of the time.

Start Small

Training to be home alone starts with simply putting a few feet of distance between you and your puppy. And the best way to start is by leaving your puppy on the other side of the child gate whilst you go and make a cup of tea, or nip upstairs to the bathroom.

When going out of sight, don't make a song and dance of it. It is a natural occurrence. Accustom your puppy to it. Do not treat your puppy like some people use Facebook, where they announce everything they do, or plan to do, to their Facebook friends. Don't be tempted to announce to your puppy that you are going upstairs for a wee, just let your Facebook friends know you are going to have one and then update them once you have finished, but your puppy doesn't need to know.

She just needs to know that you come and go. Sometimes she can see you, sometimes she can't, but you are always coming back, so there is absolutely no need for her to worry. Coming and going is a natural process. It's not a big deal…unless you turn it into one.

Start with leaving the room for a few seconds to click on the kettle, before returning almost immediately. Build it gradually to the length of time sufficient to make a cup of tea. Build it to the time required to go out into the garden for a couple of minutes. Within a week your puppy should be quite comfortable with short absences.

Separation at Meal Time

For longer absences use the crate. Remember that separation from you might mean that you are still visible, from another room, or even just a few feet away in the same room.

A good way to put this into practice and make effective use of her crate or puppy pen is to train for separation during family mealtimes.

Forget the drivel that was pumped out a few years ago about demonstrating and reinforcing your status as "Pack Leader" by eating first. What a load of nonsense. Anyone believing that guff has obviously never watched any wildlife documentaries featuring the many diverse species including wild dogs that regurgitate their food to their cubs.

Now, I know that in order to regurgitate the food, the parent must have consumed it first, but seeing as Mum or Dad's meal was taken from the bum end of a wildebeest 3 miles away, whilst the cubs were in their den, I don't know how the cubs would have got wind of it. As far as they are concerned they're getting first dibs.

See how much peace you get when your puppy, who hasn't eaten for 4 hours, sits barking when she smells what you are all having for tea. (I know some of you posh folk out there will refer to the evening meal as dinner, but you are wrong, dinner is what you have at lunchtime!)

Instead, have the children come home from school and allow for some playtime with puppy. After this play is done allow puppy to have a piddle and a poo if required, then settle puppy down and relax for at least 30 minutes before feeding. Whilst most people understand that a puppy should not have vigorous exercise after feeding, it is not good practice to give vigorous exercise and play before feeding.

Whilst your puppy is relaxing and settling down you can prepare her meal, then feed her. After feeding take her out to the toilet area, she will almost certainly have a piddle, and, if she didn't do so after the earlier play session, a poo. Reward the desired behaviour and then settle her in her crate, or in her puppy pen, which should be equipped with a bed and a secured, stuffed/frozen Kong and let the rest of the family enjoy their meal in peace. Puppy may watch from a distance, but in all likelihood she will be fast asleep by this point.

This is a good routine to develop because it takes in a number of training for life skills; playing with the kids, toileting and relaxing in her own company, whilst not learning to sit under the table waiting for a chip to drop from the end of the youngest nipper's fork, and not learning to scrounge food.

Of course, at first, if your puppy hasn't fallen asleep she may cry or bark. Please don't acknowledge this. You have already ensured that she has been exercised, toileted and fed, so you know that her needs have been well taken care of. Do not reinforce her attempts to gain your attention. This applies to all the adults of the family and to all the children as well. And remember, telling her to "Shut Up!" may well be seen as rewarding in the mind of your puppy. After all, she managed to get your attention, didn't she?

If she persists, you should outlast her, but think of ways that you can make it easier for her to get it right tomorrow. Maybe allow more time for her to settle, or alternately put some additional distractions in her crate or pen to occupy her attention.

Separation at Bedtime

What about bedtime? Where should your puppy sleep? If you have read the section on crate training, you will know it should be a draught-free, relatively warm location, in a high-traffic area, such as the kitchen.

Do not be tempted to take your puppy into the bedroom unless you are prepared to do this for the next 15 years, or go through a massive re-training programme in a year's time, when the 10lb ball of fluff that is baby Alice weighs in at 70lbs and has the leg strength of a mule, sufficient when stretching to dump you and your other half on the bedroom floor. No, don't be tempted. Start as you mean to go on.

Apart from the lack of duvet space, another reason for your puppy sleeping downstairs, alone, is that it also acclimatises your puppy to being apart from you for 7 hours or so. If she can do this at night, she is better able to cope with shorter periods of absence during the day.

Train For When You May Need It

What if you are one of those lucky people who get to work from home? Or are fortunate enough to be able to take your dog to work with you? Once again, prepare your puppy for life. You have no idea when this might change, so build short periods of separation into her life in order to acclimatise her and proof her against future change.

My last tour of duty in the RAF was as Senior Instructor at the Joint Service Dog School, Defence Animal Centre. I would commute to my unit on Monday morning and return home on Friday evening. As I had taken on a Malinois puppy, Jimmy, he accompanied me to my unit.

Much of my work was office-based and Jimmy would come with me to the office. I used to walk him from my accommodation to my office each morning, which took about 15 minutes and he would always have a piddle and a poo on his way to work.

In my office he would sleep on a small settee, and whilst small he would be crated when I had to leave the office. Once his toilet training routine had been established, which was a very quick process, and he had passed through the chewing phase, which wasn't so quick, he would lounge about in my office, with a child gate keeping him in.

He developed his own scheme for amusing himself. He would sit at the child gate with his Kong on a rope in his mouth, looking at anyone who was passing by and who had stopped to talk to him, with a sort of "Please play with me" expression. Many would stop and have a short game of tug with Jimmy for a couple of minutes before moving on.

As he grew, he became extremely strong and the game of tug was fraught with danger for the unwary. I posted a big sign on my door, which read; **"Warning! Please Don't Play Tug With Jimmy!"**

I lost count of the number of meetings with my OC that were interrupted by a noise resembling a train crash as Jimmy enticed someone into a game, before yanking his victim over the top of, or right through, the child gate. It was a skill that would help build his strength and serve him well as you can see below!

"Taste 'im, Son!" Jimmy in action BPSCA Service Dog Trial 2014 (D. Hibbert)

The main point of the story is that for at least part of each 24-hour period that we were living and working together, Jimmy had to adapt and acclimatise to me being absent and cope with a bit of solitude.

It is something I have done with all my dogs and I have never had a dog with any form of separation anxiety; a successful combination of nature and nurture.

Just a final note on this subject. As well as getting your puppy acclimatised to being separated from her human family, please remember to acclimatise her to periods of absence from any other dogs, or other pets, in the family. I have worked with more than a few dogs over the years who were unable to cope when the other dog in the family had died. So, if your home is a multi-dog household, please ensure that you spend one-to-one time with each dog individually, as well as periods together as a group, and that you train your older dog and your new puppy for periods apart as well as time together.

====

Life is a Series of Introductions

Some of the most important and formative events in your puppy's development are the occasions when she encounters something or someone for the first time.

Now we will consider the best way to see her through these events and turn our attention to a range of introductions.

We have already looked at introductions to people at the veterinary surgery, but before the vet visit has occurred, your puppy will almost certainly have already increased her circle of acquaintances.

It is likely that within hours of arriving at her new home your puppy will be faced with a barrage of new people and, if you have pets, new species of animal, that she has never come across before.

This can be overwhelming for your puppy, but by prior planning and managing each scenario carefully you can ensure each new introduction is a happy, safe and enjoyable experience for all involved, especially her.

===

Introducing Your Puppy to Children

If you have young children in the family home, or you have relatives who visit with their children, you obviously want to make sure that your puppy is childproof. Please read the following statement carefully, and repeat it as many times as necessary to make sure it penetrates and you understand it.

"Puppies and children should treat each other as playmates, not playthings."

As the adult in the family you have many responsibilities. You are now responsible for your puppy as well. Her Mum will not take responsibility. She passed that role to you when you took her puppy home with you.

You should have considered this responsibility before deciding if a puppy was the right choice for you and your family. If you did not, and you now have a puppy and child together, you must accept this responsibility without delay. If you are unable to accept this responsibility I urge you to "bite the bullet" and make the difficult decision, sooner rather than later, to put your child in the hands of a reputable adoption agency!

Emily and Charlotte with Jimmy, Tilly, Daisy May and young Alice

Puppies and children **do** mix, and the relationship between a child and a puppy who grow up together is one of the most valuable and long-lasting relationships both will ever experience. I don't know anyone who was brought up in childhood with a dog, who didn't benefit from the experience and look back on it as one of their life's most important relationships.

In this day and age, when so many people are reluctant to accept responsibility for just about anything, blaming any mishap on the NHS, police, government, or the Dagenham Girl Pipers, know this one thing; Defra will not be sending a representative around to your house to manage this situation for you. Shaping the relationship between your puppy and your children, and everyone else's children for that matter, is **your** responsibility.

It is your responsibility to teach them how to play together.

It is your responsibility to teach them the rules of play.

It is your responsibility to teach them mutual respect.

And it is your responsibility to supervise all contact between them until the respectful relationship between them is firmly established and beyond.

Your new puppy will probably have never seen a toddler or youngster before, unless you have been fortunate enough to choose a breeder whose home circumstances were similar to your own. If that was the case and the breeder was smart, your puppy will have had a few weeks of familiarisation with children. If, as is likely your puppy has never met a munchkin, then it is up to you to familiarise both species to each other.

As stated elsewhere in this book, during the visit to select your puppy from the litter you should not take your children with you, selecting the puppy being a job for adults. I would also advise against having young children accompany you to collect your puppy and bring her home in the car. That first journey is likely to be quite stressful for the puppy so having a couple of sprogs on the back seat wrestling over her probably isn't going to add to the experience.

The first meeting between sprog and dog should be after your puppy has arrived in her new home and had a few hours to settle in.

Dress Rehearsal

My **Top Tip** to ensure this important event passes off successfully for all concerned is to carry out a full-scale rehearsal a few days before the big day.

Most children have a large selection of cuddly toys. If yours don't, what sort of parent are you? You should hang your head in shame. Only joking.

Single Sprog Rehearsal

Use one such cuddly toy to rehearse this first meeting. If you have one child, let's call him Tarquin, have young Tarquin take a seat on the sofa. When he is settled, you enter the room carrying the stuffed Roger Rabbit and take a seat next to him on the sofa.

Allow Tarquin to stroke Roger gently for a couple of minutes, then get up and carry Roger out of the room. Repeat this a few times, making adjustments if required, so that you all know exactly what you are going to do at the first real meeting.

Rehearsal in the Duel-Sprog Household

If you have more than one child, you should practise this with both of them on the sofa, and a gap in the middle where you should go and sit after entering with Roger Rabbit. Allow each child to stroke Roger in turn, first young Tarquin and then young Guinevere, or vice versa.

If the rehearsals go well, then that is how you should carry out the first introduction. But if you are uncertain that they will be able to contain their excitement, then to avoid the risk of a squabble breaking out with your puppy in the middle of it, you must decide to do it with one child at a time. Multiple children are prone to squabbling because one is getting more strokes of the puppy than the other and in the ensuing bedlam your puppy may become distressed.

No plan is fool-proof and any soldier will tell you that even the best plans rarely survive the first contact with the enemy. But practising the first meeting with Roger Rabbit as a stunt double greatly improves your chances of success.

Pre-meeting Preparation

If, as I recommend, you have carefully planned events so that you collect your puppy in the morning, she will have had most of the day to acclimatise to her new surroundings before the nippers arrive home from school, or are returned home by the person who was caring for them whilst you collected your puppy.

This careful planning has given you the opportunity to let your puppy take in her new surroundings. She has found her piddling patch in the secure garden you have carefully prepared. She has enjoyed her first meal with you, nipped out for a poo and enjoyed a nice post-poo nap, in her cosy bed that has been cunningly disguised as a crate. She is now fully prepared for the potential bedlam looming on the horizon.

First Meeting

The first meetings should be quiet and controlled and adults should outnumber children so one can hold puppy and each child can be supervised by an adult, or older, calmer, more responsible child.

As per your rehearsals you will all be seated on the sofa, you have your puppy on your lap and your sprog(s) next to you. Keep puppy calm and relaxed and allow your child to gently stroke her for a few minutes, but not much longer. If you have more than one child, each takes a turn at this. Keep the first meeting brief. It can be repeated in the same manner several times before bedtime.

So, the great day has arrived and has passed off pretty successfully.

You collected your puppy and she has made her first car journey with you. She has become acquainted with her new home. She has been introduced to her crate and her bed in it. She has been feeding well. She has had several naps. She has been taken out to the toilet on several occasions and been rewarded for piddling and pooing outside. And you have carried out the first introduction with your children successfully.

Well done, you have achieved top marks and have successfully managed the major events of your puppy's first day in her new family.

Practise, Practise, Practise

Over the next few days you must practise all of these routines over and over again.

Consolidate the first successful contact between puppy and children over the next couple of days in the same manner.

When this has gone well for a few days, repeat the greeting routine, but whilst sat on the floor, with your child on your lap. Allow your puppy the freedom to approach and be gently stroked. Do not encourage her to climb up, but instead ensure that hands go down to her and stroke her. If she is calm and relaxed you may pick her up and put her on your child's lap to be gently stroked for a few minutes.

Please remember to dress your child in thick jogging bottoms and a long-sleeved top or something similar. We don't want any yelling, should baby Alice inadvertently scratch young Tarquin.

Children and puppy toilet training **do not** mix. When you are taking puppy through her regular trips to the garden to piddle and poo, young Tarquin isn't invited. He may be upset, but this is just one of the first of many disappointing events he will experience in life. Distractions during this training will set your puppy's toilet training back, and he is likely to be such a distraction. Just explain this to him and enlist his cooperation...or tell him to "Man Up!"

You will also note that the initial contact has taken place with young Tarquin seated, and for good reason. It is likely that puppy will try to climb up legs initially; we don't want an impromptu rendition of Riverdance by your favourite human child to either injure baby Alice or excite her enough to join in the performance.

Gradually allow more natural interactions between dog and sprog to occur and develop over the following days and weeks. All such contact must be supervised and managed. The key to successful interaction is calmness. Calm, Calm, Calm, Calm.

Older Children

With older children, as the relationship between child and puppy develops you should consider encouraging young Tarquin and Guinevere to take part in the online safety programme set up by The Kennel Club. The KC Safe and Sound programme for children who are a bit older involves leaflets on dog and child safety and there is an interactive online quiz that your child can do.

The programme allows them to print out a certificate in their own name for successfully passing the test. This may be the first of many certificates your child and puppy earn, should they go through the Kennel Club Good Citizen Scheme together.

Having your children help to train your puppy will help cement their relationship and provide your nippers with a sense of pride in their achievement.

Iona (10) and Saskia (1¼)

===

Meeting Dogs

Introduction

Apart from your relationship with you and your family this is probably the most important aspect of your puppy's life training. In my opinion it is even more important than her relationship with other humans. It is also the area in which most dogs and their owners struggle to cope. In my behavioural practice 75% of all my behaviour modification cases are primarily concerned with this issue, which can make life so difficult.

It makes every walk a stressful experience for dog and owner alike, often resulting in the dog not being exercised, and all the knock-on issues that result from this and, in the worst cases, the dog being re-homed.

With so many unwanted dogs in rescue centres, any dog that has issues with other dogs is extremely difficult to re-home.

Once the problem has become established it is more difficult to remedy than dog-to-human aggression, because whilst you are working with a dog-to-human case the owner rarely tells me of setbacks caused by a stray human running across the park at them in the way a loose, uncontrolled, albeit friendly dog might do.

Time to bore you again. **Prevention is better than cure**.

Being social with her own kind is part of her nature. Whilst you have taken her into your home and become her new family, you have a responsibility to ensure that you allow her to develop a healthy, comfortable relationship with her own species.

If you have selected a puppy of sound character and temperament by following my advice, and you provide her with the right kind of opportunity to meet and interact with her own kind and keep this process going until she reaches adulthood, you are likely to help her grow into a happy, social, well-balanced young lady who can enjoy life to the full at your side.

How to Meet Other Dogs

There are a number of ways you can give your puppy opportunities to be social with other dogs.

Baby Alice aged 6 months, meeting new friends at the beach. (Ms Nicholas)

Remember that other dogs encompass puppies, adolescents, adults and senior dogs. It also covers all breeds. No other animal on the planet has so many variations in the same species. This can be problematic for a puppy who only mixes with other dogs of her own breed, or size or colour. Variety is the spice of life and in this case it is essential for a happy life.

The Best Environment?

There is a lot of organised stuff out there; puppy parties, puppy classes, dog walking groups, doggy day care, doggy adventures and just about doggy everything else. Some of these are helpful and some, in my opinion, are likely to be absolutely disastrous for your puppy's development.

Your Local Dog Owner

In your street there will be a number of other dog owners who have nice, friendly, calm dogs. Go and speak with them and ask if you can accompany them on their walks to see how their dog interacts with others in the area. Be careful! This approach often requires that you make friends with some of your neighbours, something many people have problems with, but here's the truth of the matter - If you struggle to interact with people, your puppy will struggle to interact with their dogs. Remember one of the benefits of dog ownership highlighted in Part 1 was increased human-to-human social interaction. If you don't like people, perhaps you should consider getting a hamster!

On your first walk, with a few local dog owners, don't take your puppy. In fact you may not even have brought her home yet. Accompany them and get them to introduce you to other dog owners. This way you will have a ready-made socialisation network set up. Prior Planning, etc.

As soon as your puppy has completed her inoculations you will be able to take your place on these walks. Everything will be strange to her and perhaps a bit scary, but it won't be for you, because you have done a bit of reconnaissance, and time spent on recce is seldom wasted.

You already know that little Rex the Jack Russell is very calm and accepts other dogs, large and small, adult and puppy equally well.

You know Dave the Staffy is a bit excitable at the first greeting, but then settles well and walks nicely with all the other dogs.

You know that Alfie the Lurcher is a very big, but calm, gentle, fella who will introduce himself politely to your puppy.

You know Elsie the Springer is nervous and may not be able to deal with an excitable puppy, so don't put her in an uncomfortable position, until your puppy has learned to be calm around other dogs. In this instance you and your puppy will be returning a kindness by helping Elsie increase her circle of doggy friends in due course.

What about Organised Events?

Puppy Parties

I struggle to comprehend the thinking behind puppy parties and having attended quite a few, never with a dog of my own I hasten to add, I have yet to attend one that was beneficial to the puppies in attendance in any way, shape or form.

They are commonly run at the local veterinary surgery, a venue that is generally far too small to allow the pups involved to work in a space that they find comfortable. They offer little opportunity for the person running them to take stock of the individual character of each puppy attending, which is essential in order to ensure that a timid puppy is not overwhelmed, and the big bruiser doesn't learn that it is easy to pin the little pup's head to the floor with one swipe of his paw.

I am of course assuming that the person running the puppy party is capable of making such an assessment. Seldom are puppy parties run by a qualified trainer. They are usually run by a nurse, receptionist, or someone else from the practice.

With those that are run by a trainer, just bin the puppy party and get in touch with the trainer directly to enquire about their training classes. If they don't do classes, ask yourself why?

With the others; simply avoid them. Most veterinary staff are outstandingly professional in their jobs, but put simply, their job is not to train or develop puppies, just like mine isn't to scrub up and assist when your dog is undergoing surgery.

Puppy Training Classes

Selecting a puppy training class is a good idea. In this environment the primary function should be to teach your puppy to give you her attention during the classes and involve several short periods of social interaction with 1 or 2 different puppies each week, until your puppy is happy and confident with the whole group. That does not mean the whole group at once, all together in a big bundle.

In my classes we start with a short walk down the drive, to allow the pups to meet whilst exploring the area and take the opportunity for a piddle and a poo before training.

I discourage stationary greetings around the car park, which is difficult sometimes as owners seem to love standing there to chat, usually oblivious to the fact that their puppies are standing on their hind legs, pawing at each other and barking excitedly. (If you don't want your dog to do it, don't train it!)

I often have to warn owners against doing this several times before it gets through to them, but poking them with a long stick or spraying them with a hosepipe often helps to get them moving.

When the class starts all owners are encouraged to position themselves between 2 different puppies each week.

After each short period of training another walk is taken, with the pups allowed to walk alongside each other and interact, without getting over-excited.

In the course of each training session there are 2 or 3 walking breaks, plus the arrival and departure walk. Plenty of opportunities to practise polite greetings and calm interaction with their new pals.

When we get 2 puppies that simply get each other too wound up they are not permitted to interact until they have learned how to meet with calmer pups in the group who can assist them in the learning process.

Same Breed Dog Walking Groups

One of the things that have sprung up recently, certainly in my area, are breed walking clubs. Cannock Chase and the Wrekin have a number of such groups that meet up once a month or so for social walks with their fellow Dachshund/Golden Retriever/Pointer owners.

Are these a good idea for socialising your dog? In my opinion they are, but with some reservations. They are generally more suitable for the older pup and the adult dog. Be mindful about the distance these walks cover and ensure you do not allow your puppy to overdo it.

But it's the same as everything in life. It can be beneficial or not, depending upon how you use it. It is good if you use the groups to enhance your puppy's social circle with dogs of her own breed, but you must remember to make sure that you don't forget to socialise your pup with other breeds.

They should not be an excuse to let your puppy learn how to run riot in the company of other dogs. The walk should be controlled and should involve some time with your puppy and indeed all the other dogs walking with their owners on the lead, not just marauding through the woods, or across the common.

If you do get involved with a good group that meets your needs and those of your puppy, treat each of these meets as a training opportunity, not just an exercise opportunity.

Doggy Day Care

The reason I am discussing this under the "Meeting Other Dogs" heading is that a puppy or dog being cared for in doggy day care spends far more time in the company of other dogs than most dogs. The proprietors of a doggy day care should not be handed the responsibility for developing your puppy and her relationships.

If you need to employ doggy day care with your puppy because you are out at work all day or for long periods, why did you consider getting a puppy, or even an older dog in the first place?

Doggy day care may be a solution for occasional absences, but if your dog is going in every day, is she still your dog? She spends most of her time with other people and other dogs. Perhaps you have just become a sort of Travelodge for her to kip down after a long day playing with her gang. Some day cares also offer training, which is great...if you want your puppy to be obedient to someone else.

If you must be absent, please make an arrangement with a friend, relative, or a reliable neighbour who will visit your puppy, allow her to go to the toilet, spend some quality time with her and take her for a controlled walk, implementing all the things that you have learned in your puppy training class and have demonstrated to your friend, relative, or neighbour. If, like me, you have no friends, hire a reliable, recommended dog walker who will give your puppy individual attention.

In my classes I am more than happy for a neighbour or relative who will share the care of the puppy to come to the classes with the owner, watch the training and if appropriate have a practise. (At that point I normally ask the owner to retreat back to the car, so as not to put unnecessary pressure on a puppy or risk confusing her by not having her know who she should be paying attention to.)

Multi-Dog Households

Just because you already have a couple of older dogs please don't feel there is no need for additional socialisation, because your dog is already being socialised. She is not. She is merely fitting into her own little pack and if anything, she is becoming more isolated from others of her species.

Take her walking with your older dogs along with other dogs from the neighbourhood, but also take her for walks with neighbours' dogs on her own. She has to learn she is an individual, capable of standing on her own 4 paws, coping alone with the stresses of life, not just operate under the safety umbrella provided by her older doggy family.

Don't Overdo It

Do not allow your puppy the complete freedom to run off and play with all her doggy pals. If you allow her to learn that other dogs are the most exciting thing in the world, you will always struggle to get her attention in the presence of the most exciting thing she knows.

Everything should be in moderation and when the excitement gets too much for her, return her to the lead, allow a period of calm to return and make a mental note not to let things get to that stage again. You are the adult and, just as when dealing with your human sprogs, early intervention can often prevent bedlam.

A calm, friendly, older dog can be your best training partner. An excitable, manic, or aggressive older dog is your worst nightmare.

Don't Permit Frustration to Build

The reason I discourage owners standing and chatting with their puppies on my car park is that it invariably builds excitement, and as the pups are being restrained on a lead, this in turn results in frustration.

Keeping the dogs in motion and walking them together generally prevents this happening in the early stages of training them to be social with their fellow pups. Nose-to-nose greetings with puppies on a tight lead should be avoided at all costs.

Contact with other dogs should neither be too much, nor too little. And the right amount of contact and the type of contact will depend upon your individual puppy and her personality.

Too much unrestricted access to play with other pups and dogs will lead to too much excitement and an expectation of fun with every dog encountered. Too little may lead to frustration. Get to know your puppy and get the balance right.

Fearful Puppies

Please don't force your puppy into contact with other dogs until she is ready for it. If she is timid, or a little fearful, always give her the opportunity to move away and take the pressure off herself. Also make sure you explain things to the other owner, so they don't allow their dog to pursue yours when she moves away to relieve any anxiety she might be feeling. If we teach her that slowly moving away from the scary thing is permitted, it becomes a less scary thing.

Holding her in position when she is afraid will either terrify her, or cause her to respond aggressively, in order to make the scary dog move away. If she learns that taking an aggressive approach is the way to deal with such situations, she will repeat it. Puppies will do what works. Don't provide her with the opportunity to learn the undesirable stuff.

Your dog trainer, who you will have carefully selected, will be able to advise you on how to prevent aggression developing and build good dog-to-dog relationships during your initial training classes. If they can't, go to a better trainer.

Use It or Lose It

Socialising your puppy with other dogs is an ongoing process that should continue through adolescence and throughout her adult life. Like any other form of training if it isn't practised it will become weak and may break down at some point in the future.

===

Meeting New People

Meeting new people is an exciting time for your puppy. Your aim is to make it less exciting. A task that is often easier said than done. A first encounter should be a nice experience, but not an exciting one. Achieving this depends greatly upon the cooperation of the people she meets.

In the early days you have an ideal opportunity to set a really good pattern of the kind of controlled greeting, which, if made sufficiently rewarding for her, will ensure that she is keen to repeat the pattern.

Visitors to Your Home

Visitors to your home are the first people outside your immediate family who you will get to practise controlled greetings with. In the first couple of weeks your puppy will be restricted to visitors to your home, people who you meet on your visits to the vet and other places that are "clean", so a good pattern can be established before she is going to be walked in the presence of the wider public.

Unless you have removed your front door for some reason, you control access to your home. This being the case, you can set up regular meetings with visitors, whom, you can brief in advance on how they should greet puppy and allow puppy to greet them, rather than some random "Herbert" who you are going to encounter once your puppy is being walked in the big wide world.

Practise a Greeting Routine

Before carrying out a greeting with a friend or neighbour, practise the routine with members of your family. In this way you can establish the pattern with people she already knows, so the only thing new is the person she is greeting, as opposed to the person and the routine.

A Simple Routine

Place a few treats in a small plastic tub at your front door, which visitors can take out and carry when they arrive at the door. Before the practice visit begins, take a few treats and place them in your treat bag and attach it to your belt, or have it easily accessible in your pocket. Treat bag is best.

Have your puppy on a light lead or houseline and have the family member acting in the role of "visitor" ring the bell. In response, walk your puppy to the front door. Take a few treats from the treat bag and hold them in your left hand so that as you are walking her towards the door, she is not going to be concerned about where she is going. She will be more interested in what you have for her, rather than rushing to the door. On the way to the door, stop once or twice and reward her at nose level from your left hand.

When you open the door, if she is focused on you, rather than the visitor, then reward her. It isn't the worst thing in the world for her to be quite indifferent to visitors!

If she is interested in the "visitor" and she approaches her, they may reward her with a small treat delivered to her at nose level before they stand upright again. At this point you should say her name gently, but clearly, and when she looks to you, do the same; reward her at nose level.

Move back into the house and continue with the visit. If seated, have puppy next to you and reward her for sitting or standing calmly at your side.

After a minute or 2 take her over to the "visitor", still on the lead, and once again the visitor may offer her a small treat from her left hand at nose level. Once this is done, return with her to your seat and reward her for switching her attention back to you. Repeat this a few times, before ending the visit.

The visit has been really calm, quite boring really, with very little interaction by voice or hands between your puppy and the "visitor". She now thinks that visitors are a bit boring.

Repeat this routine a few times each day, with different family members, before your first session with a real visitor.

The Real Visit

Arrange this with a trusted friend or neighbour whom you can brief properly in advance. It might be a good idea to have filmed one of your practice sessions on your phone so you can show them how it is done, rather than just explaining.

Arrange the first few real visits around her daily routine, so a good time would be in the couple of hours after she has been fed and rested.

By this point your puppy should be used to having a lead fitted when she walks around your garden. Take her into your garden and let her have a mooch about, a sniff and a piddle. Give your neighbour a call and invite her round as previously arranged.

When the doorbell rings go to the door with your puppy on the lead, and carry out the same routine you have already practised many times with a family member acting as a stunt double.

Keep everything exactly the same. The only change is the person making the visit.

If for some reason your puppy is reluctant to approach the strange person, then don't force matters. A large, unknown adult towering over her can be quite a scary experience for a puppy. If she doesn't want to approach the visitor, go into the living room and have your visitor sit.

At this point see if puppy wishes to approach without encouragement, if she does, then carry on as previously rehearsed. If not, go over and sit next to the visitor and it is likely that your puppy will go with you.

If she does you should treat her and then allow the visitor to do the same. All the time at nose level and with all 4 paws on the ground.

If puppy is reluctant to greet your visitor, just relax. Don't force it. Give your puppy space if she needs it. Taking the process gently will get a result far more quickly than trying to force her to do something before she is comfortable. Take your time and allow your puppy to learn and become confident when meeting new people in her own good time.

All 4 Paws

The main rule to follow is the all 4 paws on the ground rule. This is why I have an issue with teaching a puppy to give you her paw. Once you have taught her this it isn't much of a stretch for her to put up 2 paws, and before long, about 3 minutes in fact, she will be standing on her hind legs.

Teaching to give a paw can be quite endearing, but can become a bit of a pain and quite scratchy when she is a puppy and has learned that giving the paw is a good way to gain your attention. It becomes a nightmare when she weighs in at 75lb and is tall enough to shove her tongue in your mouth.

As with everything else, if you don't want her to do it when she is big, don't let her practise it when she is little.

Meeting People Outdoors

The first person is most likely going to be a vet nurse. Go through a similar routine as you did in your own home. Obviously you have to go to the surgery first, but ensure that you and the vet nurse are equipped with some nice treats.

Make sure you have agreed the session with the nurse first and briefed her about her role.

If you are approaching the nurse, have her seated, and as your puppy slowly approaches, she may treat your puppy from her left hand at nose height. If this goes well, walk out of the room, return a few seconds later and repeat the process. Try to do about 10 such meet and greets in a 5-minute session.

If you cannot do this routine for any reason, always ensure you take your puppy to meet the nurse, rather than have the nurse bear down on your little puppy.

Repeat this experience over a few days and try to use a different vet nurse on each visit. Ensure that if you use a different nurse, you brief them correctly.

Meetings in the Street

Manage these initial encounters carefully and at your puppy's own pace. Have a few treats available that you can pass to anyone she might approach and explain to them how she has been learning to greet people. If you get the impression that the person you are speaking to is a bit of a muppet, make your excuses and move on to the first available non-muppet to practise the first few all-important street greetings.

If you are getting the hang of this training caper, your first few "street" encounters will have been pre-arranged with a well-briefed stunt stranger! (Prior planning and all that.)

Don't let the stranger maul her head, or tower over her. Patting an unknown dog's head is a bit rude and can be intimidating, not just to puppies but to all dogs. It's a bit like a stranger walking up to you and feeling your bum at the bus stop. Not something generally encouraged as far as I am aware.

Don't allow people to encourage her to jump up, or to over-excite her. Encounters with strangers in any location should be calm, relaxed and well-managed.

Set the pattern for her life. Since she may become a big, powerful young lady, you need to ensure she is a big, powerful, **well-mannered** young lady.

It used to be said: "Manners maketh the man." Well the same goes for puppies. "Manners most certainly maketh the pup."

Variety is the Spice of Life

You must remember that people are quite varied in appearance. Not as varied as the many breeds of dogs she will meet during her lifetime, but we are not all the same.

Big people and short people are different to your puppy. Men and women are different. Black people and white people appear different. Children are different from all of the above.

What about clothing and other accessories? As I am somewhat lacking in the fashion department I include carrier bags and umbrellas in the category of accessories.

Your puppy needs to be introduced to all those different people described above, and also to those in long coats, long skirts, in hats, carrying rucksacks, handbags, man bags (Surely, they are just handbags for blokes!) and umbrellas.

Remember, if it's summer your puppy may not see many umbrellas in real life, although in the UK there is always a reasonable prospect even in August. It is your job to fill in the gaps. You don't want her to have her first experience at 8 months old when you could have been getting her used to them yourself for several months already.

A relaxed, confident puppy will grow into an experienced, relaxed, confident dog, as long as you use it and don't lose it.

===

Meeting the Family Cat

The first non-human and non-canine encounter your puppy is likely to experience is a meeting with a cat.

Cats and dogs do not need to fight like cat and dog and over the last 40-odd years, for most of that period my family has had multiple dogs and multiple cats without any problems. But as with everything else, it takes a bit of thought, care and structured practice to create a good relationship between them all.

In the vast majority of cases a dog's desire to chase a cat is because the dog's owner has encouraged it to do so. The stupidity of some people never ceases to amaze me, but as they say; "The problem with common sense is, it's not that common."

Introducing Your Puppy to Your Cat

You will note that I say introducing your puppy to **your** cat, rather than the neighbourhood cats. This is because the latter are notoriously reluctant to co-operate, unless of course you live in Albrighton, where the big, black moggy who lives on the high street opposite the bank sprawls out on the pavement every sunny day, forcing pedestrians and dog walkers alike into the road as he steadfastly refuses to move.

On a sunny but breezy day, he curls up in the big flowerpot in his front garden and never wakes unless a passing dog puts his nose in to sniff him, in which case he will give the offending mutt a Thousand Yard Burmese Jungle Stare as an initial indication of his displeasure, and if this fails to achieve the desired result, a quick clip across the nose will follow, before he nonchalantly resumes his kipping session.

Prior Planning

The first thing to ensure is that your cat always has plenty of places that are designated puppy-free areas, so that he isn't being harassed constantly by a marauding puppy. Once again, this is where the child gate or puppy pen earns its corn. Prepare the environment where the initial work will take place.

The safety and well-being of both cat and puppy are your absolute priority.

Getting Started

When introducing a puppy to a cat I take a different approach than when I am introducing an older dog to one.

The first few days of the new puppy being in the house will have allowed your cat to get used to the strange sounds and smells that accompany this unwanted home invader.

The careful deployment of child gates will have ensured no encroachment by your puppy into cat territory. At this point the confident cat may have already decided to visit your puppy and gently explain a few of the ground rules. If this is the case, you may need to do nothing else other than supervise future encounters until the relationship has been firmly established, which invariably means the cat continues to rule the roost and your puppy gets used to playing second fiddle.

If this hasn't happened, then it's time for you to take the lead.

Your first step is to have the cat eat her food in the kitchen whilst your puppy is in her crate. Most cats will overcome their reluctance to cooperate in exchange for a nice bowl of food. Please bear in mind that you should be dealing with a relatively calm and confident cat. (If you have an extremely nervous cat, perhaps out of concern for her welfare, you shouldn't have acquired a puppy.)

Ensure that your puppy is not hungry, so somewhere between meals. She should have been exercised and toileted so that she is nice and relaxed. Pop your puppy into her crate, with her tied-down frozen Kong.

Place your cat's food at the furthest point from the crate on the floor of the room. Carry your cat in and allow her to eat her meal. This means that your puppy is watching an almost stationary cat. It hasn't walked in and she won't walk out. You will carry her out.

Your puppy has been entertaining herself on the frozen Kong, so the chance of your cat doing anything other than arousing mild interest is pretty slim.

This is good for the learning process and don't forget both puppy and cat are learning here.

Try to repeat this process 2 or 3 times a day. The family children are not welcome at this event, so go and lock them in the shed whilst you do this.

The next stage is to repeat the process, but whilst you carry your cat in at the start of the training, you will allow her to walk out of the room. Why in this order? Well because if your cat is hungry, she may run to her food and get your puppy excited. After eating she is more likely to stroll out, moving slowly and arousing less interest.

We have now introduced a moving cat, but a slow-moving one. When this has gone well for a few days your cat may be allowed to walk in and out of the room to eat.

The next stage is having your puppy loose on one side of the child gate and the cat on the other, eating her food, a good distance away. Once again, you should have provided your puppy with something a bit more stimulating than the cat. The frozen Kong is, once again, a good training aid.

By now puppy and cat are getting more and more accustomed to each other's presence, so it may be time to move on.

Progress

This stage needs 2 people. Puppy should be on her lead or house line and your cat should be on the lap of another adult, with whom she feels comfortable and safe with.

You are just going to spend increasing periods of time with both puppy and cat in the same room, becoming even more accustomed to being around each other. The cat is the one who dictates the pace leading towards the first close encounter. In all honesty I have never yet got to the stage of the first encounter in this way when a puppy has been involved. Events have invariably overtaken me and cat and pup have made their own introductions around about this point.

But if for some reason the close encounter has not occurred, just take it patiently. Spend time every day just gradually allowing them to be in the same room. Don't allow your puppy to fix her focus on the cat.

Keep your cat still on your lap until she is confident enough to move around. Your puppy is on the house line, so in the event your cat moves too quickly and attracts puppy's attention, you can ensure a pursuit doesn't follow.

Whilst your moggy is gaining in confidence you will be otherwise occupying your puppy's attention. You may carry out little periods of control training. Or you may provide your puppy with a treat-dispensing activity toy, or the ubiquitous frozen Kong. In a relatively short time your cat will become part of the background as your puppy engages in training or play with you. Habituation will gradually occur.

The only rule I enforce rigorously is the no chasing rule. And this is where teaching a reliable stay as described in Part 4 comes into its own, whilst the house line provides backup until reliability is established.

After all your hard work, you have successfully established a comfortable relationship between your cat and your puppy. Congratulations, you can now let your kids out of the shed.

Meeting Cats on Walks

Most encounters will be long-range ones. By this time your puppy will be used to the family cat, so others encountered will not provide a great deal of interest.

As you will already have started training your puppy to respond immediately to her name and to "Watch!", it is relatively simple to distract her from a casual cat encounter and divert her attention back to you, until the moggy has passed by.

If you don't have your own cat you will use a combination of the control skills described in Part 4, and cats will become one of the distractions you proof against during your puppy's control training.

In summary: Your puppy is easily trained to be social towards cats or to be completely uninterested in them. Don't train her to be otherwise, or allow her to train herself by neglecting to foster an acceptable relationship. It's all in your hands, not her paws.

Train, don't complain!

===

Meeting Other Species

When considering introducing your puppy to other species, safety is paramount and the law must always be complied with. The law applies to everyone, regardless of how well trained your dog is, or you think she is.

With a puppy, proofing takes a long time and so always ensure you and your puppy work safely and legally. As well as respecting the law, please respect the landowner, the owner of the animals in question and of course, the animals themselves. They have as much right to a peaceful and stress-free life as your puppy.

For many of you who live in a city this part of your dog's development might not appear to be the most important thing, but even if meeting other species is not likely to be an everyday occurrence, getting in some practice during your pup's formative period will help to give her a well-rounded education.

Whilst many of you live in cities, you will occasionally visit the big green thing just outside your town or city, that is known as the countryside, even if only on day-release. It is always wise to have prepared your dog whilst she is young and receptive to such experiences.

If you do live in the countryside, then such training is absolutely essential if future problems are to be avoided.

Commonly Encountered Animals

In this section I am really referring to domesticated animals rather than wild ones. The only way to habituate your puppy to the presence of wild animals such as foxes, rabbits and squirrels is to do so slowly, having first perfected a reliable, immediate recall and once she has been returned to her lead, maintaining a calm focus on you, as opposed to the rabbit that attracted her attention.

While she is still a puppy it is unlikely that you will have reached this level of reliability, so use your training equipment wisely and remain on the right side of the law and your local farming community.

Horses, cows, sheep, pigs, goats and, increasingly, alpaca are animals that your puppy may encounter when being walked or exercised in the countryside.

Your Goal

Alice aged 6 months meeting her Alpacas

The aim is to habituate your puppy to all species in a controlled manner, so that they stimulate little interest in her and most certainly do not arouse her predatory instinct to chase. As ever, prevention is better than cure.

Do Your Reconnaissance

The first consideration is to get to know the area and what animals are there. A bit of a recce means you are far less likely to get any unpleasant surprise encounters that may lead you and your puppy into danger and you into trouble with the law. As ever remember the 6 Ps.

Initial Encounters

As in all other things, chance encounters are not the way to achieve the desired result. A planned encounter in which you are in full control is the way. The more practice you put in, the more reliable will be your puppy's response.

It is important that you select the correct environment, which means that the animals in question should be in a secure field. If your puppy can see them at a distance through a fence, that is fine, but even if she can only smell them, that too is a good starting point.

Ideally, you may be able to meet a couple of different species in a single session, but if this isn't possible, work with whatever is closest first and when a good result has been achieved, then move further afield and repeat the whole process with another species, and so on.

At this stage, your puppy will always be on a lead and you should always ensure that there is a secure fence between your puppy and the animals in question. Only once she is showing a complete lack of interest in them should you consider walking her, on lead, along a footpath that leads through a field containing these animals.

Opt for a few walk-past encounters. If she stops to look at the animals through the fence, allow her to watch calmly, before encouraging her to move on. If she is engrossed you may need to use a treat to encourage her, but by this time she should be quite responsive to her name and quite proficient at giving you her attention.

If at any point she begins to get excited, move her on quickly and plan to make your next training session a bit less exciting. Maybe have her further away, or have fewer animals on display.

If she responds well, by showing only mild interest or complete lack of interest then on the next occasion you can let her look for longer, or take her a bit closer.

Before moving any closer, you should carry out the following test. Position yourself in an adjacent field, once again separated from the other animals by a secure fence. Clip your puppy onto a strong, 5-metre long gundog training line, or a similar secure line. Remove her short lead and walk the fence line with your puppy on the long line, observe her and let her sniff around. Practise the occasional recall, rewarding a good response. You are looking for no interest, or only mild interest in the other animals and an effective recall.

When this has been achieved increase the line to a 10-metre line and then a 20-metre line.

Finally, you should consider playing games of fetch with your puppy in the adjacent field on training lines ranging in length from 5 metres to 20 metres.

When your puppy can play these games, remaining oblivious to the presence of the animals in the adjacent field, she has been proofed sufficiently for you to walk in the same field as the animals concerned on a lead, but no longer than the 2 metres specified by law.

Words of Warning

Whilst you may have proofed your puppy to the presence of horses in a field, that is not the same as a horse on the road. Horses on the road move differently. They make a great deal of noise due to the shoes on the road surface and usually have someone in a big, fluorescent jacket sat on top of them. This is a completely different experience for your puppy. Train for it, but in the meantime when you encounter horses being ridden, keep your puppy secure and if possible warn the riders that your puppy hasn't encountered horses being ridden before.

Cows and Calves

Cows with calves can be very territorial and can be aggressive in defence of their calves when faced with a perceived threat. Many farmers will put up warning signs when cows have calves in the field. My advice is to stay out of the field when you see these signs. Whilst your puppy may have been acclimatised to cows; the cows have not been acclimatised to her.

If you enter a field and notice calves and the cows begin to approach, get yourself out as quickly as possible. In extreme circumstances release your puppy and beat a hasty retreat whilst calling her. You will not win in a physical encounter with an irate, bovine bruiser.

Sheep with Lambs

Whilst your puppy may be comfortable in the presence of boring, slow-moving sheep, lambs scampering about the field at high speed are a different kettle of fish. If you can, train her to deal with this added distraction, as described above. If you haven't done so, don't be tempted to walk with your short-leashed puppy through a field with lambs in it until you have trained her.

Use It or Lose It

Introducing your puppy to other species should be started as early as possible to obtain the best results, but it is a continuous process that should be practised through adolescence and her adult life. Like any other form of training, you must use it or lose it.

=====

PART 3

Training Principles, Theory and Method

Introduction

Training Principles, Theory and Method, phew! I wonder if I have covered all the bases there. I am not sure that I have.

Training theory, canine learning theory, or whatever you want to call it has an impact on every aspect of your puppy's life, so understanding the basics should be well up on your list of priorities.

If you don't understand the basic principles you are putting yourself and your puppy at an unnecessary disadvantage when it comes to learning all sorts of things, whilst a good understanding will ensure that you will have the ability to take your puppy's training well beyond the subjects covered in detail in this book.

It will help you to get your puppy's training programme right, and just as importantly it will help you work out why something has gone wrong, as it inevitably will at some point.

The subjects covered in this section apply equally to the way in which your puppy will acquire her life skills and learn her control training exercises. If you apply them in your practical training with your puppy, there will be no end to what you and your puppy might achieve.

In the words of that famous philosopher, Delboy Trotter: "The world is your lobster!"

===

Training Ethics

There has been a lot of talk about positive-only and force-free training. Before discussing or arguing about either concept it is essential to define the terms used. This is where a true debate gets derailed, as it is just about impossible to agree what these terms mean.

I have had many discussions with people who are ardent advocates of both force-free and positive-only training. Yet all use a lead when taking their dogs for a walk. In fact the law says that in many instances you are compelled to restrain your puppy by use of a physical means of control, i.e. the lead. If you don't you are breaking the law.

The term **"Positive-Only Training"** is something of an odd description, as the word **Positive** in terms of dog training simply means **adding** something; a consequence, in response to the dog's actions, in order to establish a pleasant or an unpleasant association.

The term **Negative** when applied in dog training just means **subtracting** something; a consequence in response to the dog's actions.

The term **"Force-Free"** depends upon what a person defines as force. Once again there are many definitions of force. Until everyone can agree what it means the discussion is pointless. As I comply with the law and use a lead when in public places with my puppy, I cannot describe my own training method as force-free.

Everyone would agree that putting a dog on a choke chain and dragging it is force. But what if my puppy is on her lead and she sees a rabbit in the park and wants to bolt after it, so leans against the lead and has to be restrained? If I do not immediately drop the lead and allow her the freedom to exercise her free will and chase the rabbit, I am using force to prevent her doing so.

If I was in this situation with Alice, I would not be in a hurry to drop the lead. I would hold the lead, try to attract her attention and instruct her to **"Sit!"**, but if she did not respond to my instruction to her, I would not drop the lead. I would prevent her from running after the rabbit by using the lead. In my opinion, in this instance I would be using force.

Similarly, those claiming to be **"Balanced Trainers"** appear to use this term in order to justify the use of training techniques and equipment that most people, in the UK at least, would regard as extremely punitive. In fact in Wales, the use of at least one such device is a criminal offence.

So where does my training philosophy sit? I will leave this for you to decide as you read through this book, but as a full member of the British Police and Services Canine Association I fully support their stance regarding non-use of pinch/prong collars and electric-shock collars by Association members.

===

Consequences Shape Behaviour

Dogs, in common with most other animals possessing intelligence, learn as a result of their experiences and the consequences attached to those experiences. In short; Consequences Shape Behaviour. If you remember nothing else from this book, remember this.

When you are training your puppy you must present her with learning opportunities and, depending upon what we wish her to learn, connect the learning experience with a pleasant, unpleasant, or completely neutral consequence.

Fortunately, unless your puppy has her own key to the front door you have almost complete control over her early experiences, and you are in an ideal position to apply the appropriate consequences to her every learning experience and action. You may create a pleasant experience, which she will wish to have again, an unpleasant experience, which she will wish to avoid repeating, or a neutral experience, which will have no impact upon her and so become inconsequential.

In some circumstances an intense experience may result in a one-hit learning experience. I have found that this is generally associated with an extreme aversive consequence that inflicts pain upon the dog, or terrifies her. Such traumatic events can sometimes result in an almost irreversible learning experience, such as gun shyness.

The consequences you apply during training are seldom so pleasurable that they result in a one-hit learning experience to your benefit, although occasionally some actions are extremely self-reinforcing, such as the adrenaline rush received from the pursuit of a cat or livestock. Sod's law dictates that such learning experiences are generally directed towards instinctive behaviours that we rarely wish to train a companion dog to perform.

When training your puppy in her life skills and control skills you try to provide her with repeated pleasurable consequences closely associated with the action or response you wish your puppy to perform reliably. And by repetition, accurately marking the desired response and reinforcing through reward, you will teach her to do so.

In many instances you provide your puppy with a neutral consequence in relation to an experience, a process known as habituation, and when training puppies in life skills this is one of the most important and often overlooked aspect of training.

You will routinely habituate your puppy to a range of people of differing appearance, pushchairs, bikes, walking near traffic, and travelling in the car. By being aware of the process you can plan effectively to ensure nothing is missed.

Never forget that Consequences Shape Behaviour. It will help you teach your puppy all the things you want her to learn and the things you most definitely don't want her to learn.

===

Operant Conditioning. Theory and Practical Application.

Before you think this is going to be some deep explanation of scientific theory, it is not. It is a very brief explanation. It is a fascinating subject and for those of you who would like to learn about it in more depth there are a number of good books, the best of which in my opinion is "How Dogs Learn" by Burch and Bailey. I would recommend this book.

The terminology used can cause quite emotive reactions from the dog training/dog owning community. Whilst everyone appears to be perfectly happy with the term "Reinforcement", many are uncomfortable with using the term "Punishment", equating it to beating or hurting your dog.

In fact some trainers and behaviourists no longer use the word punishment and instead use the term "Inhibitor", because too much time is spent explaining it or arguing about its true meaning in the context of dog training. Some might think this is a cop-out and that they should argue the merits of the terminology, but in my opinion they quite sensibly just make use of a different, less emotive word, which has the same meaning in dog training terms and allows them to get their message across without getting into an argument.

For the purpose of this book I will use the terms:

1. “Reward” or “Reinforce” your puppy’s response.

2. “Inhibit” or “Correct” your puppy’s behaviour, or response.

3. “Prevent your puppy from ‘Practising’ or ‘Rehearsing’ this behaviour.” By this I mean exactly that. You are not punishing the undesirable behaviour because, quite simply, you are not going to allow your puppy to perform it.

Good or Bad

I have tried not to use the terms “Good” or “Bad” behaviour or response. I have tried to use the terms “Desirable/Desired” or “Undesirable/Undesired” instead.

The reasons I use these terms are quite simple. Firstly, your puppy has no concept of good or bad. Secondly, it is not for me to decide on your behalf what is good or bad behaviour. Come to think of it, it isn’t my place to tell you what desirable or undesirable behaviour is. That is your decision and your responsibility, but remember, you will have to live with the consequences of your decision for many years.

Operant Conditioning

Operant Conditioning is the term used to describe a method of training your puppy effectively. It is often described as a quadrant, because it consists of 4 parts:

The Operant Conditioning Quadrant

The 4 terms used are Positive Reinforcement, Positive Punishment, Negative Reinforcement and Negative Punishment.

The terms **Positive** and **Negative** do not equate in any way to **good** and **bad**. Please remember this, or you will struggle with the whole concept. Think of them in a mathematical sense. **Positive** simply indicates that a **consequence** is **added** when an action has been performed by your puppy.

Negative means something is **subtracted** or **withheld** when an action has been performed, or not performed, by your puppy.

The term **Reinforcement** means the **consequence** is **pleasurable/rewarding.**

The term **Punishment** means the **consequence** is **unpleasant/aversive**.

The theory states that if an action results in a pleasurable consequence then the puppy is more likely to repeat it. If an action results in an unpleasant consequence then your puppy is less likely to repeat it. Consequences shape behaviour.

You Control the Consequences

Whilst in life there are all sorts of unintentional consequences that muck things up, in the controlled environment of your puppy's early training, you control the consequences. Use this opportunity wisely.

Positive Reinforcement in Practice

When your puppy performs a **desirable** action you **add** a pleasurable consequence. This may be a nice word, a treat, a ball. Anything your pup finds pleasurable and rewarding.

You ask your puppy to **"Sit!"** and she does so. You **add** a slice of sausage to your puppy.

Negative Punishment in Practice

When your puppy performs an **undesirable** action you **withhold** the anticipated pleasurable consequence.

You ask your puppy to **"Sit!"** and she does not. You **withhold** the slice of sausage from your puppy. (Just ignore those little pleading eyes, she will get another chance to earn her reward very soon.)

Positive Reinforcement and Negative Punishment work well together. Most puppy owners have little difficulty understanding these 2 concepts and are happy to implement them. What they struggle with are the next 2 parts.

Positive Punishment in Practice

When your puppy performs an undesirable action you add an unpleasant consequence. This may range from a harsh rebuke; **"No!"** to a physical act such as a sharp snap on the lead or a smack on her bum.

Whilst your puppy is in the **"Sit!"** position, you instruct her to **"Stay!"** After a second or so, she begins to stand up. You deliver a light tap to her bum, in order to punish her undesirable response to the **"Stay!"** instruction.

Negative Reinforcement in Practice

Negative Reinforcement means that you **take away** an unpleasant consequence that your puppy is experiencing whilst she is in the act of performing an undesired action. It invariably involves the removal or the ending of a Positive Punishment.

An example might be that whilst your puppy is in the **"Sit!"** position, you instruct her to **"Stay!"** After a second or so, she begins to stand up, so you firmly place a hand on her bum and push her back into the **"Sit!"** This action is uncomfortable for her and may be described as a Positive Punishment. If she resists, the push continues, until she stops resisting and returns to the **"Sit!"** position. When she does so, the push stops. She is Negatively Reinforced by the ending of the Positive Punishment, delivered in the form of the push.

So, do Positive Punishment and Negative Reinforcement have any place in puppy training? Well the Operant Conditioning Quadrant is just that...a **quadrant**, which means it comprises 4 parts, if it didn't it wouldn't be a quadrant, it would be a ... well I'm not sure what it would be, but it definitely wouldn't be a quadrant, because there would be fewer than 4 parts.

How I Used Operant Conditioning Whilst Educating Alice

Whilst educating Alice and all of my other dogs, as a conservative estimate, 90% of my training comprised Positive Reinforcement, when I rewarded Alice for performing the desired behaviour by giving her, in ascending order of value, verbal praise, physical praise, a small treat, her Kong, her tuggy, or her biggest treat ever, a bite on a bite pad.

In order to inhibit her undesired behaviour, about 9% of my training comprised negative punishment, during which I withheld the rewards listed above.

As I say, 90% Positive Reinforcement is quite a conservative estimate. This percentage has been increasing as I have become better at selecting, developing, understanding and training my dogs.

Why is it so important to me to strive for the biggest chunk of my training to be based upon positive reinforcement and reward-based training?

The main reason is that I consider that my relationship with baby Alice to be far more important than having a perfectly straight **"Sit!"**. I have enjoyed the process of working with Alice. It has been a fantastic experience for me. Why would I want her experience of working with me to be any less enjoyable?

I love watching an owner or handler and her dog working together as a team, happy and confident in each other's company. I think it's great. When I see a dog working for rather than with its owner, or handler through fear of punishment, it makes me want to go and slap the owner.

I was once criticised by another handler for training my dog with food rewards. He went into great detail about the problem of training in this way.

"You don't want your dog to work for you just to get a biscuit do you?" He asked.

"I don't mind really. Are you happy for your dog to work for you in order to avoid being punished?" I asked.

"Yes, I am." He said.

"You are a complete dobber!" I thought. I didn't say it out loud, 'cos he was about 6'4" and I am a bit vertically challenged.

The relationship is of paramount importance, but of course the owner/handler is the boss, with the dog taking the role of the subordinate, but how many of you reading this book ever enjoyed working for a boss who ruled through fear of punishment, rather than calm, clear direction, praising good work and dealing with poor work appropriately?

Did I ever use Positive Punishment when training baby Alice? Sadly, I did. But it is highly unlikely this ever went beyond a firm **"No!"** by way of reprimand, which whilst only a word, if said harshly enough, definitely constitutes an example of Positive Punishment. It doesn't have to be physical.

I can't recall an obvious example of a "physical" Positive Punishment when training Alice, but I'm sure there were a few.

If I use an imaginary incident and how I might have dealt with it, hopefully it will illustrate the point I am trying to get across to you and show how the Operant Conditioning Quadrant might have been used to achieve the desired response from Alice.

Imagine Alice is now about 8 months and I am walking her on a long line, because I am in an unfamiliar area and don't know what hazards and distractions we might come across.

She has gone into the hedgerow and is sniffing at a rabbit hole. Wanting to move on I have given her a call to return to me, **"Alice...Come!"** This is an instruction she has learned and practised over the past 6 months. An instruction that she has clearly heard and knows must be responded to immediately and which usually results in her being positively rewarded with a fuss, treat, or Kong.

But on this occasion Alice keeps her nose firmly to the rabbit hole and does not return to me. She has just chinned me off!

I make the call once more, **"Alice...Come!"** and after one second of noncompliance I correct her by a single, small, but sharp tug on the lead. As soon as she responds by turning towards me I immediately revert to gentle, nice, encouraging tones to ensure she returns to me. Which she does.

When she gets back to me she has completely forgotten that she did not respond to the initial instruction and she is now being a good girl. I cannot retrospectively punish her, why would I want to? In any case she received her Positive Punishment at the moment she failed to respond and now she is complying, so I have to Positively Reinforce her for coming back, but as it was the result of a leash correction, this would only comprise a little verbal praise and a stroke.

But here is the important bit: I do not leave it at that.

I immediately take her back to the same spot. I let her sniff and, instead of calling her from the end of the 20-metre training line, I go closer, so as to make it more likely she will comply, and give the same command again; **"Alice... Come!"** and when she responds immediately, I **mark** her correct response with a **"Yes!"** and Positively Reinforce with a treat, praise and maybe her Kong.

Why? Because she has just performed a response in difficult circumstances. She would very much have liked to continue sniffing rabbit poo, but she chose to respond. That is worthy of a bigger reward.

I also reflect that perhaps my training regime is not as clever as I thought it was and that I need to improve Alice's response in situations where she is distracted by a strong scent. Over the next few days I practise this dozens of times, in various distracting circumstances, until baby Alice is consistently performing the desired behaviour.

I may end up doing a similar recall 50 times, which on just a single occasion resulted in a Positive Punishment, with the remaining 49 providing a Positive Reinforcement for baby Alice.

And this is where training works. It isn't the correction that really taught her anything of great value, it's the 49 positive experiences that did that. But the single correction ensured that she didn't learn that ignoring my instruction could ever result in a self-rewarding experience courtesy of little Peter Rabbit, because I nipped that in the bud at the outset.

So yes, Positive Punishment has its place, but if you train well you need hardly ever use it.

I'm sure that 95% of you reading this book, like me, have ABS braking fitted to your car. Despite the fact the majority of us hardly ever need it, I'm sure none of us would tell the manufacturer to remove it, or make a conscious decision to buy a car without it. This is because it is a tool that may be required, even if only very occasionally, or in extreme circumstances.

That is how I consider the use of Positive Punishment. You are free to disagree and if you do, you simply have to adjust your training process with your puppy accordingly.

===

Sensitization and Habituation

Sensitization and **Habituation** play a major role in your puppy's development and training. Both are invaluable when educating your puppy, but you must manage both processes carefully.

There are many things that you want your puppy to become **sensitized** to and even more things you want her to become **habituated** to. I do not intend to discuss **de-sensitization** here, because if you sensitize your puppy to the things she needs to be sensitized to and habituate her to the things she needs to disregard, then you won't need to concern yourself with de-sensitization.

Habituation

When you want your puppy to ignore something and become oblivious to it, you will **habituate** her to it. In order to achieve this you will take every opportunity to expose her to it on a regular basis, ensuring that she does not make either a pleasant or unpleasant association with it. It should become something of no interest and of no consequence to her, so she will learn to ignore it.

The way to achieve this in practice is to introduce her to the thing at an extremely low level, so that she barely notices it.

An example of this might be habituating your puppy to traffic. The best way to do this is not to take her to the hard shoulder of the M6 motorway, but to begin at a reasonable distance from a minor road, which is used by a moderate amount of slow-moving traffic, so that your puppy can barely hear it.

You should occupy your puppy with some other activity, so that the traffic noise fades even further into the background of her consciousness. Having practised this, gradually move closer to the road. By the time your puppy gets to walk along the pavement next to the traffic she should be hardly noticing it.

Sensitization

When you **sensitize** your puppy to something you want to achieve the opposite effect to **habituation**. You want the thing to become extremely important to her, either because it is nice for her, or it announces the arrival of something else, which may also be nice, for her at least.

Sensitization works for things you want your puppy to learn. For example, when she sees you put on the treat bag and pick up her lead, you want her to be sensitized so she pays attention to you, because she knows she is going to have a nice time training.

Whenever I take Alice's tracking line and harness out of my van, I have to ensure that I keep her calm as she has learned that tracking is an extremely rewarding activity and the sight of the line and harness indicate the fun is about to begin. She has become sensitized to it.

Providing that her excitement remains at a manageable level, I am happy for her to remain sensitized, because it means that regardless of whatever other distractions are present, her mind is already focused on the forthcoming exercise.

There is always a danger that your puppy will become sensitized to stuff that is exciting but distracting, and even more worryingly, she may become sensitized to things that cause her to be afraid.

There is also a risk that she will become habituated to stuff that you definitely want her to remain sensitized to. An important example of this will be discussed later in this book.

The Bottom Line

Sensitization and Habituation are essential elements of your puppy's development and training. If you manage each process carefully they will help you to produce a well-balanced and well-trained dog.

===

Timing, Markers and Consequences

Regardless of whether the consequence is a reinforcer or a punisher it is essential that the dog can link the consequence with the behaviour. In order for this to occur it must be delivered skilfully and accurately for maximum effect.

Compare the effectiveness of a Royal Marine sniper with that of an RAF Airman employed on his once-yearly guard duty. When the situation demands, the former will deliver a single, well-targeted consequence quickly and accurately, leaving no room for ambiguity, whilst the latter might be on his 3rd magazine of 30 rounds before hitting the target in the foot, or giving him a nasty scare!

Delivering an appropriate consequence immediately when the desired or undesired response occurs ensures that Thorndike's Law of Effect will come into play and the desired behaviour can be achieved in a remarkably short period of time. (Phew, how scientific was that?)

As you are going to be concerned predominantly with reinforcing desired behaviour, I will focus on this.

It is essential that the **marker** is given as close as possible to the precise moment your puppy performs the desired response. The more accurate you are in marking it, the quicker she will learn. The marker should be delivered verbally, with the word **"Yes!"** delivered in a clear tone, or, if you have decided to use the Clicker, with the **click**.

The **marker** is always followed by a **reinforcer**, usually in the form of a treat, but for more demanding exercises it may be in the form of a toy reward. This

reinforcer must be given within 2 seconds of the **marker**, in order for your puppy to make the connection between her **action/response**, the **marker** word and the **reinforcer**.

This is the case even when you make a mistake. If you give the marker too early and she fails to complete the desired action as you expected, then that was your mistake. You must still reinforce with a treat, because you gave the marker. Just make sure you get it right next time. Don't dent her faith in the system.

In the case of a **Positive Punishment** being the consequence, the same rule applies. It must be delivered within 2 seconds of the undesired behaviour.

This 2-second period is the main reason why punishing your puppy for a toilet-training failure is certainly doomed to failure. If you were close enough to punish your puppy within 2 seconds, why didn't you just interrupt her, you Muppet! If you can't punish her within 2 seconds, then your puppy can't associate the punishment with her piddling, and will just view you as an unpredictable lunatic. So don't do it!

Accurate marking of your puppy's actions/response is one of the fundamental skills you need to develop to train her successfully. The delivery of the subsequent, appropriate consequence completes a cycle, which will lead you both towards success in training.

Top Tip: When I have a human who is struggling with timing the marker correctly I take them to one side. No! I don't do that! I take them aside and throw a tennis ball about 6 feet in the air and ask them to mark the exact moment when the ball hits the ground. I repeat this about 20 times.

Once they have mastered this, I then start to throw it a bit higher or lower, so the time it takes to touch down is longer or shorter. Most usually get it very quickly, and using this method they can improve their timing without allowing their puppy to become confused or de-motivated.

===

The Value of a Reward (Reinforcer)

The value of any particular reinforcer may vary from puppy to puppy. In the same way as we humans have preferences for different reinforcers, so too do dogs. Some puppies are fanatical about any old toy. Others have very strong preferences for just one particular toy.

The value of a food reward varies depending upon the puppy's fondness for food. It may vary depending upon the type of food and it will certainly vary depending on how hungry your puppy is at the time of the training session. If she is not hungry, food might not be a great reinforcer. If she is too hungry, it might be too strong and cause her to become over-excited.

Some puppies will perform for a low-value food reward, whilst others need high value. Often your pup's performance and response will be affected by the nature of the task, so you should take this into account when deciding upon what value of reinforcer you should use.

For a relatively simple routine task a low-value reward may suffice. But for a difficult task, or one which your puppy is less keen to perform, the delivery of a high-value reinforcer might be required to motivate her and retain her attention.

Even the value of verbal and physical praise can be altered by the manner in which it is delivered. It can be delivered in an exciting manner to your puppy in order to gee her up and hold her attention, or it can be delivered in more measured tones to keep her performing steadily and calmly.

Some trainers begin training with a high-value reinforcer, whilst others always start with the lowest value of reinforcer that they can get away with. I tend to favour the second approach. I do this on the basis of trying to match the reinforcer to the difficulty or complexity of the exercise being trained.

For example, when training my puppy to walk at my side, in my garden, with no distractions, I would reinforce a desirable response with a small piece of puppy food. But when proofing this exercise by performing it in a field full of chickens, I want to make sure I hold her attention. I am competing with a strong distraction, so I will use a high value reinforcer to achieve this, especially during the early stages of training this exercise.

Performing in my garden is her usual level of work, but doing it in the chicken pen is the canine equivalent of working a Bank Holiday Monday - she deserves to be paid at the double-time rate! A good boss always pays the going rate for a job well done.

Just to give you some food for thought, I have graded baby Alice's reinforcers in ascending order:

1. Piece of puppy food.
2. Piece of hard cheese.
3. Piece of liver cake.
4. Ball.
5. Kong.
6. Ball or Kong on a rope.
7. Bite pad.

For simple tasks I start at #1 and as her tasks become progressively more challenging I work up to #6. I reserve her bite on the bite pad for her giving a clean response to the instruction to cease attacking the criminal.

===

Reinforcement Schedules

When you are training your puppy you need to know how often to reward her in order to teach her the desired response to a signal or instruction, and to have her perform it reliably. Having started training her correctly, your puppy may now be performing the exercise you are teaching her quite well, but there are 2 ways to make a response worse rather than better.

The first is to **under** reward it. This is when you do not reward it frequently or sufficiently enough to improve her response, or to maintain it at the level you are happy with.

The second way to weaken her response, surprisingly enough, is to **over** reward it. By doing this, the outcome of the exercise becomes too predictable, a bit boring. As it is almost impossible for her to perform each response to exactly the same level, some responses will be better than others, and if you reward all of them you will end up with a puppy that produces a mediocre response. Whereas if you selectively reward the very best responses by varying her reinforcement schedule, she will produce much better work for you.

The key is to get the balance just right, and this varies from puppy to puppy. It depends upon what stage of training you are at with your puppy, your puppy's character and the difficulty of what you are training her to do.

As you become more knowledgeable about your own puppy, her strengths and weaknesses, you will be able to make the right decisions about when to reward her responses.

How often you reward your puppy is known as the **Reinforcement Schedule.** There are 6 types of reinforcement schedule used in dog training, but for training your puppy you only really need to concern yourself with 3 of them. These are:

1. Fixed Ratio.
2. Variable Ratio.
3. Fixed Duration.

Fixed Ratio

This means that the reward is given at set times, say after every 1st, 3rd or 5th repetition of the behaviour. Whilst it is easy for you to remember, it is not a good way to train as the predictability can lead to boredom and poor standards from your puppy.

But, when you begin to train your puppy you will use a **Fixed Ratio**, because in the early stages of training, you will reward every correct response from her. This is a Constant Reinforcement Schedule, which, as it is given after every correct response, is **Fixed Ratio**.

In order to improve her response and make her work better and harder for you, once she is performing the desired response reliably, you will quickly move to a **Variable Ratio**.

Variable Ratio

In this schedule the reward (reinforcement) is delivered unpredictably. Because of this unpredictability, it has the tendency to keep your puppy working over a longer period. The only thing that your puppy has to do is perform her response to the required standard and wait until the **marker** is given and the reward is delivered.

It does mean that she will **not** be getting a marker and reward after every successful repetition. Each success will be acknowledged with a "Good Girl", but the **marker** and subsequent reinforcement will be delivered randomly, or after an especially pleasing response.

Fixed and **Variable** Ratio Schedules are very useful in control training.

Fixed Duration Schedule

This is employed where continuous performance of a behaviour is required. A good example of this is when teaching a 30-second **"Sit! Stay!"** your puppy must perform the exercise correctly for the whole duration of the exercise in order to earn a reinforcer. (Although it should be pointed out that to keep your puppy on her toes, you would not always ask her to "Stay!" for 30 seconds. You would vary the length of the stay on a regular basis.)

===

The Keys to Success

The key to success involves relatively few golden rules. A bit like the first rule, they are fairly simple.

Simplicity

Keep your training simple. Teach one thing at a time and be clear in your own mind precisely what single, simple lesson you want your puppy to learn in this training session.

Motivation

Find out what motivates your puppy. Does she like toys, food, or praise? She probably enjoys all of these things at different times and in different situations.

Communication

You will communicate with your puppy consciously by verbal instructions and by hand signals. Ensure this communication is consistent.

Your body language will also communicate with her and her body language will communicate with you. You must try to become aware of both conscious and unconscious communication. This will help you to understand each other.

Discipline

Self-discipline and training discipline. Be self-disciplined by carrying out regular training sessions and be disciplined in applying the rules of training consistently. Lead by example. If you are disciplined in your training, it will help your puppy produce consistent results.

Consistency

Be consistent when applying consequences to her behaviour and responses. That doesn't always mean that every time your puppy sits, for the rest of her life, she will get a sausage. But she should know that performing the correct response to an instruction or a life skill, will be acknowledged and reinforced at some point.

Be consistent in what you allow and don't allow her to do. Don't stop your puppy from jumping on you today and allow her to do it tomorrow.

Patience

Patience means accepting regular, small pieces of progress in training, rather than going for a big leap. By taking small steps you simplify each little step for your puppy and run less risk of leaving gaps in her understanding of what you are trying to teach her.

Perseverance

To persevere is to keep going, when progress is apparent but slow. Good training is often slow. You can have good, or you can have quick. Good is better!

Understanding

Understand your puppy's limitations. Be sympathetic and understanding of your puppy's limitations in regard to her levels of concentration, emotional and physical limitations. She is a living puppy, not a robot. Respect her limitations, she will develop and push the limits of her abilities as she develops.

Knowledge

The knowledge you acquire about your puppy and how you can help her to learn, if applied correctly, will ensure that the training process will be a rewarding experience for you both. Take every opportunity to learn and give your puppy the same opportunity.

And always remember, as you learn and improve, so too will your puppy. Just do your best. A wise lady once said, "Until you know better, do your best. When you know better; do better."

===

Applying Core Skills

In the RAF there is an element of training that relates to proficiency in military skills, which must be achieved by all members of the RAF, be they RAF Police personnel operating in Afghanistan, or an Officers Mess Steward, serving pink gin in Surrey.

Both trades must be able to perform first aid, strip their personal weapon in a specified time, fire it to an agreed standard of marksmanship, must be able to carry out effective respirator drills and many other things, I am desperately trying to forget, I mean, remember.

These are known as Common Core Skills.

It is much the same with puppies. All puppies must be able to toilet appropriately, to walk properly on a lead, to come when called. This is equally true for Attila the Police dog as it is for Trixie the toy poodle.

We can minimise the amount of learning your puppy needs to take in by making the most effective use of her simple core skills.

When I train owners for the Kennel Club Good Citizen Silver award, 3 of the exercises included are: Stay in one place for 2 minutes, which is self-explanatory; The Controlled Greeting, where the dog meets another person and does not jump up on them; The test of Food Manners, where the dog must be made aware of the presence of food being handled or consumed in her presence without begging or trying to steal it.

I have seen instructors and students come up with all sorts of elaborate ways to train these 3 exercises. I don't bother. I simply teach my dog to **"Sit!"** and **"Stay!"**

If she can **"Sit!"** and **"Stay!"** for 2 minutes she passes. If she can **"Sit!"** and **"Stay!"** in the presence of a person, who I may have a chat with and who may want to give her a little stroke, she passes. If she can **"Sit!"** and **"Stay!"** when someone nearby is eating a pie, or drops a packet of crisps on the floor, she passes. Alice is particularly good at this as it is normally me eating the pie!

As you progress through this book you will see that in almost all instances, training for one part of your puppy's education has links with many other aspects. That is as it should be. We don't need to think up a completely different solution to each thing we want our puppy to learn.

If you always make use of the core skills she has already acquired and see how you can incorporate them into the next thing you are trying to teach her you will significantly reduce the amount of learning that your puppy needs to absorb.

Don't clutter her head with lots of unnecessary information. Keep it simple and let her absorb the important stuff with the minimum of effort. It is your puppy's job to acquire knowledge. It is your job to simplify the task for her.

===

The Importance of Discipline

Discipline is an essential factor in puppy training. It must be rigorously enforced. If you don't exercise discipline, you will fail your puppy.

So where does discipline begin? With **you!** Forget your puppy and enforcing discipline with her. Start with yourself.

All forms of training require practice. It is you who decides when this is to happen. It is you who must decide how frequently it happens.

If you are disciplined and prepare well, you will be amazed at how quickly you can train a puppy in just 3 to 5 minutes, 3 times a day.

Discipline is for every day. Not just sunny ones. It is very easy to be disciplined on a nice sunny day and carry out her control training and life training, but it is not so easy to do it when it's cold and wet. By way of example, consider how your self-discipline affects your puppy's toilet training.

Each night following your puppy's little bit of supper you take her out for a last piddle and poo before settling her down for the night in her nice, warm comfortable crate. But tonight it is pouring with rain, so you decide to put baby Alice out on her own, because you don't want to get your brand new velour slippers wet.

So you open the door and push her out. After 5 minutes you open the door and in she scampers. A little bit damp, but nothing that a quick towelling down can't put right. After drying her off, you pop her in her crate, lights out and then off you go to bed.

In the morning you get up at your normal time, which during toilet training is a bit earlier than usual, and go into the kitchen. Baby Alice has been clean and dry for three nights now, so the funny smell you note as you enter the kitchen is a bit unfamiliar; that's right, it's puppy poo. A nice Mr Whippy that baby Alice has deposited in the middle of a piddle pond, in her previously pristine crate.

How did this happen? Well guess what, just like you don't like getting wet, neither does she. As soon as you popped her out last night, she shot into the only bit of shelter available at the side of the shed. She was only concerned with staying dry, not going to the toilet.

This is the time for a bit of Positive Punishment! Take yourself outside and give yourself a good hard slap, you feckless individual! Then come back in and apologise to your puppy for your idleness and lack of consideration for her. Your indiscipline has really let her down.

Now place your hand in the small of your back and poke your fingers into your flesh. If you're a bit less porky than me, you might feel something hard and a bit knobbly. It's called a backbone, and it's time you showed a bit of it when training your puppy.

Here's what you should have done. Give your puppy her supper as usual and whilst she is eating it, remove the velour slippers, get your waterproofs on and fetch your big umbrella. (If you haven't got one go to your local retail park and find the sports outlet with the big bin of massive golfing umbrellas that they flog off for £2.99 each, or two for a fiver. These are not golfing umbrellas. They are puppy training umbrellas, because there is plenty of room under it for a large human and a small squatting puppy!)

Open the back door, open the umbrella and go outside for as long as you need to for baby Alice to perform her customary toilet routine. If it's really piddling down, remember it is more important to keep your puppy dry. You already have your waterproofs on, so you don't really matter.

Another option is to provide a comfortable toilet area for puppy for use during periods of rainy weather. Consider rigging up a tarpaulin, or a cheap gazebo.

Do whatever it takes to make toileting in the garden as comfortable as possible for your puppy. Discipline is a 24-hour-a-day activity in the formative period of your puppy's life. If you maintain discipline, you will be aware that every time you are with your puppy you are training her, for better - or for worse.

I have always believed that training a companion puppy is a lot harder than training a Military Working Dog. (MWD).

A MWD spends a lot of time in her kennel or run and when she is taken out of her kennel for work, she is happy to see me because she has been deprived of my company for a long period of time.

When I go to collect her I am in a different frame of mind. In effect I have put my dog training hat on. I will only be spending a limited amount of time with her and it is relatively easy for me to remain focused and guide her learning in the right direction.

When training has finished I may spend some additional time bonding with her before returning her to her kennel. The time together is special for both of us and the time can be structured and directed towards learning only what I want her to learn.

When we are on duty I have my working hat on. She soon gets to understand this and quickly becomes accustomed to operating at a slower pace, but always waiting for the opportunity to go into action. If she can point me towards the action, so much the better.

At other times I might just be enjoying play and companionship with her, but it's not a 24/7 deal like it is with a puppy that shares your home and most of your life.

With a companion puppy it is different. My companion puppy spends most of her time in my company **not** being trained. Or so most people would think. But this is where problems occur. Whilst I may not be actively training her, make no mistake, she is being trained all the time. It's just that neither baby Alice nor I are aware of it. But learning is taking place all the time.

She is learning about her environment, she is learning that when I am working on the computer I am not giving her my full attention, so this is the best time to chew the mat by the front door without the chance of being disturbed.

She is learning that when I am watching football, this is the best time to sneak onto the sofa next to me, because when I am otherwise engaged and she snuffles at my hand, I respond to this snuffling by tickling her behind her ear.

Learning is a continuous process and during the early months my puppy is like a little sponge. I need to be aware of this and maximise her opportunities to rehearse and learn the things I want her to do in later life - all the desirable stuff, and eliminate, as far as possible, opportunities to rehearse and learn the undesirable stuff.

Be disciplined and keep your wits about you, because your puppy will have her "mischief radar" on just about all of the time.

===

Giving Your Puppy Direction

I have lost count of the times when I see a puppy or a dog rehearsing undesirable behaviour. A classic example is when one puppy owner stands 6 feet away from another puppy owner, with both pups up on their back legs barking like lunatics and with each trying with all their might to get to the other one for a wrestling match.

Whilst this goes on, both owners stand oblivious, allowing their pups to practise this behaviour.

Another classic is the 12lb puppy who decides to pull her owner off her feet to go and sniff a piddle patch, whilst her owner goes with the puppy to accommodate her and reinforce the puppy's undesirable behaviour.

Be in no doubt that if you allow your 10-week-old 12lb Rottweiler to pull you towards an object that she is interested in, having learned that this is the way to behave, it is exactly what she will do when she is 70lb. If you don't want her to do it when she is big, don't allow her to rehearse it when she is little.

Many trainers will tell you to correct (punish) your puppy when she does this in order to teach her not to do it. The problem is that by the time you have given the correction she has already done it.

Surely the key is to give your puppy direction before she does it? Keep her close to your leg, encourage her and reward her for remaining there. If being sat next to your left leg is a nice and rewarding place to be, why would she want to go elsewhere?

Your puppy needs to sniff, so you should permit this and allow her to enjoy doing it, but it must be you who makes the decision to allow her to go for a sniff, or have her sit quietly and attentively for just a little longer.

Remember, she is only a puppy and cannot sit quietly for long periods, so be realistic. As with everything else, practise it in short bursts. If this means you cannot stand and chat to your neighbour in the street for 15 minutes because your puppy cannot cope with sitting still for that long, so be it. If you feel this is beyond you, go and have a long chat and leave your puppy at home, snuggled in her crate with her favourite frozen Kong.

Giving your puppy clear direction makes it easy for her to perform the right behaviour and be rewarded for it. It prevents her getting into mischief, so she doesn't learn how nice mischief can be, and as an added bonus she also avoids being punished for making undesirable choices.

And remember, training doesn't just take place on the training field. It takes place everywhere.

===

My Name is Alice...Don't Wear It Out!

Unless you plan to remain attached to your puppy by way of her lead for the whole of her life, the best means of communication are hand and body signals and your voice. In the initial stages you should use both means of communication together, but as your puppy learns to respond to your voice, this will become the main means of communication. The more effective your verbal communication is with your puppy, the better you are able to get her to respond.

The most important thing you will ever teach your dog is to respond to her name. For 99.9% of owners this will be the first thing you try to teach her, closely followed by the word "Sit".

Unfortunately, whilst her name is nearly always the first thing you will teach your puppy to respond to, it may also be the first thing you teach her to cease responding to.

Sensitize or Habituate?

Habituation and **Sensitization** are almost polar opposites when it comes to educating your puppy.

To recap; when you want your puppy to ignore something, you will **habituate** her to it. This means that you will expose her to it on a regular basis, ensuring that she doesn't develop a pleasant or unpleasant association with it. It becomes uninteresting and of no consequence to her, so she learns to ignore it.

When you **sensitize** her to something you want to achieve the opposite effect. Ensuring the thing becomes extremely important to her, either because it is nice for her, or it announces the arrival of something nice.

Sensitize Your Puppy to Her Name

In relation to your puppy's name we want to achieve sensitization; the last thing we want is for her to become habituated to it. In the vast majority of cases new owners quickly start on the right track, but lose their way.

So how do we do this in practical terms? Simple; make her name important to her. It is very special. It is the only one she's got, so treat it like something precious.

A highly successful competition trainer I know gives her working dog 2 different names. The first is a pet name for use at home. She does this because she has children and visitors who will use her dog's name excessively and reduce its importance. So she has given her dog another, working name, which only she uses and which she always uses appropriately, so her dog is highly sensitized to it.

It also acts as a good signal to the dog that he is now working and has to pay careful attention. Is this an effective way of doing things? Well I think the number of successes she has consistently achieved with her dogs over the years shows me that it is.

Perhaps giving your puppy 2 names is taking things a bit far for the average puppy owner, but I use a similar system with my own dogs. I don't know when I started to do this, but I can't exclude the fact that I may have nicked it from her and then just modified it, because I am a bit dim, and it was easier than remembering 2 names.

Starting Out

If you want to sensitize your puppy to her name, how do you start?

You start by getting her attention. Surprisingly enough the first way I taught baby Alice to give me her attention was by using anything other than her name. Then introducing her name only after she was responding quickly and enthusiastically to some other signal or sound, and once her name had been introduced, using it very sparingly.

The reason I don't use her name from the start is because she doesn't know it, or what it means. So I start calling her without using her name.

I get down on my knees in the living room and call to her, "Here puppy, good baby, here puppy!" I use my voice to call her softly and in a friendly enticing way. There is no room for any mumbling, I am calling to my new puppy, not auditioning for the role of Mumbling Phil Mitchell in EastEnders.

If my body posture is right and my voice is pleasant she will come, because that's what puppies do. She is a social animal and there is nothing better than me on offer. How do I know there is nothing better on offer? Because I made sure that when I first did this I removed all distractions such as toys, shoes, socks, other people from the room. It was me or nowt!

When she came to me I cuddled her and loved her and talked to her nicely. (At least until she drew blood whilst sinking her teeth into me. Joking!) As if the voice and cuddles weren't enough, sometimes I also gave her a tiny, tasty treat.

Within a day or so, I was her very best friend. I had sensitized her to my voice and to me, particularly when I was kneeling down. As soon as I did this I barely got the chance to call "Puppy!" before she was all over me, like fur on a weasel. Why would it ever occur to her not to come to me? Coming to me was very rewarding for her.

I made sure that I practised this routine many times a day and I also did it in different rooms of the house as I wanted her to learn that this response was not just something that happened in the living room. No, it was a magic trick that worked in all the rooms, in the garden and also on the training field. When the fat bloke kneels, get over there pronto for a cuddle and a sausage. Simples.

Introducing Her Name

Now that I had this response I could introduce her name; **Alice**. It is a very important name. It is the only one she has got and the only one she will ever have.

Once again I started on my knees and called her; **"Puppy!"** As soon as she saw me and was making for me at top speed, when she was almost on me and was so close she could not possibly fail to get it right, I introduced her name for the first time. But I extended the syllables so it almost sounded like **"Aaaaa...liiis"** being sung to her.

The response was great, but obviously she had no idea what she had just done. That would take hundreds of repetitions. (Did he just say hundreds? Yes he did!)

After a few days of this successful routine I began to put her name into the sequence a bit earlier.

The routine is now me being down on my knees and calling; **"Puuuppy"** clap, clap, and when she is just **halfway** towards me; **"Aaa...liiiis"** and upon making contact with me, she gets cuddles, tummy tickles and sausage time. Alice also got something nice at this point!

More practice followed over the next few days with baby Alice always responding well until she was ready to answer the call to her name.

Introducing Her Name Earlier

I made sure there were no distractions that could lead to failure. I waited until she was looking elsewhere then got down on my knees and waited. Even the cracking of my now creaky knee joints didn't give the game away. After snuffling about for a minute or so she turned, looked at me, realised I was on my knees and knowing that when I am in that position and she runs towards me something nice always follows, she was about to set off, but this time **before** she made the first step, I called her; **"Aaaa...liiis."** She took off like a shorter and furrier version of Usain Bolt and piled into me like a lunatic for a cuddle and a sausage. It was a routine we would practise over and over again.

Making Progress

Of course I was getting a bit hacked off with kneeling down all the time. I knew I needed to get upright, or audition for a role in "Planet of the Apes". She needed to learn that if she responded to her name when called, it didn't matter what position I was in, the response expected from her was the same, and the consequence for a desirable response was still the same.

I had to get her to respond when I was standing. But I did not want to risk her becoming confused by my new position and spoil the developing response to her name.

I started on my knees when she was a little distance away. **"Puu...ppy!"** and as she turned and started towards me, I stood up, although not fully upright and kept the encouragement going. Once again, I only called her name; **"Aaaa...liiiis,"** when she could not fail.

I repeated this until I was able to do it when I was standing upright before making the call and achieved the same response from baby Alice.

Soon Alice had worked out that whether I was kneeling or standing, it made no difference to the outcome. Her response was still reliable. I began to insert her name into the sequence a bit earlier, until I was able to use it at the very beginning, just before she made the first step.

Progress

The sequence was then practised when she wasn't looking. Again, I went back to simplify it, first calling **"Puuuppy!"** and adding her name when she had responded, was approaching like a missile and couldn't possibly fail.

Finally, I called her name when she wasn't looking. I waited and checked all around to ensure there was nothing that could distract her once I had called, then gave her the call **"Aaal...iiis!"** It was amazing; she completely ignored me and ran away! No, I'm kidding, but it would have made this bit more interesting, wouldn't it?

Baby Alice spun around, locked on to me and came hurtling back for the best ever tummy tickle, loads of snogging and some extra bits of sausage. After all she had just passed her first exam and I was very proud of her. It was only right that I should let her know.

More than just teaching her to respond to a word, we had just completed the first step to building a relationship for life and for any working role we might perform together in the future.

How Long Does it Take

Reading that breakdown it might seem like it is going to take a long time to achieve this level of response. How long does it take? Well that depends upon you, your puppy, and how often you practise.

This whole process took Alice and me less than 3 days to achieve. After 2 weeks we had successfully generalised her response so that she performed it reliably in about 6 different locations.

Why is it So Important?

As you progress through your puppy's training, following the methods described in this book, your puppy's name will be the word that alerts her to the fact that you are just about to give her some important information. Information she must respond to in order to experience a very nice consequence.

It will be used before almost all instructions that you give to her. It is vital to her progressing from a response to her name delivered at close quarters to an effective, reliable recall regardless of distance.

Establishing it as something special is essential. Once learned, treat it like it is precious and only use it when you have something important to tell her, never frivolously.

===

Other Words Used When Training Alice

Cue or Command?

You will notice that the heading for this subject is "...Words Used in Training Alice." I haven't referred to them as "Commands" or, as is often used in dog training circles, "Cue" words. There are a number of reasons why I have not referred to the words as either commands or cues.

The first reason is that dog trainers always disagree on terminology, and are happy to argue the point at length; resulting in 3 days spent discussing something that is fairly irrelevant. (I have noted over many years that those who spend most time arguing over terminology generally don't spend much time actually training dogs!)

The second reason is that it doesn't really matter to your puppy. She doesn't even know what a word is. To her, it's just a sound that her Mum or Dad makes. Later she will learn that if she responds to this sound in a certain way something nice will follow. If she doesn't, it won't.

The third reason is that you, the proud owner of a fantastic puppy, don't care either. You just want to teach her to **"Sit!"**

I have used the term **instruction** for verbal communication and the term **signal** for communication given by hand or body movement. I may have forgotten occasionally and slipped up to use the word Command or Cue, so I apologise in advance. You will be able to follow what I am telling you, because you are human and you understand that different words often have the same meaning.

But please remember, your puppy doesn't understand stuff like that. Words only have a single meaning to your puppy. They are not interchangeable.

Small Vocabulary

The words I used to train Alice are the same as I use in all my initial training and it is a remarkably small vocabulary. The fewer words for her to learn, the easier it is for her. I want to make it as easy as possible for her to get it right, so she can earn her reward.

The better she learns that this training lark is a game worth playing, the more she will want to do it. Everybody likes a game that they are good at and win **most** of the time. I say most, not all, because there needs to be a challenge in order to maintain interest. In this respect puppies are remarkably similar to humans.

Tell Me the Words!

The words I use are few and simple. No, I don't mean that those are the actual words. I mean, I don't use a lot of words and the ones I use are simple to remember.

If you can remember these few words, their meaning, as understood by your puppy, use them consistently, appropriately, and at the right time, you will succeed in training your puppy. If you can't, you won't!

The words are:

Alice. This is the most important word. It is her name. It's the only one she has. It is special, so don't wear it out. (But please remember to insert your own puppy's name here; calling them all Alice will just result in confusion, particularly if your puppy is a boy!)

Your puppy's name is usually the first word you will train her to respond to. Make sure it is not also the first word you train her to ignore!

The other words are **Yes, Watch, Come, Heel, Sit, Down, Stay, Good Girl or Good Boy**.

The more astute amongst you will have noted that I have missed the word that many of you are saying more than any other at present; **"No!"**

There is a very good reason for this. It is not that you shouldn't use this word, but it doesn't actually tell your puppy what you want her to do. So whilst it might be important to you, it is not a great puppy training word. It might be OK to interrupt something that your puppy is doing, but then you have to tell her what you want her to do instead.

For example, I am walking Alice on the lead, when a rabbit pops out of the hedge. Alice immediately locks on to it and wants to chase it. I tell her; **"Alice...No!"**

So she stops looking at it. But what does she do next? I have to tell her to do something, such as **"Come, Sit** or **Down!"** because if I don't, she will stop for a second and then, given the absence of any further guidance from me, she will just go back to looking at the rabbit and wanting to chase it.

Using the word **"No!"** just seems a bit pointless. I could have just said; **"Alice, Sit! Stay!"** If Alice has been sufficiently trained, she will do exactly as I have instructed her to do. She doesn't need to know what I **don't** want her to do, she needs to know what I **do** want her to do.

Perhaps the reason we all use this word so much is because we had it said to us so much. It's a bit monkey see, monkey do. We do as was done to us.

Some might disagree with my thinking and training methods in this regard, but then I have 4 dogs that live on a 10-acre smallholding alongside 5 horses, 2 cats, 26 alpacas and 3 chickens, which, despite the absence of the word **"No!"**, none of my dogs chase.

There are undoubtedly other methods that other trainers use, but I use the ones that work for me and my dogs and which I have tried and tested. As I said earlier, this is not a "How To" book, it's a "How I did it" book, and the methods explained for you have worked time and time again.

Other Words Used

"Watch!" is the word used to tell your puppy to follow your left hand and touch it with her nose. Teaching your puppy to touch your left hand with her nose is called Hand Targeting. It is an excellent signal for your puppy to respond to, because when she is targeting your left hand she is giving you her attention, rather than anything else that you might not want her to focus on.

It also ensures she is focusing on you, so you can follow it with a further instruction such as **"Heel!"**

"Come!" is the word used to instruct your puppy to return to you immediately, from wherever she is, so that you can take hold of her collar.

"Heel!" is the word used to instruct your puppy to take up a position at the side of your left leg. Then to walk alongside you in the same direction, at your pace, in order to maintain this position until you give her a further instruction.

"Sit!" is the word used to instruct your puppy to immediately place her bum on the ground. I will explain 2 different **"Sit!"** positions in detail.

"Down!" is the word used to instruct your puppy to lie flat with her elbows and tummy on the ground.

"Stay!" is the word used to instruct your puppy to remain in the position that she is in when the instruction is given, until she receives a further instruction from you.

"Yes!" is not a word used to give an instruction to your puppy. It is the word used to **mark** your puppy performing an act in response to one of the words of instruction listed above. It is extremely important.

It is given at the exact moment when your puppy responds to the instruction or signal correctly, according to the standard that you have set. This **marker** word is then followed by some form of reinforcement, most commonly a small treat delivered from your left hand. It may also be a toy delivered to her, verbal praise, or physical praise.

As well as marking the desired response and letting your puppy know that the reward she has earned is on its way, the **marker** word also **ends** the need for her to continue performing the desired response.

For example you ask your puppy to **"Sit!"** she immediately adopts the correct position, at which point you **mark** the desired behaviour with the word **"Yes!"** Your puppy may now move in order to receive her reward.

If you had instructed her to **"Sit!"** then added the instruction to **"Stay!"** before walking away from your puppy, the word **"Yes!"** would not be given until you had returned to your puppy and you wished to indicate to her she had performed the **"Stay!"** part of the exercise correctly and she had earned her reward. The exercise is ended not when you return to your puppy, but when the word **"Yes!"** is given.

Good Girl/Good Boy. These words are neither **instructions** to your puppy, nor are they **marker** words indicating successful completion of the desired response. Rather, they are words of encouragement that convey to your puppy that you are pleased with her and for her to keep going with the response she is giving for a bit longer yet.

It is human nature to regularly tell your puppy she is a **"Good girl!"** She should enjoy hearing these words because of the way they are delivered, but they are given in such varied circumstances that they do not make good marker words.

"No!" If you feel you can't possibly survive without having a word to instruct your puppy to stop performing an undesirable act then just use the word **"No!"**

"No!" means only one thing. Stop whatever you are doing immediately. For it to be effective it must always be followed by a clear instruction to tell your puppy what you want her to do instead. That being the case, as I said earlier it would have been more effective to have simply given that instruction in the first place! Still, if something is important, it is worth saying more than once. Unless of course it is your puppy's name!

===

Planning, Goal Setting and Recording

Planning Your Training Session

Planning your training is essential to success. Many will say you don't need to take such a methodical approach. This is the stated opinion of 2 categories of trainer; absolute training geniuses, who are very rare, and those who consistently produce mediocre results and then claim their dog was a poor student. Those people are abundant.

Set Time Aside

Plan how many training sessions you are going to do each day and set time aside for them. Your actual training time is probably going to be only 3 to 5 minutes per session, with 3 training sessions performed each day.

But with planning, preparing your equipment and allowing your puppy time to absorb what she has just learned, you are probably looking at 15 minutes of your time spent on each session.

That is quite a time commitment and you really do need to organise your time to fit it in. That said, real life often gets in the way of training and it is far better to miss a session rather than do a rushed one because of time constraints, or a bad one because you are not in the right frame of mind. If you have just had your backside chewed by your boss, and your car got a puncture on the way home, you are unlikely to have sufficient time or be in the right frame of mind to train your puppy. Just spend some nice bonding time with your puppy instead and leave training until your puppy's next scheduled session.

Set a Precise Criterion

Be absolutely clear what you are going to train your puppy to perform in this specific session. Don't vary from it. Don't elaborate. Stick to it accurately and be patient. This might be something as simple as **"Sit!" front, by following a clear, slow hand signal.** That's it. That's all. She doesn't need to sit straight, or close, she just has to put her little bum on the floor in response to your clearly delivered hand signal.

Plan the Different Exercises

In the early stages this is quite simple, as each session will focus on a single exercise, such as **"Sit!"** As you both progress you will train 2 or 3 different exercises in a single session, with breaks in between, but don't be in too much of a rush to do this. Alice is quite the young lady now, but I still train a single exercise in a training session the majority of the time. Even with my most advanced and experienced dogs, I very rarely train more than 3 different exercises in a single session.

3 Sets of 5

Keep your training sessions structured on the basis of 3 sets of 5 repetitions. This may be a 1st set of 5 x **"Sit!"** Break. 2nd set of 5 x **"Sit!"** Break. 3rd set of 5 x **"Sit!"** End session. Relax and absorb.

Or, as you progress; 1st set of 5 x **"Watch!"** Break. 2nd set of 5 x **"Sit!"** Break. 3rd set of 5 x **"Down!"** End Session. Relax and absorb.

It's really not that tricky, unless you choose to over-complicate matters.

Goal Setting

You can divide your goals into immediate goals, weekly goals, or monthly goals. It may go even longer into the future if you are training a working dog, such as a Service dog, in which case you will be working towards a big goal, maybe a year in the future.

For most owners of a family dog, it is generally enough to set shorter-term and more modest goals. Your daily session should take you slowly towards the weekly goal and the weekly goal should take you towards your monthly training goal.

For example, your weekly goal might be to have your puppy "Sit!" in front of you, on the first hand signal with a minimum success rate of 80%.

Your monthly goal might be to have your puppy **"Sit!"** in front of you, **straight** and **close**, on a hand signal and verbal instruction with a minimum success rate of 80%.

Your 3-monthly goal might be to have your puppy **"Sit!"** in front of you, **straight** and **close** on just a **verbal instruction** and do so in at least **6** different locations with a minimum success rate of 80%.

Recording

You don't need to be an Excel spreadsheet Ninja in order to chart your puppy's progress. If you are a bit of a technological dimwit, like me, a simple notebook is absolutely fine for the job. For those who regard themselves as computer geeks, design a simple table that you can complete, and keep the completed sheets in a little folder.

It can be as simple or elaborate as you like, as long as you can understand it and chart your puppy's progress, or identify patterns showing when it all goes a bit pear-shaped.

If you note that every Friday evening, the results of her training sessions always seem to be a bit poor, then you might consider missing that session each week, or not going to the pub before coming home to train her! That might be a bit drastic though - better to miss the training session.

===

Generalisation and Proofing

Why is it important?

A lesson learned by your puppy must be of value throughout her life, and in real-life situations.

It is of little value to have your dog recall reliably in your garden, but nowhere else, unless of course she will spend her whole life in your garden. Likewise, your puppy will not live her whole life in a vacuum, there will be outside influences that affect her level of performance and reliability. You must train her to deal with all these influences.

So what do the terms mean?

Generalisation

When the term Generalisation is used in puppy training, it means that anything you have taught your puppy can be performed anywhere, anytime, to the same level of proficiency.

It means that your puppy knows that when instructed to **"Sit!"** on the training field, she has to give the same response to the instruction as she does when being walked in the street.

It means that when the same instruction is given in the same way outside the pub, the response required is exactly the same as is required on the training field, or at the kerb on the high street.

It also means that the same instruction given in the same way outside the pub…oh, we've already done that one, haven't we?

Regardless of the location, time of day, weather conditions, whenever your puppy is given the same instruction, she is required to give exactly the same trained response, and in return she expects the same reinforcement from you.

The bit where Generalisation usually goes wrong is when your puppy gives the same response in the street, then looks to you, glowing with pride at her cleverness and you fail to mark her success with a **"Yes!"** and then you fail to reinforce it in the same way. Shame on you!

A simple example of Generalisation might be: You have taught your puppy a reliable 20-second **"Sit, Stay!"** when you are 5 paces away in your garden.

You then teach her to do the same on the training field. You then teach her to do the same when you are walking her around your usual walking route.

You should consider that the exercise has been successfully generalised when she is performing the same exercise, at the same distance, for the same length of time in half a dozen different places.

You will note I specified the exact same exercise. Don't move to a different location and expect her to stay for twice as long or at twice the distance. If you do, and she fails, then it may not be a failure to generalise, it may just be that she hasn't learned to **"Sit! Stay!"** for that long, or at that distance.

You have forgotten the important rule. Whenever you are training your puppy, only change or increase one criterion at a time. That way, if it goes wrong, you have a good idea of why it has gone wrong, and you should then be able to remedy the problem without too much difficulty.

Of course I am far too good a trainer ever to make such mistakes...

Daisy May and the Dumbo, er, Dumbbell

When you are teaching your puppy any new lessons, she is taking in the information you are consciously teaching her, but she is also picking up information from the environment where you are training. Most of this information is irrelevant to the lesson you are teaching her, but of course she doesn't know this. She is taking in a lot of information that you need to filter out in order to make the picture clearer for her.

Let me give you an example of how your puppy might take in information.

This is Daisy May. She is a 10-year-old German Shepherd. When Daisy was a puppy I was teaching her to perform a formal retrieve for Working Trials competition.

Daisy May (Normal head)

I decided to train her to do it by breaking the exercise down into small, precise component parts, **marking** each tiny, correct action, and following the **mark** with a treat to **reinforce** it in Daisy May's mind.

Only after she had learned a number of individual elements would I begin linking them together to form the whole exercise.

With many other dogs I have successfully trained this exercise by chucking a dumbbell, having my puppy chase it and bring it back to me in a casual manner, before slowly refining it into the final, sharp, precise exercise I required her to perform.

Both methods work well and I have used both successfully with many pups since, but this was to be the first time I had used the first method described with a 12-week-old puppy.

I began training in my kitchen, because it was dark when I came home from work. It was a quiet place away from my other dogs. (I'm not scared of the dark or anything, it was just easier.)

I started with Daisy in the **"Sit!"** position, right in front of me, in what would be her final position when presenting the dumbbell to me. I showed her the dumbbell and when she looked at it **marked** it and **reinforced** her for doing so.

Once this was reliable I wiggled the dumbbell to stimulate her to touch it, but being a bit cocky, she grabbed it. As she did so, I let her hold it for a second or two, then marked her for the hold. At this point, from experience, Daisy knew that a mark was followed by a treat and she was never going to fit a treat in her gob whilst holding the dumbbell, so she released it into my hand.

The next stage was to repeat this until she would sit looking up at me and hold the dumbbell comfortably. I could put my hand on the end of the dumbbell and hold it, but Daisy did not release until she received the marker for the correct behaviour.

The dumbbell was then offered to her in a progressively lower and lower position, until I was able to place it on the floor between my feet, just in front of her paws, whereupon on the command; **"Hold it!"** she would dip her head down, take the dumbbell in a firm grip, but without chewing it and sit looking up at me in a beautiful **"Present"** position, holding it for anywhere between 5 and 20 seconds, before I put my hand on it whilst she retained it in a firm grip, until the desired response was marked.

This routine was practised and Daisy May performed it to a very high standard over a period of about a week, practising it and building it for 3 sessions of 5 minutes each evening. I was very proud of little Daisy May. (I still am.)

Anyway, I decided to show off my great little puppy and demonstrate my great training skills, so I decided to give a command performance to Carol.

I set up the scenario. The treats were prepared, the dumbbell fetched by me. I took Daisy out for a short walk and a piddle and we were good to go.

I called Carol into the kitchen and began the well-rehearsed demonstration.

I started the training session with a 3 of 5 routine and then set up for the command performance.

I had Daisy May in front of me and I placed the dumbbell on the floor directly between us, just in front of her little paws. She was looking directly at my face and all was set. **"Daisy, hold it!"** Daisy looked down at the dumbbell, at me, at Carol, at the dumbbell and back at me again. But did not move, nor did she attempt to pick it up and hold it.

I was sure she must have been struck deaf, so after a short pause, during which little Daisy May never took her eyes from me, I repeated the instruction, **"Daisy, hold it!"**

Once again Daisy looked at the dumbbell, at me, at Carol, at the sink, then back to me.

Daisy May (Big head)

At this point Carol, who before she met me had no sense of humour whatsoever, but now regards herself as something of a comic, asked; "Are you teaching her to leave?" "No." I replied. "That's a pity, because if you were, it would have been really good." And with that, Albrighton's leading stand-up comedienne walked off sniggering.

I looked at little Daisy May, with her outsized head, and wondered if her breeder would take her back, as she was clearly defective.

I then noticed she kept looking past me towards the sink. I suddenly realised that every night when we had practised, I had stood with my back towards the sink. Now, in my haste to show off, I was standing on the other side of the kitchen.

When I had given the **"Hold it!"** instruction to Daisy she must have thought, "Well this is all very familiar Dad, but surely we are in the wrong place. I don't want to get it wrong, so I will just wait until you move to the correct place, you plonker!"

In Daisy's mind the sink was an important element of this exercise. What I needed to do was to go back to the first stage of training in a slightly different place and build it up to the point I was at now.

I then trained the whole process in a different place, then another, then another. Each time starting at the beginning and building it up to the point she had achieved in front of the sink.

It soon dawned on Daisy May that the sink had absolutely nothing to do with the exercise. And regardless of where we did it, if she got it right, she would be marked and rewarded for it.

This doesn't mean that when teaching your puppy to perform a skill you should not do it in the same place whilst she is learning it. I would encourage you to do exactly that. But what it does mean is that once your puppy has learned to perform an exercise in one place you need to train it again in another place, then another and so on.

Top Tip: Whenever you are generalising any exercise, the first few times you do it in the new location, drop 1 criterion, just a touch, and maybe increase the value of the reinforcement the first couple of times.

So when I ask baby Alice to perform her reliable 20-second, 5 pace **"Sit! Stay!"** in a place we have never been to before, I always make it a bit easier for her. I may reduce the time to 10 seconds whilst keeping the distance at 5 paces, or I may reduce the distance to 3 paces and keep the time at 20 seconds.

Note that even when making a reduction, I only reduce a single criterion, not both.

Proofing

Proofing is similar in some ways to Generalisation, but it isn't the same.

Proofing takes place when your puppy has reached a good standard of proficiency in a particular exercise on the training field and has successfully generalised it, so that it is performed equally well in a wide range of different locations.

You then proof the learned behaviour by testing it in the presence of progressively stronger distractions.

A simple example of proofing might be something like this:

You have successfully trained your puppy to perform a reliable recall on the training field. You can release her from the lead and at any time, when she is 20 yards away, you can call her; **"Alice, Come!"** and baby Alice will immediately change direction and run straight to you, making a beeline for your left hand - you remember that, it's the left hand which you have been teaching her to target when you have trained her to **"Watch!"**

Returning like a little missile she contacts your left hand and you mark her success with a **"Yes!"**, then you reinforce it with a treat and perhaps a cuddle and tummy tickle as you take hold of her collar for a brief moment.

You have generalised this exercise, so she will perform it equally well in your garden and at least half a dozen different places where you take her for walks, play and training.

But she hasn't yet learned to do it when there are distractions. So this is where proofing comes in. If you do it at the right pace, only increasing the level of distraction, or changing the type of distraction very slightly, until she has successfully mastered it, it should go well, with very few mishaps. You never increase the level of distraction and change the type of distraction at the same time.

If you are concerned, consider attaching a very light training line in the initial stages, so that if she gets it wrong, or looks like she is about to, she won't be able to self-reward.

Start with very mild distractions. It may just be a stationary, single person standing 30 yards away. You call her from the same distance, or a distance slightly less than that at which she has proved reliable. You call her in exactly the same way.

When she performs the exercise successfully you **mark** it and **reinforce** it in the same way. As I said before, you may consider making the reinforcement a little bit more special, but don't kick the backside out of it. A slightly bigger or tastier treat will suffice - she doesn't require a whole leg of lamb!

Work at this level of distraction, then raise the bar a bit. Increase the level of distraction by having the person walk. You now have a moving distraction to contend with.

Having achieved reliability with 1 walking person, you should increase the level of distraction by using 2 people. If you think that this might be a step too far, have the 2 people stand still, then achieve reliability, before having them walk.

As you can see, all the time it is a gradual progression. The progression may differ from puppy to puppy. Some pups may find people a remarkably interesting distraction, whilst others don't really care.

Some puppies will find a slow-moving, adult dog to be a bit boring and not worthy of their attention, whilst others will be drawn to anything on 4 legs like the effect of an electro-magnet.

The point is, make it progressive. Take your time and consolidate before making progress with your puppy. You can have good, or you can have quick. Good is always better.

===

The Training Environment

This section was going to be titled "The Perfect Training Environment", but then I realised it would be the shortest section ever, because quite simply, the perfect training environment just doesn't exist...well not in a single place anyway.

Earlier in the book different types of puppy training schools and training programmes were discussed and you may by now have decided what type of establishment you wish to use. But this is just the place where you learn the theory and technique of training your puppy. It is where she learns the basics. She truly learns during your 3 daily training sessions and these short sessions should take place just about everywhere you go with her.

Don't be under the illusion that you can use a single environment to carry out all your puppy training, because if you do her training may fall apart in different places, because you will have failed to generalise the training and your puppy only associates what she has learned to do with the specific place in which you have trained her.

You also need to seek out different environments to practice different skills as and when your puppy's progress requires it. For instance, when you are teaching the initial stages of a skill such as lead walking you want to begin in the quietest place imaginable, with no distractions.

Having mastered the basics you want to take her to different places that are equally quiet and secluded. Now she will learn that this exercise can be performed in different places and if she gets it right, has the same rewarding results. It works on the grass training field. It works on the tarmac of the local car park. It works on the pavement around the corner from her house.

The next stage is to teach her that it also works when other things are going on.

It works when there are cars passing by. It works when there are people walking towards you carrying shopping. It works when Kevin the teenager is jumping off his school bus and it works when trucks are unloading their cargo near the shops.

This may mean that you have to go to a number of different locations to generalise her response and proof it against any number of distractions, but often, by using a bit of initiative, a single location can provide different challenges at different times of the day. It just takes a bit of Prior Preparation. I know; you've heard it all before.

In my local high street I was able to achieve the vast majority of baby Alice's training needs without moving more than 200 yards in any direction, depending upon the time of day.

At 7am the village is very quiet apart from the odd car. I can practise some heelwork on different surfaces and teach her to sit at kerbs, with few distractions.

At 8.30am Kevin the teenager and his mates are heading for the bus stop, or waiting at different pick-up points around the village for school bus pick-ups. I can practise having her focus on me in crowded places.

At 8.45am the buses arrive and depart. Bedlam ensues, with quite a lot of double-decker buses coming and going. This is good for her work near traffic.

At 8.50am the primary school run takes place. There is an increase in vehicle traffic, which close to the school is generally moving quite slowly. There is an abundance of little squealing sprogs, their Mums, and their even smaller siblings being pushed around in buggies. This provides a golden opportunity to acclimatise her to buggies and sticky-fingered munchkins.

At 9.30am it is time for the old giffers to make their way to the community centre for a bit of light exercise followed by a cup of tea and a sponge finger. This provides plenty of work around slow-moving people who may be carrying sticks or using walking frames.

By 10am all the other businesses are open and the village is becoming a busy place. The pavement by the shops has a lot of people going in and out of the shops and cars parked directly outside with people getting in and out. There are plenty of doors slamming and baby Alice can be biffed on the head by heavy carrier bags at 5 pence a throw.

At 11.30am a couple of horses will usually pass and if we are particularly lucky we get the added distraction of a liberal dollop of horse poo.

At 1pm the pub is doing a decent trade in meals, and in summer, which usually falls between 11am and 4pm on 10th of July each year, there are people eating their meals in the beer garden. I can sit and have a pint. Don't get me wrong, I don't enjoy it. I have to force myself in order to further her education, so she can learn to relax when there are people eating nearby.

As you can see, the same location provides a completely different training environment for Alice depending upon the time of day I train her. I even have a railway station about 500 yards away.

I am in the extremely fortunate position of being able to find all but the most unusual training areas within 1 mile of my home. You might have to travel further afield, but in all honesty, unless you are reading this book in a Yurt in Outer Mongolia, with a bit of imagination you will be able to find similar areas within a 10-minute drive of your home.

Alice still struggles relaxing at the pub. This remains a work in progress, but having impressed upon you the need for discipline when training your puppy, I must practise what I preach, so I will stick at it until she gets it right!

=====

PART 4

Training for Control

Introduction

By the time you get around to starting to train your puppy in her basic control exercises, you will have already spent a fair bit of time putting what you have learned so far into helping her acquire her life skills. You will also be well on the way to building a good relationship with her.

In this part of the book I will explain how to train your puppy to perform a range of control training exercises and then how the exercises learned on the training field should be incorporated into your puppy's daily routines.

I assume that's why you are training your puppy. You probably don't want to enter the Cruft's obedience championships, just to take her to the shops, for a walk in the park, or to accompany you when you walk the kids to school.

This is also the bit when I come over as a bit of a mentalist by going over the same stuff again and again. As I said previously, when training your puppy, if it works, do it.

Well, this is the reason I will repeat myself to you. Because it works, so I do it. I will consistently emphasise the need to stick to routines in order to train your puppy. Keep it simple, and whenever possible, keep it the same. Don't change things that don't need changing.

By practising a routine yourself, so it becomes second nature to you, it enables you to focus on your puppy, because your own routine will be so well embedded that you will be able to perform it automatically.

On a technical note, throughout Part 4 I will assume that your puppy will walk on your left-hand side. I make this assumption because the standard **"Heel!"** position for working dogs and competition dogs is to walk on the left-hand side.

I understand that historically the reason for **"Heel!"** being on the left of the handler goes back to the early gundog trainers. Most people being right-handed, they would hold the shotgun in their right hand and fire it from their right shoulder. That being the case it makes sense that they would wish their dog to be on the opposite side, away from the gun.

I have no idea if this is actually true, but I tell everyone attending my classes that it is, so I see no reason to depart from that story at this late stage.

Anyway, on the basis of the dog being on the left, I will describe training your puppy to target your left hand and holding the lead and other stuff in your right hand. If any of you require your puppy to walk on your right side because of physical constraints, or on religious grounds, such as being raised a Welsh Tobacconist, or just because you regard yourself as a free spirit, then please just reverse the instruction I am describing and use the opposite hand or leg.

Training your puppy should be an enjoyable experience for both of you, and it is a better experience when shared. Enrol with a good trainer or training school to help you succeed.

You will have good training days and not-so-good training days, but remember, you always get to take the best puppy home with you.

"Time for work, reader!"

===

Choosing a Training Programme

There are a few established puppy training schemes in the UK and for most owners they are a good place to start with their puppy. They have advantages and disadvantages, but their effectiveness in helping you develop your puppy into a well-behaved and well-balanced dog still depends upon the qualities of your instructor.

The advantage of such schemes is that the schedule of what subjects you will be covering is set out at the start of the course, as is the standard you will be expected to attain. Another attractive prospect is the specially printed certificate you and your puppy receive upon successful completion of the course. This will look great on your wall, but given the choice between a poorly run course that gives you a smart-looking certificate, but a poorly trained puppy, and an independent course that gives you a home-made certificate and a well-trained dog, go for the second option.

Unless you are a bit odd, you won't spend much time looking at the certificate, other than to dust the frame, but you may be spending the best part of 15 years looking at your dog. A certificate doesn't show that you have a well-trained dog, her behaviour does.

So the choice you have available is to follow an established training scheme or an independent training programme designed by a good trainer. The second choice to be made is whether you wish to join a group training class, or have one-to-one training. Each option has its own merits and I will discuss these with you later.

The most well-known and widely available national training scheme is the Kennel Club Good Citizen Dog Scheme.

This scheme has been running since 1992 and currently has over 1800 organisations that offer training and testing for the scheme. The scheme aims to provide the owner with the ability to control their dog and be able to provide a good standard of care and husbandry for her.

The scheme is regulated to ensure as far as possible that the standards are maintained. Courses and testing can only be provided by Kennel Club Registered Clubs and Societies, or Kennel Club approved Good Citizen Dog Scheme listed organisations.

The scheme is modular and progressive, beginning with the Puppy Foundation and moving through Bronze, Silver and Gold levels. I understand that the Kennel Club is considering introducing a Platinum course at some point in the future.

Progressing through all the levels currently available is likely to take you about 14 months, as your puppy must be over 12 months before she is eligible for the Gold award. If undertaken in group classes, then in addition to providing your puppy with stimulation and guiding her learning through the period when she is most receptive to training, it also keeps her in contact with other dogs, thereby continuing her socialisation with her own species throughout this crucial time.

Is the scheme the perfect way to train your dog? Absolutely not, but if anyone has the perfect format for doing so please let me know.

Details of the scheme can be found on the Kennel Club website, http://www.thekennelclub.org.uk/training/good-citizen-dog-training-scheme/

The British Institute of Professional Dog Trainers also runs a similar scheme in the form of its National Codes. These codes were devised in the early 1990s, but due to the launch of the Kennel Club Scheme, which the BIPDT helped formulate, the BIPDT did not launch its own scheme until 1997, and limited the code to BIPDT- registered clubs, meaning finding somewhere offering the code often required the assistance of Inspector Morse.

In 2013, the National Code was opened to any club, organisation or individual who wished to run it. The National Pet Code is comprised of three levels each awarding a certificate; Bronze, Silver and Gold. These must be undertaken in order. The guidelines appear more flexible than the Kennel Club scheme, and in my opinion some of the exercises are positioned in the BIPDT scheme in a more logical manner. For instance, getting your dog in and out of a car safely and in a controlled manner takes place in the BIPDT Bronze course, the first course offered, whereas it isn't undertaken until the Silver course, the third level, under the KC.

The main problem with the BIPDT course remains finding somewhere that provides it. Further details of the BIPDT National Pet Code can be obtained at http://bipdt.org.uk/national-code

The Association of Pet Dog Trainers does not as an association offer a training scheme. The APDT has a code of practice for its members and strongly promotes positive reinforcement as the primary training method. The association provides a list of instructors offering puppy training. To obtain more details of APDT members offering puppy classes in your area, send a SAE to APDT, PO Box 17, Fairford, GL7 4WZ or visit its website: http://www.apdt.co.uk/dog-owners/local-dog-trainers

Independent Programmes

Many independent trainers who offer their own group training classes and one-to-one training belong to one or more reputable professional organisations, but wish to have a bit more flexibility in setting their own course content, whilst some are members of none.

But whilst professional memberships may be an indicator that the person has usually been though some sort of application process, it is not a guarantee of quality.

Just because a person holds no professional memberships it doesn't mean that they don't offer excellent, structured, progressive training for your puppy, so please don't dismiss such trainers without finding out more. But find out more by doing some proper research. Don't take it from a few recommendations on their website or Facebook page. Let's face it, they are not going to leave negative comments displayed for all to see.

When you think you have found your trainer, don't base your decision on the content of the phone call. Go and visit them and have a face-to-face chat. Ask if you can go down and see them training a group class and see if you like what you see. But please remember that the class is for the benefit of the owners and puppies in training, not for visitors.

The trainer will not be giving you any attention when they are instructing, so be prepared to watch quietly and ask questions when the class is ended and the group has dispersed. Be prepared to stay for the full session, it is the height of bad manners to ask to watch a session and then leave after 10 minutes.

If for any reason you can't view a class, ask to see the trainer with their own dogs out on a walk. If they can't control their own dog(s) effectively, they won't be much good at helping you with your puppy.

And remember, claiming to be a dog trainer and appearing to be so has never been easier. A website, business cards from Vistaprint and a shiny van... Bob's your uncle. Being a dog trainer takes a lot more. Do your research!

Residential Training for Your Puppy

What is the point? Really, I ask this in all seriousness. You have decided that a puppy is the right companion for your family, invested time and effort in research and selection, prepared your home and now you want to send her away to be trained by, and bond with, someone else.

This might sound harsh, but devoting time and effort to training your puppy for life skills and control is one of the main things for you to consider when thinking about getting a puppy. If you want an older, trained dog, then this is what you should opt for, not a puppy.

Training is a massive part of the bonding process between you and your puppy. You are setting a foundation for her future as an important member of your family.

This training should take place with you, and other members of your family, in your home, garden, local streets and local parks where she will live her life.

There is very little point sending her to a strange place, with a person she doesn't know, and whom she might never see again, to be trained using techniques that you have no knowledge of.

Unless you and your family have been fully involved in all aspects of her training you will have wasted the once-in-a-lifetime chance to develop your relationship during her most formative period. Having no knowledge of how she has been trained, and sharing this learning period with her, when things go wrong - and trust me they will go wrong - you will have no idea how to rectify the problems.

Choose your training programme wisely. Good puppy training sets you and your puppy up for the rest of your lives together. That will only happen if you are fully involved, and that means **you** must be her trainer.

===

Equipment

The equipment I use for training my dogs and in real life is relatively simple. A few years ago I was contracted, along with another company, to provide training for a press event at Battersea Dogs and Cats Home on behalf of Churchill Insurance.

Now in fairness the other company did have to bring a number of agility items with them, whereas I didn't.

When I arrived at the centre the other company was already there and had installed a very large van/small lorry outside the training hall.

I reported to the training hall, just in time for lunch, my favourite time of day. I popped my head in and spoke with the person organising the event. She asked if any members of staff could help to bring in and set up my training equipment. I requested 2 people to assist. A couple of hefty fellas promptly appeared, and accompanied me outside.

Once outside, they appeared a bit confused as there was no van. I pointed to the Tesco carrier bag and suggested if they each took a handle, they would probably be able to move the kit without having to attend a Health & Safety course to learn safe lifting techniques.

Now whilst the story is a bit of a mickey take, it does illustrate the need for very few items of equipment to successfully train your puppy for life and control skills.

Equipment List

Crate

This should be of suitable size for your puppy.

Child Gate

If you have more than one of these it can be helpful, but a single gate will usually suffice when used in conjunction with the crate.

Puppy Pen (Optional)

As I use crates and child gates, I have only ever used a puppy pen when I have bred puppies, not when I have acquired a single puppy, but many trainers swear by them.

Collar

Your puppy's collar should be appropriate to her size. As your puppy grows you may need to replace this item, but most collars these days have a great deal of adjustment built in to their design.

Check it for fitting and security every day whilst it is on your puppy. You should be able to get 2 or 3 fingers down the inside of the collar. You should not be able to get your whole arm down there.

Remember that regardless of the fact that your puppy is microchipped you must have a name and address tag securely fitted to her collar when she is outside your home.

Lead

Select a lead that can be used for general walking and also for training. I recommend the use of a double training lead, which can be adjusted to 3 feet in length when walking your puppy at **"Heel!"** and can be extended to 4 feet, 5 feet and 6 feet in length as required.

Kong

A Kong toy appropriate to the age and size of your puppy is an excellent aid for use when crate training, for keeping her occupied when home alone and as a retrieve toy.

An additional Kong on a rope can be used a tug toy.

Long Line

I recommend a loose, long line of the type used to train gundogs. The type I use comes in 5-metre, 10-metre and 20-metre lengths and I use each length for different exercises, but you can get away with using just the 20 metre length by tying a small knot at 2 metres, 5 metres and 10 metres.

Treat Bag

You have invested a lot of money in your puppy, so don't come over all "Scrooge like" now. Invest less than a fiver in a decent, washable treat bag. Pet shops and t'interweb are full of them.

Treats

Don't buy them. Make them yourself. Don't worry, you don't need to be Gordon 'kin' Ramsay; you just need to be able cut up a sausage, or some small pieces of hard cheese.

If you are feeling like a contestant for the Great British Bake Off, why not have a go at baking some liver cake, or pilchard cake. It's not difficult and it can be frozen for storage. Just make sure you defrost it properly before use.

Clicker

A piece of equipment that is used as a marker when you train your puppy. It fulfils the same function as saying **"Yes!"** but in a very fetching plastic design.

Target Stick

If you are slightly less mobile and may struggle getting down to a smaller puppy on certain training exercises you should consider buying a target stick. This is used as an alternative to training your puppy to target your left hand.

They are also obtainable with a remote treat-dispensing device at the end, so you can have your puppy **"Watch!"** the end, **mark** her when she performs the desired action, and then by pulling the trigger dispense a treat at low level. Clever eh?

===

Teaching a Simple Exercise

From Lure and Reward to Voice Command

There are a number of stages to go through to train your puppy to respond reliably to a single clear voice command.

Later in the book each individual exercise will be explained in detail. The exercise described here is just an example used to illustrate the process you will employ each time. The actual exercises and criteria will vary.

Don't worry about holding her lead at present, this will be fully explained when training **"Watch!"**

What follows covers a relatively simple, step-by-step guide to achieving this. The same technique works regardless of the control exercise you are teaching your puppy to perform.

Decide What You Want Puppy to Do

This sounds very simple doesn't it? It should be, but very often it isn't. Where it goes wrong is when you change your mind about what response you require from your puppy halfway through the exercise, or between repetitions, so that what you expect your puppy to do in the 1st and 2nd repetitions changes by the time you have reached the 3rd repetition. This results in confusion for your puppy and frustration for you.

Be very clear in your own mind what you want your puppy to do and exactly where you set the benchmark for success.

Tell Her It's Time for Work

When I train Alice everything has a beginning and everything has an end. I am clear in my own mind when I am starting to work with her and I want her to be equally clear. It doesn't get any more complicated than me clipping a small treat bag, containing some very attractive-smelling treats to my belt and saying to her, **"Time for work, Alice."**

Keep it Simple

In this example you are going train your puppy to **"Sit!"**. When you are first training your puppy to **"Sit!"** the only thing you should expect is that in response to a lure, your puppy goes from the standing position to placing her bum on the floor.

That's it, nothing more.

She doesn't have to do it quickly. She doesn't have to do it very close to you. She doesn't have to do it facing straight towards you. She just has to touch her bum down in order to have her response marked and then rewarded.

(Don't panic if this description appears to be a bit basic. I will soon explain how to achieve a perfect **"Sit!"** in mind-numbing detail!)

Lure It

You will be able to lure your puppy into any position you want, in this case the **"Sit!"** position, by using the following method.

Take 5 treats from your treat bag and hold them in your right hand. Not some crappy treats from the supermarket, some nice sausage, cut up very small. Now take 1 treat in your left hand and place it on your puppy's nose. Allow your puppy to sniff it and draw it away from your puppy, very slowly and gently. She will follow the treat a very short distance in order to be marked and reinforced. (More about those things later.)

Imagine that you have a tiny piece of thread connecting your hand to her nose and you don't want to break it. That gives you an idea of how you should move your hand.

To lure her into the **"Sit!"** have her follow your left hand with her nose, and gently raise the lure upwards slightly, just higher than her head. In order to follow it, she will look up. There is a very simple rule of canine physiology, head goes up, bum goes down.

You have just lured her into her first **"Sit!"** although she doesn't know that. But she now knows that following your left hand results in nice stuff.

Mark It

So how does your puppy know when she has got it right? Because you are going to tell her! You are going to do it clearly and decisively, so there is no room for doubt in her mind. Of course you can only achieve this if the correct response is clear in your mind.

I recommend that you mark the desired response with the word **"Yes!"** Say it plainly and clearly and pronounce it at sufficient volume to ensure your puppy hears it. There is no room for a mumbling Phil Mitchell impression here. **Mark** her response clearly and precisely with the word **"Yes!"** and do it at the exact moment that your puppy completes the desired response; in this case the exact moment her little bum touches down.

Reinforce It

You have successfully lured your puppy to place her bum on the floor and you have **marked** the exact time of touchdown with the word **"Yes!"**

Now **reinforce** it by giving her a single small treat from your left hand. That's it! At this stage it really is as simple as that.

In the initial stages of training, each time your puppy follows the lure correctly, she is given the marker; **"Yes!"** and then her response is reinforced (rewarded) with a single treat.

1 lure, 1 desired response, 1 marker, 1 reward.

Repeat the Whole Process

Take a small step backwards and taking another treat from your right hand into your left hand, once again place it in front of her nose, draw her towards you, then gently raise the lure upwards. In order to follow it she places her bum on the floor.

Mark the behaviour clearly and precisely with the word **"Yes!"** at the precise moment that your puppy completes the desired response; when her little bum touches down, then **reinforce** it by giving her a single small treat from your left hand.

Repeat the whole process until you have done the exercise 5 times. Then take a short break. Let your puppy relax for a couple of minutes. Then set up the whole cycle again.

Repeat

Repeat this whole process until you have completed 3 sets of 5 repetitions with a short rest in between each set of 5.

Finished

You have now done 3 sets of 5 repetitions. After 3 sets of 5, tell your puppy that you have finished by telling her; **"Finished!"**

You started your training session with a clear beginning. You have now given your puppy a clear ending.

Latent Learning

After telling your puppy she has **"Finished"**, allow her at least 5 minutes to quietly reflect upon what she has just learned. Don't go into a mad period of play, just allow her to come out of the session slowly and allow the lesson to be absorbed. Play can come later, or at a different time.

Practise!

Practise this same routine 3 times a day. Each time you practise it complete 3 sets of 5 repetitions exactly as above until your puppy is proficient at it. She should be getting it right at least 4 times out of 5 before you consider progressing to the next stage. This 80% success rate is very important.

Conceal the Treat

Within a day or so of starting to lure your puppy, begin to conceal the treat in your left hand. She doesn't need to see it. It is a nice smelly piece of sausage, she knows it is there.

Everything else remains the same, it's just that the treat is concealed behind your left thumb. See the photograph in **"Watch", Teaching Your Puppy to Hand Target.**

Setting the Bar Higher

You have now succeeded in teaching your puppy to give the simple desired response at least 80% of the time. Now it's time to move on. You need to raise the bar a little. Not too much, but just enough to see progress.

Your puppy follows the hand lure and performs the **"Sit!"** reliably. But the only criteria you have been training for is to get her bum on the floor. As she has been closely following your hand as it lured her, it is likely that she is already sitting quite straight in front of you, but she might be sitting a few feet away, so you want to bring her closer.

You have now added another criteria. She now needs to **"Sit!"** but she needs to do it **close** to you. You will continue to lure her into position and **mark** the new standard with a **"Yes!"** and **reinforce** with a small treat delivered from the left hand.

If she does not achieve the new standard, the marker is not given and the reinforcement is withheld. In this case, quickly set her up again and slow the luring down a bit so she can follow and get it right the next time.

Practise the New Standard

Repeat the whole process until you have completed 3 sets of 5 repetitions in each session. As ever, train to this new standard 3 times every day.

Stick, Drop or Push

How do you decide when your puppy is performing well enough to consider raising the bar again?

Before raising the bar you should be achieving a minimum **80%** success at your current standard for at least 3 consecutive training sessions. If you are, **push** on and raise the bar a little further.

If you are hitting a **60%** or **70%** success rate, you should continue to practise at the current level, until you have reached the 80% mark. In effect you should **stick**.

If you are only getting a **50%** success rate at the beginning, you are probably not luring your puppy sufficiently well, so pay more attention to your technique.

If you drop to **50%** just after you have done a **push**, and have raised the bar, you may have raised it too much. Consider **dropping** the standard back a little until you hit the **60%** or **70%** mark again, **stick** and consolidate for a little longer before pushing again and raising the bar.

Adding a Verbal Instruction

Once you have been training an exercise by using the lure and your puppy is reliably performing the behaviour to the desired standard 80% of the time, you should consider adding a **verbal** instruction to the almost complete action.

You will note I have said "**Adding the verbal signal** to the almost complete action."

What you are doing in effect is adding a **label** to an action that your puppy is performing reliably. You add the word at the point when your puppy cannot fail to complete the desired action correctly.

In the case of the **"Sit!"** your puppy is lured as before and just as her bum **is about to touch down**, you add the word **"Sit!"**. As her bum touches down, **mark** the correct response with a **"Yes!"** then **reinforce** as before.

Bring It Forward

You will gradually give the verbal instruction earlier in the sequence. Continue to lure her as before, but now when she is **halfway** to completing touch down, add the word **"Sit!"** The second her bum touches down **mark** the correct response with a **"Yes!"** then **reinforce** her success, with a small treat as before.

Practise until your minimum 80% success rate is being achieved. When this is the case you will progress to giving the lure and verbal instruction at the same time.

You will add the verbal instruction to **"Sit!"** at the **same time** as you begin the lure, before **marking** success and **reinforcing** it as before.

Having practised and consolidated this new standard you are ready to work towards fading out the lure and then slowly reducing the significance of the hand signal, whilst increasing the significance of the verbal instruction.

Fading the Lure

The method I have explained involves the treat being concealed from your puppy's view right from the early stages. Using this method, right from the start your puppy is not responding to the sight of the treat, so removing it from your hand is not a big deal for her.

With a treat no longer held in your hand, give the usual hand signal at the same time as the verbal instruction. When your puppy responds as she has been trained to, **mark** her success with a **"Yes!"** and then, with your left hand, take a small treat from your treat bag and deliver it to your puppy, just as you have always done.

In the words of the famous Meerkat, **"Simples!"**

Reduce the Hand Signal

Let me say from the outset that there is no reason whatsoever why you really need to reduce or eliminate the hand signal when training your pup or when giving her instructions in a real-life scenario.

Even with a working dog I only reduce the hand signal, I don't eliminate it. If anything, I reduce the verbal instructions and train my dog to work effectively on hand and body signals, particularly at close range.

When working with a military working dog or police dog it is a distinct advantage to have your dog respond to a silent hand signal rather than a sharp **"Sit!"** or **"Down!"** command. In some situations, giving such a verbal instruction is likely to alert some 'orrible individual to your presence, which might have adverse consequences for you and your dog.

That said, for the sake of completeness, I will explain the method of fading out the hand signal. This can be beneficial in certain scenarios such as the recall, when your dog may be facing away from you, or her line of sight is obstructed.

Reduce Gradually

As with everything else you do when training your dog all change should be in small stages, so reduce the movement of the hand in small, manageable steps, working on the principle of at least an 80% success rate before you **push**.

You should only consider reducing it when you are successfully giving the verbal signal at exactly the same time as the hand signal.

Now, instead of drawing your left hand up quite high above your puppy's head, start the action as before, but don't take it all the way. Just take it about ¾ of the distance it would usually travel. **Mark** and **reinforce** the desired result as before.

In a series of small steps, gradually reduce the range of movement of your hand, until it is little more than a small twitch as the verbal signal is given. The last step is to keep your hand perfectly still when the verbal instruction is given.

As ever, progress by reducing the hand signal in small increments, always working to at least the 80% mark before pushing on.

Avoid Contradictory Messages

It can take a bit of time for you to fade out hand signals in favour of verbal instructions. In the meantime you should ensure that your voice and hand signals are delivering exactly the same message to your puppy.

Even when you have stopped using hand signals, be in no doubt that just because you aren't consciously using hand signals, your puppy hasn't forgotten them, so don't be surprised if you find your puppy performing certain acts when you haven't asked her to. She may well be watching what your hands are inadvertently doing and responding accordingly.

Similarly you should take care that when you are trying to fade out a particular hand signal you aren't inadvertently giving her another, which is contradicting what your verbal instruction is telling her to do.

I usually see this when an owner is performing the **"Sit! Stay!"** exercise. When this exercise is first trained a flat hand signal like a policeman stopping traffic is often given. As the puppy becomes more proficient and can perform a 30-second stay at about 10 paces, owners begin to fade out the hand signal and just use the verbal **"Stay!"** instruction.

The problem arises when, not knowing what to do with their now redundant left hand, the owner either drops the left hand to their side, into a position similar to the one it will be in when their puppy is being trained to walk at **"Heel!"** or they bring it up in front of their tummy in a manner that closely resembles the hand signal to **"Sit!"** to the front of the owner.

In the confusion, the puppy ignores the verbal instruction to **"Stay!"** and decides to follow the inadvertent hand signal to either **"Heel!"** or **"Sit!"** to the front of the frustrated owner.

Top Tip: Whenever your puppy performs an exercise that you have not consciously signalled, do a double check to make sure that she has not responded to a signal you didn't know you were giving.

Pitch and Tone

You must ensure that the tone of your voice matches your intent. For instance, if you wish to praise your puppy then there is very little point doing so in a dour, monotone way. It doesn't matter how nice your words are if delivered in a harsh or boring tone.

Similarly, when giving your puppy encouragement, the words themselves matter very little. Once again it's the tone used that matters. Your puppy will be far happier if you use a nice tone to say; "You're a horrid little mutt and I would like to bake you in a pie," in a nice voice, rather than; "You are a precious little princess and I love you," in a miserable or harsh tone.

It's not what you say; it's how you say it! Now, how many times has that got me into trouble?

Move Naturally

When training your puppy you should try to move in a natural manner and at a pace just a little slower than your normal pace to begin with, but progressing to normal pace as soon as possible. Remember normal pace differs from person to person. If you are training in a group class, work at your own natural pace and be consistent.

For example, when teaching your dog to **"Stay!"** you should avoid moving away from your puppy like an Olympic sprinter, or like Basil Fawlty taking great, long strides, or like Tom Cat creeping after Jerry Mouse, or like... well you get my point.

One Instruction, One Meaning

Regardless of whether you use a verbal instruction or a hand signal, each instruction has only one meaning to your puppy. She does not understand that humans sometimes use different words to convey the same meaning.

"Sit!" means put your bum on the floor. **"Down!"** means lie flat with your elbows and tummy on the floor. **"Sit, Down!"** is just nonsense. If your puppy makes a stab at what is required, she will almost certainly follow the last part of the instruction, which is the **"Down!"** part, when in all likelihood, you just wanted her to **"Sit!"**

If you repeatedly make errors like this, your puppy will come to regard you as something of a buffoon, stop listening to you and enlist in the Foreign Legion.

Cadence

The term Cadence relates to how you space your words, in this case your instructions to your puppy. You puppy will find it much easier to learn if you are consistent, there's that word again, in the cadence as well as the verbal instructions or signals you use.

To illustrate, I will use the dashes to indicate the length of pause between words when training. In this scenario I want Alice to **"Sit!"** at my side. Then walk at **"Heel!"** for a few paces, then when I stop, **"Sit!"** at my side again. The routine goes:

"Alice - - - Sit!" Her correct response is marked and rewarded.

"Alice - - - Heel!" I then set off at a natural speed for 6 or 7 paces.

Alice is walking nicely and before I stop, I say;

"Alice - - - Sit!" As I give the **"Sit!"** instruction, I come to a stop, and as I do so, I draw my left hand back and over Alice's head, so she sits right at my side, with her bum touching down, just as I stop. I then mark and reward the desired response.

As you can see from the 3 dashes between my words I have kept the spacing even. If I am consistent in the length of pause, my instructions and signals, I will achieve success much more quickly as Alice will be able to anticipate when my next instruction will be given.

Consistency and simplicity are extremely important when training your puppy. Her business is to learn, your business is to make it as simple as possible for her.

===

How to Structure a Training Session

If something works, stick with it. If it doesn't work, don't.

With that in mind I will now explain how I structure my own training sessions and encourage you to use the same process to train your puppy. Yours might differ slightly due to your own circumstances. This one worked and continues to work when I am training Alice. That is why I stick with it.

Starting and Finishing

When I am training Alice and my other dogs I always ensure that every single training session has a clear beginning and a clear ending.

If the session is going to cover several different exercises, which is quite rare when I am training a puppy, I would always ensure that each individual part has a distinct start and finish.

I prepare for each session in the same way. I go and collect my treat bag and Alice's lead. I allow my puppy 5 minutes or so to go to the toilet, have a sniff and a scamper about. When she is done and I am ready to begin, I call her to me, **mark** and **reinforce** her response. I then attach the lead to her collar and tell her, **"Time for work, Alice."**

3 Daily Sessions of 5 Minutes

I have disciplined myself to carry out 3 training sessions with my puppy each day. These are spaced at least a few hours apart and take place after Alice has been rested and toileted, but not within a couple of hours of her last feed.

Each control training session usually lasts for approximately 5 minutes. I keep it short and snappy. I aim to finish the session whilst my puppy wants more, then schedule in a short period of reflection and calm to allow for latent learning to occur at the end of each session.

3 Sets of 5

Having started the session by telling her, **"Time for work, Alice!"** I quickly go through a warm-up. At the start of Alice's training, the warm-up routine is the whole training session, but as we progress it becomes the warm-up and lead-in to the main exercise(s) we are going to train.

The 3 sets comprise:

1 set of 5 x **"Watch!"** - Short break.

1 set of 5 x **"Sit!"** - Short break.

1 set of 5 x **"Down!"** - Short break.

Following each set, we take a short break, only 30 seconds up to 1 minute, no longer. This gives me time to reload with treats and gather my thoughts for the next set.

Once we have started the session with this routine, Alice knows she is working. Your puppy will learn the same.

Train the Exercise

I then begin to train the exercise that we are going to focus on in the main body of the session, being absolutely clear in my own mind **exactly** what I am training my puppy to do in the session, exactly what I want to **mark** and **reinforce**, and what goal is to be achieved in the session.

I am going to train just 1 exercise. I keep the session simple and brief. It comprises 3 sets of 5 repetitions with a short break between each set.

At the end of the session, I leave no doubt in Alice's mind that the session is over by telling her; **"Finished!"**

Reflection

Although her work is finished, her learning hasn't, so I don't let her tear away at that point, or throw a ball or Kong for her. Instead, I allow her a period of maybe 5 or 10 minutes to reflect upon what she has just learned, sitting quietly with me before I take her for a short walk and a piddle, have a gentle play session, or take her home.

This need for reflection was something I learned the value of when training baby Alice's Uncle Jimmy.

Jimmy was one of 6 litter mates I bought whilst I was working at the Defence Animal Centre. The other 5 were destined to be Military Working Dogs and were accommodated in the kennel complex with a number of other pups and young dogs. Being so impressed with the quality of the puppies, I bought Jimmy to keep myself.

Unlike his litter mates, who were being trained to a timetable, I was able to train Jimmy at the time when he was most receptive to training. This was usually when he woke up from his place on the settee in my office and came over to see me for a bit of attention.

Jimmy "The Jimster" (Three nines Ace of Clubs) at 11 weeks

I would take him out to the toilet, have a short play with him and allow him to stretch his legs. I would then carry out 5 minutes of training as described above. A very short session, always starting with 3 sets of 5, before completing **3 sets of 5** repetitions of the exercise we were training during that session.

Nothing too intense, keeping it simple and fun, and at the end I would give a clear **"Finished!"** We would then go and climb a small grass bank, where we would sit together and watch the world (and 200 Military Working Dogs) go by.

After another 5 minutes I would take him for a piddle, a short walk, or a game of chase the Kong, before returning with him to my office, where he would rest and relax.

It was a regime I tried to implement with the next few litters of puppies undergoing training on the Young Military Working Dog Programme. It wasn't always possible due to time constraints of the development programme, but it was built in whenever possible.

Did this routine work with Jimmy? Well, you can be the judge of that.

Jimmy aged 3. British Police and Services Canine Association Victor Ludorum 2015

Training Multiple Exercises

As I said, in the early stages of training, I only train for a single skill in each session. My early stage goes on for quite some time, at least until my puppy is 6 months old and in many cases, as dictated by my puppy, often until about 8 months.

Even though I often got excited by Alice's progress I fought the urge to carry on for too long, or move to a different skill. I did struggle at times, but I was self-disciplined enough to stick to the rules and only train a single exercise in each session.

As baby Alice grew into little Alice, I sometimes trained 2 exercises in the same session, but always with a clear break, during which she was told; **"Finished!"** and allowed a short period of reflection in order to absorb the training she had just completed.

After this period of reflection I would move on to training the next skill, but you will note there has been no play session yet. That will come later, when training the second exercise has ended, she has been told **"Finished!"** and she has had a second 5-minute period of reflection.

Avoiding Confusion

One final point that I will mention is this. When Alice and I have moved on to training more than one skill in the same session, I am very careful what skills I combine. I do not train 2 exercises that are very similar, in case this leads to confusion.

Take for example these 2 exercises and how similar they are:

In the **"Sit! Stay!"** exercise, I leave Alice in the **"Sit!"** position, walk 10 paces away and turn to face her, then pause for 5 or 10 seconds.

I then return to her to complete the exercise whilst standing at her side.

In the formal **Recall to the Front**, I also leave Alice in a **"Sit! Stay!"** position, walk 10 paces away then turn to face her, but instead of returning to her side, I call her to join me.

As you can see, the start of both exercises is identical and I believe that in the early stages of training this is likely to lead to Alice making mistakes and becoming confused. Getting it wrong results in her not being rewarded/ reinforced and if repeated regularly it will de-motivate her.

This is definitely not how I want to her to feel. I want her to feel highly motivated to play the training game, a game in which she nearly always wins, particularly at this stage in her education.

Keep it Simple

I hope you agree that what you have just read is a simple, easy-to-remember training pattern. I'm sure it is, after all, it works for me and I won't be troubling Mensa for a membership application any time soon.

It is a routine and pattern of training that has served me well over the years and has helped me to produce some excellent dogs. It will serve you and your puppy well too, if you keep it simple and are self-disciplined enough to stick to it when you practise with your puppy each day.

===

"Watch!"- Teaching Your Puppy to Hand Target

The hand target is the most basic of exercises you will teach your puppy, and apart from her name and **"Come"** it is probably the most important word she will learn, yet the number of trainers who do not teach it is absolutely incredible.

Teaching your puppy to target your left hand serves 2 really important functions:

Firstly, it ensures that you have a means of immediately grabbing and holding your puppy's attention. When she is targeting your hand, she cannot be doing a lot of other stuff you don't want her to practise and learn.

Secondly, having her target your hand and follow it closely gives you an essential means of having her follow it into all sorts of positions, which will later become the control exercises we are teaching her to perform. It forms the basic element of the **3 sets of 5,** which you will use throughout your puppy's control training sessions.

Starting and Ending Your Puppy's Training Session

Before training, go through a little ritual of going to fetch your puppy's treat bag, and, if required, her lead. For many of your early training sessions there is no requirement to have your puppy on her lead, but as this is the first time you are going to teach the hand target it is important to start at the beginning, so your puppy will be on her lead.

Before every training session you must spend at least 5 minutes giving her some gentle exercise and the opportunity to have a piddle and a poo if required.

Every training session has a beginning and an end, so after her leg stretch and piddle call her back to you and attach her lead to her collar. You are now going to tell her something important; **"Time for work, Alice."**

This simple statement will begin all your training sessions from now on, so make sure you remember it. Please make sure you insert your own puppy's name in the phrase, I don't want too many Alices knocking about out there. One is more than enough!

Starting Position

Take your lead and put your right hand through the loop of your lead, or if you are using a 6-feet-long training lead, loop it over your right wrist.

Take 5 treats from your treat bag, which should be attached to your belt in a position that will enable you to reload with treats easily and without undue delay.

Hold the 5 treats in your right hand. You now have the lead over your right wrist and the treats in your right hand.

If you have selected really nice, smelly treats, by now your puppy will be paying a lot of attention to you.

Take a single treat from your right hand and hold it in your left hand. Place it in the palm of your open hand. At this point it is essential that the palm of your hand is facing upwards, or the treat will fall from your hand into your puppy's open mouth. Don't laugh, I have seen this done a few times.

Anyway, you have the treat in the palm of your upturned left hand. Now place your left thumb on top of the treat so you can hold it in position and conceal it from your puppy in a few seconds' time.

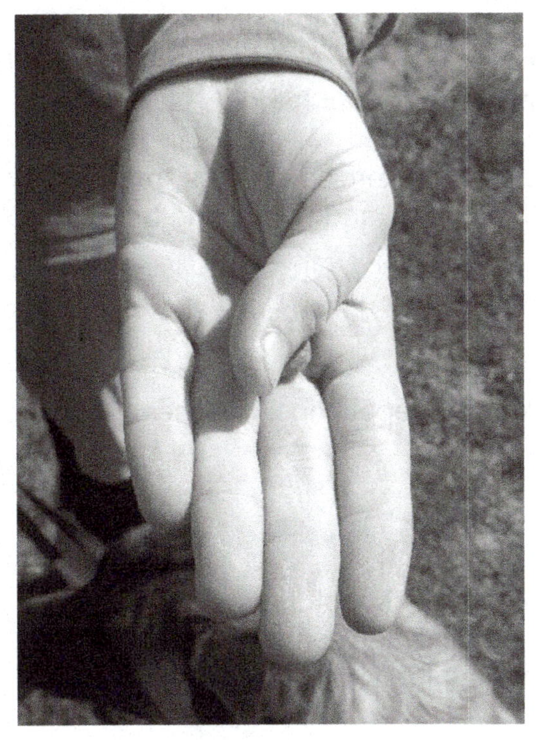

Concealed treat

Present it to your puppy

With the treat securely held in place by your left thumb, gently say your puppy's name; **"Aaa...liis,"** and as you say it, lower your left hand to your now fascinated puppy. With the palm of your hand facing her, put it right in front of her nose.

As soon as she puts her nose onto your palm, in order to snuffle whatever is hidden behind that thumb, **mark** her action by saying a nice clear **"Yes!"** then form your palm into a little cup, move your thumb out of the way and allow your puppy to eat the treat from the palm of your hand.

Repeat

Stand upright, take another treat from your right hand and hold it in exactly the same way in your left palm, held in place by your left thumb.

Gently say her name; **"Aa...liis,"** and as you do so, lower your left hand to your puppy, with the palm of your hand facing her, and put it right in front of her nose.

As soon as she puts her nose onto your palm, **mark** her action with a **"Yes!"** then form your palm into a little cup, move your thumb out of the way and allow your puppy to eat the treat from the palm of your hand.

Continue until you have performed the whole exercise 5 times, marking a successful response by your puppy with a "**Yes!**" and reinforcing her action by rewarding her with a delicious treat.

Take a Break

Your little pup has now completed 5 successful repetitions. Give her a minute to rest.

2nd Set of 5

Once she has been rested, prepare for your next set of 5 repetitions. Ensure that you are holding her lead and treats in exactly the same way, and perform 5 more repetitions in exactly the same way as the first 5.

Take a Break

Your little pup has now completed 10 successful repetitions. Give her another minute to rest.

3rd Set of 5

After a rest, prepare for your next set of 5 repetitions. Ensure that you are holding her lead and treats in exactly the same way, and perform 5 more repetitions in exactly the same way as the first 10.

Ending the Session

Your puppy has now completed 3 sets of 5 repetitions. The whole session including breaks should have taken only about 5 minutes or so.

You will now tell your puppy she has finished her work by simply telling her **"Finished!"**. You started with a clear beginning, you now have a clear ending.

Latent Learning

After being told **"Finished"** your puppy is still reflecting upon what she has just learned and trying to make sense of it all. Give her the opportunity to do so by allowing her 5 minutes to quietly reflect upon what she has just learned.

After the period of reflection I also like to take my puppy for another piddle before returning her to the house. In the early stages, I do not go into a period of play. Usually a puppy is quite tired by using her little brain. I like to allow her a chance to rest. Play can come later, kept separate during her early training.

Progress

After 2 or 3 training sessions that follow exactly the same pattern, you are now ready to raise the bar just a bit. Your puppy now has to take a few steps forward to make contact with your left hand.

Collect your training equipment, exercise and toilet your puppy and get ready to begin.

Starting Position

Take your lead and put your right hand through the loop of your lead, or loop it over your right wrist.

Take 5 treats from your treat bag, which is attached to your belt. Hold the 5 treats in your right hand.

Take a single treat from your right hand and hold it in your left hand, exactly as you did during your previous training sessions.

With the treat securely held in place by your left thumb, gently say your puppy's name; **"Aaaliis,"** and as you say it, lower your left hand to your puppy, with the palm of your hand facing her, close to her nose, but this time take a small step back and slowly sweep your left hand away from your puppy, so she has to take 1 or 2 steps forward to follow it.

Sweeping the target hand

You are now luring your puppy to follow your left hand, which has become a moving target. In order to gauge the correct speed to move, imagine that you have a tiny piece of thread connecting your left hand to your puppy's nose and you are carefully drawing her towards her target without breaking the thread.

As soon as she puts her nose onto your palm, **mark** her response with a clear **"Yes!"** and **reinforce** her success with a treat.

Repeat

Repeat this exercise for 3 sets of 5 repetitions. Ensure that each set has a short period of rest at the end of it.

Ending Your Session

After 3 sets of 5, inform your puppy that her training has ended by telling her; **"Finished!"** then allow her a 5-minute period to reflect and absorb the lesson.

Practise!

Practise as described for several sessions. The only progress you are aiming for is to gradually move your left hand slightly quicker, which requires a faster response from your puppy.

Remember, you must achieve a minimum 80% success rate before pushing on.

Progress

Having established a reliable response to the hand target from your puppy, you are now going to introduce the verbal instruction to accompany the hand signal.

Introducing the **"Watch!"** Instruction

Prepare your puppy for her training session in the manner previously described. Ensure she has been exercised and toileted and that you are properly equipped and ready to go.

Take a single treat from your right hand and hold it in your left hand.

Say your puppy's name; **"Aaa...liis!"**. As you say it, lower your left hand and sweep it away from your puppy. Your puppy knows the drill, and she will target your left hand and move towards it. Just before her nose makes contact add the verbal instruction to **"Watch!"** when it is inevitable she will complete the action successfully.

When she makes contact, **mark** it with a **"Yes!"** and **reinforce** it with a treat.

Continue for the remaining 4 repetitions of the set, and then until you have completed your 3 sets of 5 repetitions, with breaks at the appropriate times.

After the 3rd set, tell her the training session has **"Finished!".** Then allow the 5-minute period for latent learning.

Progress

As you carry out your regular practice sessions you are going to gradually bring the **"Watch!"** instruction further forward in the sequence.

Having started to insert it in the process just before your puppy completes the action successfully, the next stage is to insert it earlier.

Everything else remains the same. There is no change to the hand movement, but now you will insert the **"Watch!"** instruction when she is **on her way towards the target. Mark** and **reward** a successful exercise as before.

Before making further progress you should be achieving the 80% success rate.

Progress

Everything else remains the same. The hand movement remains the same, but now you will insert the **"Watch!"** instruction **just after she first moves** towards the target. **Mark** and **reward** a successful exercise as before.

Before making further progress you should be achieving the 80% success rate.

The Finished Exercise

You are working towards the complete exercise as you will soon perform it, as part of her "Warm-Up" at the start of almost every training session you carry out with your puppy.

Every aspect of your preparation is the same. Your hand movement is the same, but now you will say her name, **"Alice!"**. As you begin to sweep your hand, you will give the instruction, **"Watch!" before she makes a move.**

The **"Alice...Watch!"** and the hand movement should all become one single smooth event to which your puppy responds by targeting and making contact with your left hand.

Performing the **"Watch!"** Without the Treat

This is not as difficult as it sounds. In fact if you have been carrying out the exercise as described, your puppy will not have seen the treat in your left hand, because after the first couple of exercises it has been concealed behind your thumb.

To perform the exercise without the treat in your left hand simply follow this process.

Prepare for the exercise as before. Hold the 5 treats in your right hand, but do not take one in your left hand.

Say her name and give the verbal instruction; **"Alice...Watch!"** and as you do so, present your left hand in exactly the same way that you have always done, making sure to have your thumb on the palm of your hand as though there is a treat there. If you don't do this, you are changing the presentation of the hand target to your puppy, so don't be surprised if she doesn't respond correctly.

If everything is done as described, she will target your left hand as she has always done. When she makes contact, mark her success with a **"Yes!"** Then take a treat from your right hand and give it to her from your left hand.

Progress

When your puppy is successfully performing to her 80% success rate the next stage is to perform exactly the same process, but this time the treats remain in the treat bag.

Everything else is performed the same way and as she successfully targets your left hand, mark it with a **"Yes!"** then take a treat from the treat bag with your left hand and deliver it to your puppy to reward her successful response.

Generalise It

To generalise this exercise you and your puppy should perform it in at least half a dozen different places. Your puppy needs to learn that this **"Watch!"** caper is very rewarding whenever she gives the desired response, regardless of where she is asked to do it.

Proof It

As her response becomes solid and reliable, you need to proof her response in the presence of gradually increasing distractions.

At all stages of the generalisation and proofing process, ensure your puppy meets the 80% success rate before pushing on.

The Final Test

Whenever I have successfully trained a puppy to carry out the hand target on the verbal instruction, I do one final test. I did it with baby Alice and I have done it with most puppies I have trained over the past 10 years.

I sit on a small chair, or kneel down, so I am lower down in relation to the puppy for reasons you will soon understand. I usually do this off lead and quite informally.

I take a small handful of treats in my right hand, closed in a fist.

I allow the puppy to sniff my closed right hand and then I open my empty left palm, sweep it to my left away from my puppy and give the instruction **"Alice...Watch!"**

If I have carried out this test after training a reliable response by following the instructions set out above, my puppy will invariably move away from the right fist and target the empty left hand.

As she does so I **mark** her response with a "**Yes!"** then I take a treat from my right hand into my left hand and **reinforce** with a treat reward.

I repeat this several times, and with each successive repetition, I slowly open my right hand, so my puppy can clearly see that the treats are in my right hand, but she understands that the key to unlocking them is to target my empty left hand when I instruct her to **"Watch!"**

When the exercise is over I tell her; **"Finished!"** then give her a big, mental snog before allowing her 5 minutes to reflect. (Disclaimer: Do not snog your puppy if she has recently been eating horse poo.)

===

Alice... Come! Training an Effective Recall

Canal bank recall

A fast, reliable response to recall is the only non-negotiable part of your puppy's training. Your puppy must be trained to perform an effective recall. It is non-negotiable. If your puppy does not learn this, she will have a life of missed opportunity. She will be unable to take part in many family activities simply because she cannot be relied upon to return as soon as she is called.

What is the worst thing that can happen if your dog doesn't **"Sit!"** on the first command? Nothing too awful!

But if your puppy fails to recall it could have serious consequences for puppy herself, other people, and in this litigious age, you and your bank balance!

Failing to recall may in certain circumstances cost your puppy her life and will almost certainly cost her her freedom, as she won't be let off the lead again in a hurry, leading in turn to lack of exercise, reduced health and your puppy growing into an unfit, under-exercised dog, prone to frustration due to an abundance of energy she cannot use up.

Am I beginning to impress upon you the importance of starting training early and establishing a fast, reliable recall with your new puppy? Good. Because, no pressure, but teaching her this is your responsibility, and yours alone!

Build on Her Core Skills

As with each control exercise you teach your puppy, consider how you can build upon the stuff she has already learned from you; her core skills. By the time you are able to take your puppy out into the big wide world you should already have begun training 2 essential parts of the recall: the first being an effective response to her name and the second being the hand-targeting response to the **"Watch!"** instruction.

Training your puppy to respond to the "**Come!** instruction is little more than adding a different word to your puppy's name and having her target your left hand from a longer distance. See, I told you this dog training lark was simple. As long as you don't over-complicate it.

Early Generalisation and Proofing

Without doing so consciously, you have probably already begun to generalise her response to her name and the **"Watch!"** to a limited extent, by practising both in different locations. Granted, you will only have begun to do them in maybe 2 or 3 places, but it's a foundation.

You may even have already started proofing both the response to her name and the **"Watch!"** by training both in the presence of your partner, or children, or maybe even the family cat. Your puppy is beginning to realise that when she is given a clear instruction, and she responds to it, she will be rewarded, regardless of where it happens, or whoever else is present.

On the flip side, you may by now have realised that whilst she will usually respond to her name and the **"Watch!"** instruction, she can't yet perform either reliably in a strange place, or when there are other things to distract her. In this case, drop back a bit and practise more in familiar places and without distractions until each lesson has been thoroughly learned, before raising the bar a little bit.

Starting Your Puppy's Formal Recall Training

Start in the place where your puppy is already responding enthusiastically to her name.

This is usually the garden or in the house. You should start in the garden as it gives a little more space to work and usually, unless the kids are playing football, there are fewer human distractions, although there may be a few scent distractions.

Prepare in the same way as for any other training session.

Begin training with her "Warm-Up" of 3 sets of 5 repetitions; **"Watch!"** **"Sit!"** and **"Down!"** to get her in the mindset to work.

Before beginning the session you should decide whether you are going to train this exercise alone, or with the help of an assistant. Both methods have their merits and it is very much down to your puppy's character, what motivates her and the availability of an assistant.

I will explain both methods for you. In both methods you build upon the core skill of your puppy's trained response to her name and the **"Watch!"**

With an Assistant

It is a very simple exercise. Have your puppy on a light line, which can loosely trail as she runs to you.

Have your assistant hold the line as you walk backwards from your puppy. As explained, you have already trained her to respond to her name. Make sure she is looking at you by showing her your left hand and holding it with your palm facing towards her as in the **"Watch!"** position, with a treat behind your thumb, but say nothing to her yet.

If your puppy is very small you may have to bend over for this, but you should not kneel. You have already moved beyond this stage in teaching her to respond to her name, so try not to regress.

As you walk backwards and make a little noise, **"Pup, Pup!"** she should now have well and truly locked onto you and be leaning quite hard into the line. She should be released when she begins to put pressure on the line. But - this is important - please ensure that your assistant doesn't just release the line, or puppy will nosedive into the grass.

Your assistant should step forward a pace or 2 with your puppy and then release the line. This should prevent grounding of the snout.

As your puppy runs towards your left hand, call to her; **"Aaaliiis...Come!"** The word **"Come!"** should be given just before your puppy makes contact with your left hand.

When contact is made, mark her success with a clear **"Yes!"** and then reward her with a small treat. Having given the treat, you should go down to her level and give her some more physical praise and tell her she is a **"Good girl!"** You may also give her another treat.

This continued praise and extra reward keeps your puppy in close contact with you, which enables you, whilst giving her the additional praise, to gently take hold of her collar. This will prove essential in the future, avoiding the development of a "Fly Past" recall, when she merely snaffles the treat and clears off again.

Teaching her to accept you taking hold of her collar as part and parcel of a nice experience will prevent her from becoming wary of this as she gets older. Pups that develop this problem, and view their owners taking hold of their collar after recall either as a game or something to be avoided, have not been trained by this method.

Training Alone

Once again, start in the garden. Begin with a short "Warm-Up" session of 3 of 5.

She may or may not be wearing a light line. Ideally, she should be, but if you think this may distract her, because it is lying on the floor, then you may dispense with it.

Wait until she is looking in your direction and move backwards from her, but do not make any sound until your movement has attracted her attention. At that time, give the **"Pup, Pup!"** sound. At this point she should now be moving towards you.

As you retreat show her the treat in your left hand and hold it with your palm facing towards her as in the **"Watch!"** position.

As soon as she moves towards you, call her name; **"Aaaa...lisss!"** and as your puppy runs towards your left hand, deliver the word; **"Come!"** Once again, the word **"Come!"** should be given just before your puppy makes contact with your left hand.

As before, when contact is made with your left hand, mark her success with a clearly delivered **"Yes!"** then reward her with a small treat. Having given the treat, go down to her level and give her some more physical praise and tell her she is a **"Good girl!"** Then give her another treat while you briefly take hold of her collar for the reasons outlined previously, before releasing her and setting up to play the recall game again.

Progress

If you have begun to train the recall with an assistant holding the long line and releasing it, when your puppy is locked on to you, your next progression is to carry out the exercise as described for a person training their puppy on their own. Carry it out exactly as described.

Puppies trained by either of the methods explained are now at the same stage of training.

Practise!

The recall should be practised as an exercise at least 20 times per day. And it should be just that; **an exercise**. Do not slip into the trap of becoming too casual at this point. She is still learning.

In these early stages of training, do not call your puppy unless you have prepared by taking the treat, facing your puppy, being ready to give the hand signal and call in the right sequence and in the right manner.

Initially, still use your movement and the **"Pup, Pup!"** call to get her moving. **Mark** and **reward** the desired response.

This is a simple process, but you must remember it and perform it consistently. If you lack this consistency in your method, you will not get a consistent response from your puppy.

Progress

The next stage is to have your puppy respond to your call when she is not looking at you. I do not mean when she is engrossed in some great big distraction, like eating a discarded leg of lamb, just when she is mooching about. Try to time it when she is between sniffs.

Prepare yourself for action, by positioning yourself in the correct manner and taking the treat in your left hand as previously described. Watch her closely as she mooches about and as she lifts her head, between sniffs, call; **"Pup, Pup!"** and move backwards with your left hand acting as a clear target.

When she is committed to returning, deliver the **"Aaaliiis...Come!" Mark** and **reward** her for a successful response.

You now have your puppy responding when she is not looking at you. Practise until you achieve the 80% success rate.

Progress

You are now going to gradually bring the **"Alice...Come!"** instruction into the sequence earlier.

Everything else remains the same, your preparation and actions are the same. The **"Pup, Pup!"** call is still made just as before. But now, instead of waiting till your puppy is fully committed and hurtling towards you, you are going to give it when she has made the first couple of steps. **Mark** and **reward** a successful response.

Practise this until the 80% success rate is achieved.

Progress

You are now ready to dispose of the **"Pup, Pup!"** call. But that is the only thing that will change. Your preparation and movement is still the same.

Again, wait until she is mid-mooch, so to speak, with her head up, then give her the call; **"Aaaliis...Come!"** If you have progressed at the right pace, and have delivered the call at the optimum time, the little fur ball will soon be bearing down upon you. **Mark** and **reward** her success as before.

Remove the Long Line

I would anticipate that the majority of you have been confident enough to remove your puppy's long line before this stage has been reached. If not, it is now time to remove it, and continue your daily practice sessions.

Congratulations, you have established a fast reliable recall to a voice instruction in your garden with minimal distractions. This is the foundation for all further progress.

Increase Distance

Your early training will probably have been carried out at about 10 paces or less. You now need to increase this distance in gradual steps over several training sessions.

Increase from 10 to 15 paces and consolidate. Increase from 15 paces to 20 paces, and so on. Never increase the distance until the 80% success rate has been achieved.

Generalising - Different Locations

Having succeeded in your garden you need to repeat the above steps in a different place. It may just be a friend's garden, or another clean, secure area, free from distractions.

When you go to a new place, go back a few stages in training and reduce the distance. In a few short sessions your puppy will be performing to the same level in several different places and this is ideal preparation for the big wide world, which she will encounter as soon as her inoculations are complete.

Proofing It

As most of the work will have been done alone with your puppy, you should now take the initial steps towards proofing it by introducing very small distractions. Initially this may just be another person, standing still and watching.

If she copes with this distraction successfully, have the person move about slowly, and having successfully ignored this bigger distraction, progress to the person sitting on the grass.

All the time you are gradually increasing distraction levels, so that your puppy understands that the instruction; **"Aaliss...Come!"** is always given in the same way and if responded to successfully ends in a rewarding experience for her.

This is only very basic proofing, but it will stand your puppy in good stead when you both venture to pastures new.

The Big Wide World

Your puppy will have now completed her inoculations and you have established a reliable recall at about 20 paces in several clean, secure locations.

Her first recall session in the great outdoors should take place in a relatively un-exciting place, but you have to understand that every new environment is exciting to your puppy and you may not be able to see the distractions that she can from her level. You certainly won't be able to smell them, unless you have unwisely taken her to a poo field.

When going to new, unfamiliar or exciting areas, you may have no idea what challenges or distractions your puppy might encounter, unless of course you have acted upon my earlier advice with regards to the importance of carrying out a bit of reconnaissance beforehand. Prior Preparation and all that!

Progressing to the wider world is a big step, but you must do your best to make it a series of smaller ones, rather than a great big one.

If you need to, drop back to 5-pace recalls and build again. If you feel more confident by reverting back to the long line for the first few sessions, then do so.

As with everything else, make slow and sure progress and do not put your puppy in situations she is not yet trained to cope with.

Success in the big wide world depends largely upon your puppy's early training, turning what is potentially a massive step into a pretty small one.

The last challenge you face is ensuring that **you** are more valuable and interesting to your puppy than the environment is. This is crucial.

Take the Fox Poo Challenge

If you have conducted your early recall training outdoors, even if only in your own and other people's gardens, your training will have prepared you reasonably well for the great outdoors.

If, however, your early control training has been conducted solely in your house, or as is common, your puppy training classes have taken place in a church hall or community centre, you may both be in for a rude awakening when venturing further afield.

Unless your pup has a fetish for floor polish, scent distractions will have been few and far between, so even if you have the personality of a bullfrog, you have probably managed to hold her attention, albeit with a pocket full of treats.

Even the step up from your safe, outdoor training area is likely to be a bit of an eye-opener. You now need to be prepared to hold your pup's interest in a more challenging environment.

On the first true outdoor recall your single call of **"Aaa...liiis, Come!"** should have succeeded in grabbing her attention, and she has started back towards you, but there are a lot of distractions out there, so you need to keep reeling her in, like a little, fat, furry fish.

Do not repeat her name, or the **"Come!"** instruction, but keep the encouragement going, by telling her; **"Clever girl! ... Here, Pup, Pup! ... Good Pup!"** until she has safely completed the recall and you can **mark** and **reward** her successful response.

You must use this encouragement to let her know just how good she is being, to maintain her interest and focus on you, until she arrives safely at your left hand to have her success marked and rewarded.

If you switch off, and go too quiet during her journey back to you, she is likely to think that you have changed your mind, or there is no rush, and so a short detour to investigate the fox poo she has just caught a whiff of is entirely in order.

You must be more interesting and enticing than that fox poo, or you will struggle to train your pup. In fact if you are less interesting than a fox poo, you may struggle in life generally!

End Your Training Session

As ever, at the end of each training session tell your puppy she has **"Finished!"** You started with a clear beginning, you now have a clear ending.

Latent Learning

After being told she has **"Finished!"** allow her 5 minutes to quietly reflect upon what she has just learned.

===

Teaching the "Heel!"

Alice at Heel

Teaching your puppy to walk at **"Heel!"** is a very useful control exercise, but in my opinion its use should be limited to those times when closer control is required than is offered by loose lead-walking, such as when passing pedestrians, close to livestock and when you meet other dogs, especially in confined spaces.

For those of you who might wish to train your puppy for competition later in her life, it is an essential control exercise, but for the average dog owner its value is as an addition to loose lead work, to be used sparingly, as required.

Prior Training

Before beginning to teach your puppy to walk in the **"Heel!"** position, it is essential that you have built a firm foundation by training a reliable response to the **"Watch!"** instruction.

She should also be quite well-practised at the loose lead-walking exercise, even if only in your garden, so having her lead attached for learning the **"Heel!"** shouldn't be an issue.

Before Training

Before beginning the session spend at least 5 minutes giving your puppy some gentle exercise and the opportunity to have a piddle and a poo if required.

Carry out your pre-training routine, fetching your puppy's treat bag and, for this exercise, her lead.

Getting Started

After your pup's leg stretch and piddle, call her back to you and attach her lead to her collar. Tell her it's **"Time for work, Alice."** Don't start forgetting this bit already!

Begin your training session with 3 sets of 5 to "Warm-Up".

You are now ready to begin training the **"Heel!"**

The Heel Position

In the heel position your puppy should walk in the same direction as you, at the same pace as you are travelling, on your left-hand side. Her right shoulder should be close to your left leg. Not so close that she is bumping into you, but not so far away that someone can ride a bike through the gap.

Depending upon the size of your puppy, this position might be slightly different. Variations between different dogs are fine, but what you are training your own puppy to do is take up and remain in a consistent position. The position is consistent between you and her, it doesn't matter if it is a bit different from everyone else's version, as long as you and your pup are consistent.

Starting Out

Hold your lead and treats as per training for the **"Watch!"** and with your puppy in front of you, give the **"Watch!"** instruction. When she makes contact with your left hand, mark with a **"Yes!"** and **reinforce** with a treat reward. Continue until you have completed 5 repetitions.

Progress

Repeat the process, but this time, as she contacts your left hand, **do not mark** with a **"Yes!"** Instead, slowly take a couple of steps backwards with her nose in contact with your hand. Remember to imagine the piece of thread connecting her nose to your hand, so you move slowly enough. If she maintains contact for a couple of steps, **mark** with a **"Yes!"** and **reward** her success.

Repeat this routine until 3 sets of 5 repetitions have been successfully completed.

Tell your puppy she is **"Finished!"** Your session is now over. Allow her 5 minutes to reflect upon what she has just learned.

Practise, Practise, Practise!

Progress

Over the next few sessions you are going to gradually increase your number of backward steps, with your puppy targeting your left hand. When you have successfully mastered 5 good accurate steps, with a minimum success rate of 80%, you are both ready to move on.

Progress

The next stage is to add the instruction **"Heel!"** to the movement. As with your other exercises you have already achieved success in having your puppy follow your hand on the **"Alice...Watch!"** instruction.

You continue to begin with the hand signal and verbal instruction to **"Watch!"** but now as your puppy makes contact with your hand you are going to **add** the new instruction; **"Alice...Heel!"** and step back 4 or 5 steps before **marking** her success with a **"Yes!"** and reinforcing with a treat.

Repeat for 3 sets of 5 with appropriate breaks. Finish the session and allow for a period of reflection as usual.

Progress

The next stage is to ditch the reverse gear, unless of course you are happy to walk backwards with your puppy for the next 15 years. You are now going to train your puppy to walk forward in the **"Heel!"** position.

Begin with the hand signal and verbal instruction to **"Watch!"**

But this time, instead of stepping backwards as your puppy makes contact with your hand, give the verbal instruction; **"Alice...Heel!"** and make a small anti-clockwise circle with your hand, nice and slowly, so as not to break the imaginary thread.

Your puppy will have completed a small circle to follow your hand. Now, slowly step forward just 1 or 2 paces with her following your hand.

After these few paces, **whilst you are still moving, mark** her response with a **"Yes!"** then stop and deliver the **reward**. Then start the whole process again.

It is absolutely essential that you do not step off and move forward with your puppy until you have given the verbal instruction; **"Alice...Heel!"** and she is locked on to your hand.

It is also essential that you deliver the marker, **"Yes!"** whilst you are moving and your puppy is still following your hand.

Repeat this process until you have completed 3 sets of 5. Remember you are only going 1 or 2 paces. You are just training the setting-off movement at present, not distance.

Progress

Over a period of about a week gradually increase the number of steps until you can comfortably complete 10 -15 paces. But remember what you read earlier about reinforcement schedules, and ensure you vary how many paces she needs to successfully complete in order to earn her reward.

If you consistently reward after 5 steps you will never increase the distance. If you consistently reward after 15 steps, you puppy will not really focus on you at the beginning of the exercise, as she will soon work out the reward only comes some time later.

The key to building a reliable response to **"Heel!"** is to vary when the reward is given. Your puppy's only clue to when the reward is coming is that it only ever comes when she is in a nice **"Heel!"** position; the position which you have consistently **marked** and **reinforced**.

In a relatively short period you and your puppy will be comfortably completing 25-30 steps between marks and reinforcement. But take your time. Don't sacrifice accuracy for distance. You can have long, or you can have good. Good is better!

Dispose of the "Watch" Instruction

Once your puppy is happily performing 10-15 paces of accurate **"Heel!"** you can dispose of the **"Watch!"** instruction. It is highly likely that around this time you will have also trained your puppy to **"Sit"** at heel and that is likely to become your regular start position for much of her **"Heel!"** training.

Combining Control Exercises

Whilst training the **"Heel!"** you will have also been training other exercises, albeit in different training sessions. Now is a good time to combine 3 of these control exercises; the **"Watch!" "Sit!"** at heel, and the **"Heel!"** itself. Before attempting to combine these exercises, make sure each individual exercise is being performed proficiently.

Prepare yourself and your puppy for the training session in your usual manner. Carry out 3 of 5 to "Warm-Up".

You are now going to start combining a few simple exercises.

Face your puppy and, with a hand signal and verbal instruction, tell her to **"Watch!"** As she targets your hand and steps forward to make contact with it, whilst ensuring you don't break the little imaginary thread, perform the little anti-clockwise circle with your left hand. Your puppy will follow it and will now have completed the little circle and be facing the same direction as you, close to your left leg.

You are now going to give her the hand signal and verbal instruction to **"Sit!"**, another exercise you have both been practising.

To recap, you will lure her into the "Sit!" position by gently drawing your left hand backwards over her head. As her head goes back and she looks up at your left hand, her bum will go down onto the ground. As her bum is about to touch down, deliver the "Alice, Sit!" instruction.

Your puppy is now sitting at your side.

Take your left hand down onto her nose and as she makes contact with it, give her a verbal instruction; **"Alice...Heel!"** then step off and complete a couple of steps with your puppy in the **"Heel!"** before **marking** her success with a **"Yes!"** and **reinforcing** it with a treat as a reward.

Practise, Practise, Practise!

Repeat and practise this whole movement for 3 sets of 5, with appropriate rest breaks. At the end of your training session, tell your puppy the session is **"Finished!"** and let her have 5 minutes of quiet reflection to take in all she has learned. This has been a big session, so give her time.

Progress

Progress until your puppy is reliably performing 25 to 30 steps of accurate heel work on a variable reinforcement schedule.

Top Tip: Don't forget that the sequence I have just described consists of 3 separate control exercises. Just because you have begun to combine them, you must not forget to train each element individually on a regular basis. If you don't practise the individual elements, the whole sequence will soon begin to deteriorate.

Verbal Encouragement

In the early stages of training, until you are successfully getting 5 steps of accurate **"Heel!"** from your puppy, you probably won't need to give her any verbal encouragement. But as the distance increases, she is likely to become a little unsure that she is doing the right thing, as she is having to wait for so long for her reward.

This doubt is easily dispelled by delivering a little quiet, pleasant, verbal encouragement to keep her working happily. Don't be a parrot and don't keep just telling her to **"Heel!"** She is already doing that.

Have a proper, quiet little conversation with her. **"Alice…Heel!…Good Girl… Keep it going my little sausage…You really are a clever little puppy… YES!!!"**

After **marking** her **success**, reinforce with a treat as a reward.

At the end of your training session tell your puppy she has **"Finished!"** and allow her 5 minutes to quietly reflect.

Generalise and Proof

As with every other exercise, the **"Heel!"** must be generalised and proofed, so that your puppy performs to the same level of proficiency in different locations and in the presence of gradually increasing distractions.

===

Teaching the "Sit!" Front

The **"Sit!"** is the exercise that many owners regard as the most simple to teach. The main problem is that what you think you are teaching your puppy may not be what your puppy is actually learning.

This was the first practical lesson I always used to teach at the Defence Animal Centre in the practical session to accompany the Canine Learning Theory lessons.

The question I would first ask the handlers and trainers was: "When you ask your dog to **"Sit!"** what do you expect her to do?" When I asked this to a class of 6 students, I would get at least 4 different answers. If 6 professional handlers can't decide what it means, how the hell could a Military Working Dog? How could your puppy know?

Rather than go into some lengthy philosophical discussion about canine learning, it is far easier and quicker to tell you from the beginning what teaching the **"Sit!"** should mean to you, so you can teach it to your puppy.

I will divide the **"Sit!"** into 2 separate exercises to avoid confusion.

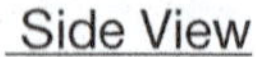

Side View

Rear View (a bit wonky!)

Sit Front

The first position to train your puppy to adopt is the **"Sit!"** front. This is because it follows on naturally from the hand target in the **"Watch!"** exercise. As you can see in the photos, in the "Sit!" front position your puppy should be right in front of you, facing straight towards you, quite close to your legs, with her bum on the floor looking up at you. That's quite a lot of stuff.

Starting to Train the Sit Front

Begin your session as usual. After your "Warm-Up" your puppy will be focused on your left hand and you will use your left hand as the lure to draw her towards you. The only words you will use in this exercise are her name; **"Alice,"** at the beginning and the marker word; **"Yes!"** upon her taking up the desired position.

With a treat in your left hand, touch your hand on her nose. (1) Then say her name; **"Aaaliiis!"** as you gently draw her towards you using the imaginary thread. (2)

Draw your hand back in towards you. Your puppy will be following the delicious smell of the treat. As your hand comes into contact with your legs, slowly draw it up your body.

Keep your hand positioned centrally, between your knees, and then draw your hand upwards. Imagine you are doing up the zip of your trousers, and then up to your tummy. (I understand that even ladies now wear trousers in these liberated times.)

By now your puppy should be close to your legs and looking up at your hand, getting a crick in her neck. In order to relieve the crick in her neck, she is likely to put her bum on the floor to look up at the treat in your hand. (3)

The second her bum touches down, mark the desired behaviour with a clear **"Yes!"** then **reward** her with a treat.

Take just 1 or 2 steps backwards and repeat the whole process.

Complete 3 sets of 5 repetitions. Mark and reinforce each successful response.

At the end of your 3 sets of 5, end your session. Tell your puppy she has **"Finished!"** then allow her 5 minutes to reflect on what she has learned.

Touch nose (1) Draw in (2) Draw up (3)

Practise!

Practise until your puppy is performing the desired **"Sit!"** front reliably (80%) on just her name and the hand signal. Your puppy is now ready to have you introduce the verbal instruction.

Progress

You are now going to introduce the **"Sit!"** instruction, which will be added to the hand signal that is still luring your puppy into the desired position.

Carry out the exercise exactly as before. Say her name and lure her into the desired position. But this time, **just before** her little bum touches down you are going to **add** the word **"Sit!"** Her bum will touch down as before and you will **mark** and **reward** as before.

Each repetition of the instruction to **"Sit!"** is inserted just before touch-down. Nothing else has changed. Just a verbal instruction has been **added** at the point where the action was certain to be completed.

Complete your usual 3 sets of 5 with breaks. Finish and reflect.

Practise, Practise, Practise!

Progress

Your next task is to bring the verbal **"Sit!"** instruction forward so it occurs earlier in the process.

Instead of giving the instruction just before she touches down, you are going to insert it in the process a little bit earlier. When her bum is **halfway down**, add the **"Sit!"** instruction.

The "Sit!" instruction is now beginning to get absorbed into her little head. But she is still not responding to the verbal instruction, it is still just accompanying the hand signal.

Keep practising your 3 sets of 5 in this manner.

Progress

Having achieved the 80% success rate, you are now going to bring the **"Sit!"** forward, so it comes earlier in the sequence. The hand signal is still in effect, but now the hand signal is accompanied, at exactly the same time, by the verbal instruction **"Alice...Sit!"**

Fading the Hand Signal

In the same way that we gradually increased the prominence of the verbal instruction, you are now going to gradually reduce the prominence of the hand signal, by making the range of movement progressively smaller and smaller. It will be gradually faded out completely over a number of training sessions.

There is no rush to do this. Take your time. When training pet dogs there is no reason why you should try to dispose of it altogether. Even when not actively luring her into the **"Sit!"** position most people still end up with their left hand in front of their tummy as their puppy completes the **"Sit!"** Unless you are taking part in an obedience competition there is no problem with this.

If it helps your puppy...do it!

Generalisation and Proofing

Generalise and proof this exercise as with all others. Train in at least 6 different locations and proof against a variety of distractions. Not least of your considerations should be practising on different surfaces for her to put her bum down on.

===

Teaching the "Sit!" at Heel

Whilst the **"Sit!"** front is probably the simplest response to teach your puppy, the **"Sit!"** at heel is one of the most practical exercises. It is the position you want your puppy to adopt when you reach a kerb, when you talk to a neighbour in the street, or when you go through a door or a gate.

Teaching your puppy to **"Sit!"** at heel is a relatively simple matter, especially as you have already trained her to target your left hand and you have successfully trained her to take up a number of positions by this simple hand-targeting technique.

Before Starting to Train the "Sit!" at Heel

Before teaching your puppy to **"Sit!"** at heel, it is a real advantage to teach her to **"Heel!"** even if only for a few steps. She does not need to be able to do any more than about 10 good accurate steps in the **"Heel!"** position.

As with all other exercises you need to be clear exactly what you want your puppy to do and how you are going to mark and reward her for the desired action. Remember, in this exercise you are teaching the **"Sit!"** at heel, not your puppy's performance of the **"Heel!"** itself.

It is absolutely essential that you understand this and that you remember it.

Front View

Side View

The Correct Position

As you can see from the photographs, the completed action means that your puppy sits on your left side, close to your left leg. She is facing the same way as you and is sitting parallel to you. Her right shoulder is in line with your leg. Her bum is flat on the floor and her legs are perpendicular to the floor. Phew! How complicated is that. (Check out Alice's Yoda ears in the pics!)

Starting to Train It

Before training, exercise and toilet your puppy. Strap on the treat bag and tell her it's **"Time for work!"** Carry out 3 sets of 5 to "Warm-Up" and focus your puppy.

Even if you have been training other exercises without a concealed treat in your left hand, as ever, when you first begin to train any new exercise conceal a treat behind your left thumb.

Remember, when you are teaching the **"Sit!"** at heel, you are marking and rewarding the **"Sit!"** in the correct position, and that is all.

Start with your puppy loosely on your left-hand side. Begin by giving the **"Watch!"** instruction and as she moves to make contact with your left hand, give the **"Alice...Heel!"** instruction and step forward, but do so in slow time. Your puppy will initially have her nose against your hand, like she has the little piece of thread attaching her to your hand.

You will only complete 2 or 3 slow steps, then, whilst she is still in contact with your left hand, say her name; **"Alice!"** and then halt. As you come to the halt, slowly draw your left hand backwards and just over the top of her head. Imagine the thread. If you go too fast it will break.

If as you come to a halt you draw your left hand in the correct way, at the right speed, she will stop with you and as her head goes backwards a little to follow your hand, her bum will touch down. **Mark** her response with a **"Yes!"** and **reward** with the small treat from your left hand.

Repeat the whole routine until you have completed 3 sets of 5 repetitions, with breaks between sets, marking each successful repetition with a **"Yes!"** and reinforcing with a small treat.

Having completed your 3 sets of 5, end your session. Tell your puppy she has **"Finished!"**

Latent Learning

Allow 5 minutes for your puppy to reflect upon what she has just learned.

Top Tip The key to this exercise is to co-ordinate your feet, left hand and voice at the same time. Don't be surprised if you need to practise this a few times to get your co-ordination right. If you are really switched on, you will practise your own movement, alone, without your puppy. Once you have got it right and can perform the correct action without falling over, then it's time to invite your puppy to the party.

Practise!

Practise a short session of 3 sets of 5 sits for the next couple of days until your puppy is performing the desired **"Sit!"** at heel reliably as you come to a halt on just her name, **"Alice!"** and the hand signal.

Increase Speed

Over these sessions increase your speed, so that you are moving at normal pace over the 2 or 3 paces you are covering with her in the **"Heel!"** position.

Increase the Number of Steps

Having increased the speed to normal walking pace, you are going to gradually increase the distance covered up to a maximum of about 10 paces. You are only doing this to make the whole exercise more natural, you are not training the **"Heel!"** You are still training the **"Sit!"** at heel so don't kick the backside out of it by going too far.

Your puppy is now responding to the **"Alice! Heel!"** and following your left hand at normal pace, before you say her name, **"Alice!"**, just a step before you come to a halt and lure her into the **"Sit!"** at heel position. She is now ready to have you introduce the verbal instruction.

Progress

You are going to introduce the verbal **"Sit!"** instruction, which will be added to the hand signal, that is still being used to lure your puppy into the desired position.

Carry out the exercise exactly as before. Say her name and as you come to a halt lure her into the desired position. But this time, **just before** her little bum touches down you are going to add the word **"Sit!"** Her bum will touch down as before and you will **mark** and **reward** as before.

Repeat the whole process and continue until you have completed 3 sets of 5 repetitions, with a short break between sets.

On each repetition the verbal instruction to **"Sit!"** is inserted **just before** touch-down. Nothing else has changed. Just a verbal instruction has been added at the point when the action was certain to be completed.

Practise, Practise, Practise!

Progress

Your next task is to bring the verbal **"Sit!"** instruction forward so it occurs earlier in the process.

Instead of giving the instruction just before her bum touches down, you are going to insert it in the process a little bit earlier. When she is **halfway down**, add the **"Sit!"** instruction.

As with the **"Sit!"** front, the **"Sit!"** instruction is now beginning to sink in. But she is still not really responding to the verbal instruction, it is still being added to the hand signal.

Keep practising your 3 sets of 5 in this way, always aiming for the 80% success rate.

Progress

You are now going to bring the **"Sit!"** forward, so it comes even earlier in the sequence. The hand signal is still in effect, but now the hand signal is accompanied, **at exactly the same time**, by the verbal instruction **"Alice... Sit!"** as you come to a halt.

Fading the Hand Signal

In the same way that you gradually increased the prominence of the verbal instruction, you are now going to gradually **reduce** the prominence of the hand signal. It will be gradually faded out over a number of training sessions.

Once again, there is no rush to do this. When training pet dogs there is absolutely no reason why you should dispose of it completely. If it helps your puppy...do it!

You must also remember that whilst you may fade the hand signal, the biggest signal of all to your puppy is the fact that you come to a halt. You will find that after practising this exercise, even for a short time, your puppy will automatically begin to **"Sit!"** when you are walking her in the **"Heel!"** position and you come to a halt. When training a pet dog this presents no problem that I can think of, so encourage it, by **marking** and **reinforcing** her actions on a **variable** schedule.

Generalise It

Having established a reliable response to the **"Sit!"** at heel you now need to generalise it. You should carry out the same exercise in a different place, but once again without too many distractions. The change of location is more than enough for her to deal with and you never change 2 criteria at the same time.

Repeat this whole process in up to 6 different locations. Having achieved reliability in 6 places you can consider the exercise has been generalised.

Proof It

Having trained the exercise to a reliable level, and having generalised it, you need to proof it by carrying it out in the presence of progressively stronger distractions. As before, when you increase the distractions, consider simplifying the exercise a little for the first few sessions to help your puppy achieve success.

Different Surfaces

When considering generalising and proofing this exercise, also consider different surfaces for her to put her bum down on.

Latent Learning

Don't forget your puppy's 5 minutes of quiet reflection after each training session, before engaging in play.

===

Teaching the "Down!" Front

The **"Down!"** exercise generally follows on straight after the **"Watch"** and the "**Sit! front**, because it is the natural progression from those 2 exercises and, once trained, it will form part of your 3 sets of 5 that will begin your future training sessions.

Teaching the **"Down!"** front has very little practical value, other than as a part of the "Warm-Up" and as a stepping stone to the **"Down!"** at Heel, which has more practical value, especially in real-life situations.

As with the **"Sit!"** I will divide the **"Down!"** into 2 separate exercises to avoid confusion.

First Position

The first position to train your puppy to adopt is the **"Down!"** front and it should be trained soon after the **"Sit"** front has been mastered.

Carry out your pre-training exercise and toilet routine, get your treat bag on and tell your puppy it's **"Time for work!"**

Start the training session by carrying out 3 sets of 5, mixing **"Watch!"** and **"Sit!"** front exercises.

Starting to Train the Down Front

Start by instructing/signalling your puppy into the **Sit!**" front position, so she is nice and straight and looking up at your left hand. If you have used your left hand to signal your puppy into position your left hand should be on your tummy, about where your belly button is.

If you have brought her into the **"Sit!"** front on just the verbal instruction, bring your left hand to your tummy now.

Say her name, nice and gently, **"Alice."** With the treat in your left hand put your hand to her nose. Once again, imagine you have a little piece of cotton attached to her nose. Draw your left hand downwards, nice and slowly, so she can follow you.

"Yes!" and **reward** her by giving her the treat from your hand.

Stand upright and step back, so that she follows you out of the **"Down!"** position and repeat the whole process again. Instruct her to **"Sit!"** front, then say her name and slowly lure her to the ground with your left hand. **Mark** and **reward** a successful touchdown.

Carry out the remainder of the session to complete your 3 sets of 5 repetitions, **marking** and **rewarding** success.

At the end of your session tell your puppy she has **"Finished!"** Allow 5 minutes for your puppy to reflect upon what she has just learned.

Practise

Practise a short session of 3 sets of 5 **"Down!"** front for the next couple of days until your puppy is performing the desired action reliably on just the hand signal. Your puppy is now ready to have you introduce the verbal **"Down!"** instruction.

Introducing the Verbal Instruction

You are now going to introduce the **"Down!"** instruction, which will be added to the hand signal that is still luring your puppy into the desired position.

Carry out the exercise exactly as before. Start in the **"Sit!"** front. Say her name and lure her down to the ground and into the desired position. But this time, **just before** her elbows and tummy touch down you are going to add the word **"Down!"** She will touch down as before and you will **mark** and **reinforce** as before.

Continue until you have completed 5 repetitions. Take a short break before continuing to complete the whole training session comprising your usual 3 sets of 5.

Each time the instruction to **"Down!"** is inserted **just before** touch-down. Nothing else has changed. Just a verbal instruction has been added at the point when the action was certain to be completed.

Practise, Practise, Practise!

Progress

Your next task is to bring the verbal **"Down!"** instruction forward so it occurs earlier in the process.

Instead of giving the instruction just before she touches down, you are going to insert it in the process a little bit earlier. When she is **halfway down**, insert the **"Down!"** instruction.

The **"Down!"** instruction is now beginning to be absorbed by your puppy.

But she is still not responding to the verbal instruction, it is still being added to the hand signal.

Keep practising your 3 sets of 5 in this manner. Ensure you give a short break between sets and tell her she is **"Finished!"** at the end of the session, before her 5-minute period to reflect on what she has learned.

80% proficiency means you are both ready to move on.

Progress

You are now going to bring the **"Down!"** forward, so it comes earlier in the sequence. The hand signal is still in effect, but now the hand signal is accompanied, at exactly the **same time**, by the verbal instruction **"Alice... Down!"** Success is **marked** and **reinforced** as before.

Practise until your required level of proficiency has been achieved.

Fading the Hand Signal

In the same way that we gradually increased the prominence of the verbal instruction, you are now going to gradually reduce the prominence of the hand signal. It will be gradually faded out over a number of training sessions.

Whilst there is no rush to do this, unlike the **"Sit!"** instruction, where there is little benefit to fading out the hand signal, in this case, unless you want to be touching the ground every time you give this instruction you definitely want to fade the hand signal, or at the very least, reduce it to a tiny hand movement.

Fading the hand signal is a very good idea unless you fancy a future career as an extra in Planet of the Apes.

Method of Fading

Everything begins in exactly the same way and all goes as usual, until you take your hand down to the ground. Instead of taking it all the way down, stop it a couple of inches from the ground. At first your puppy will hardly notice the difference because as you have been practising this exercise you will have both been doing it progressively more quickly and in all probability she is already getting down well before you do. If she is, then that is good.

Mark the touch-down with a **"Yes!"** and reward.

Top Tip: Although according to the Operant Conditioning model once the marker is given your puppy is free to change position and be reinforced, I recommend that when you are teaching the **"Down!"** you should reward her in that position. So rather than letting her come up to receive her treat, you should take it down and deliver it to her whilst she is still **"Down!"** at least until a high level of proficiency has been achieved. In my experience this helps to cement the idea of the down in her head much faster.

Progress

Over the next week of training slowly reduce the distance you move your hand when giving the **"Down!"** instruction.

Try to reduce the distance your hand moves by just a couple of inches each day. It is important to observe the 80% rule before pushing on to reduce the hand signal.

Within about a week, with regular practice you should have reduced your hand signal to little more than a minor hand movement to accompany the verbal **"Down!"** instruction. But remember, you can have quick or you can have good. Good is better!

Generalise It

Having established a reliable response to the **"Down!"** front, you now need to generalise it. You should carry out the same exercise in a different place, without too many distractions.

With the **"Down!"** the main thing that will have an impact on your puppy's performance is the type of surface that you are training her on. Take this into account when you are carrying out generalisation. You wouldn't be too keen to lie down on a gravel path, frozen grass, or in a puddle. Neither is she.

In due course you need to train your dog to perform the **"Down!"** on all surfaces, hard, cold, wet, etc. but be reasonably sympathetic to your puppy's needs, take it slowly and introduce new surfaces to the generalisation process steadily, at a pace she can cope with.

Proof It

Having successfully generalised her response to the **"Down!" front** in different locations and on different surfaces you now need to proof it in the presence of increasingly strong distractions.

Latent Learning

Don't forget to end each of your training sessions with 5 minutes of quiet time for her to absorb the lesson.

===

Teaching the "Down!" at Heel

Why Train an Alternative **"Down!"** Position?

Whilst I refer to it as the **"Down!" at heel,** it doesn't mean a bit scruffy, it means having your puppy lie down in the **"Heel!"** position.

Whilst the **"Down!"** front is the first **"Down!"** you will teach your puppy, the **"Down!"** at heel is the best practical application of the exercise and is one of the most effective exercises you can teach your puppy to equip her for many situations.

When to Teach It

Teaching your puppy to **"Down!"** at heel follows her training to **"Watch!", "Heel!", "Sit!"** front**, "Sit!"** at heel and "**Down!** front.

Front View

Side View

She is proving to be a clever little pup, and enjoys her training sessions with you. Your training skills have come on in leaps and bounds and you are turning into a proper little team. You are both ready for the **"Down!"** at heel.

Before Starting to Train the **"Down!"** at Heel

As with all other exercises, have a clear picture of exactly what you want your puppy to do and how you are going to mark and reward her for performing the desired action.

Remember, in this exercise you are teaching the **"Down!"** at heel, not your puppy's performance of the **"Heel!"** itself. It is essential that you understand this and remember it. When training the **"Down!"** at heel, you are **marking** and **reinforcing** the **"Down!"** in the correct position, nothing more.

The Exact Position

The completed action means that your puppy performs a **"Down!"** on your left side, close to your left leg. She is facing the same way as you and is lying parallel to you. Her right shoulder is in line with your leg. Her elbows and tummy are flat on the ground.

Starting to Train It

Before training, exercise and toilet your puppy. Strap on the treat bag and tell her it's **"Time for work!"** Carry out 3 sets of 5 to "Warm-Up" and focus your puppy.

It's a new exercise, so you should have a small treat concealed in your left hand.

Start with your puppy in the **"Sit!"** at heel position. Place your left hand on her nose and give her the **"Watch!"** instruction.

Using your imaginary magic thread take your left hand down the front of her chest and all the way to the ground. **Mark** and **reinforce** a successful touch-down.

Instruct her to **"Watch!"** then lure her straight up into the **"Sit!"** at heel position again. It may be easier if you take a small step forward as you do this. Do whatever works best for you and your puppy. (Although this is not the aim of the exercise, I recommend marking and reinforcing the return to the **"Sit!"** position.)

Repeat this routine until you and your puppy have completed 3 sets of 5, with appropriate breaks.

At the end of your session tell her she has **"Finished!"** and allow her a period of reflection.

Progress

You will now introduce the verbal instruction, **"Alice...Down!"** Nothing else changes at this point. You still begin with her in the **"Sit!"** at heel. You still instruct her to **"Watch!"** and lure her towards the ground, but this time you **add** the verbal instruction to **"Down!" just before** she touches down.

Practise, Practise, Practise!

Progress

Everything remains the same, but slowly, you are going to bring the verbal instruction to **"Down!"** into the sequence progressively earlier and earlier. Instead of adding the instruction just before she touches the ground, you are going to add it when she is **halfway down**.

After practising sufficiently and achieving the 80% success rate you can begin to insert the **"Down!"** instruction at exactly the same time as the hand signal begins to lure her to the ground.

Dispose of the "Watch!" Instruction

When your puppy has demonstrated her proficiency (80%), you are going to dispose with the **"Watch!"** instruction. Now you will be taking her from the **"Sit!"** at heel into the **"Down!"** at heel on the hand signal and verbal instruction; **"Alice! "Down!"**

Fading the Hand Signal

The hand signal is gradually faded over a number of training sessions. Nothing else changes. You are just going to reduce it in small stages.

At first you will simply take your hand down to a few inches above the ground, instead of all the way. Then you will stop the hand signal a few inches higher, then halfway down and keep reducing the signal slowly but surely until it has been dispensed with, or is little more than a wiggle of your finger.

Remember to achieve the 80% success rate at each stage of the reduction.

"Down!" at Heel from a Moving Position

Having mastered the **"Down!"** at heel to the level described previously when stationary, you are now going to teach your puppy to do it whilst on the move. This is a big step.

Starting To Train It

As ever, carry out your pre-training routine with your puppy.

As it is the first time you have trained your puppy to do this new exercise, you will simplify it for her by holding a treat in your left hand and reverting to using hand signals and voice instructions together.

Begin with your puppy in the **"Sit!"** at heel and give the **"Heel!"** hand signal and verbal instruction at the same time as you step off. You are only about to perform about 3 or 4 **very slow** steps, then you will halt.

As you halt, perform the **"Sit!"** at heel with your puppy, simplify it a little by giving the hand signal and verbal instruction at the same time. Your puppy will perform this part of the exercise as she has been trained to.

But this time when her bum touches down, **don't mark the "Sit!"** at heel, instead immediately lure her with your left hand to the ground and as she is about to touch down, add the verbal instruction **"Alice...Down!"** As soon as her elbows and tummy touch down, **mark** her response and **reinforce** with a treat.

Repeat for your usual 3 sets of 5, with breaks. Finish and allow time for reflection at the end of the session.

Practise, Practise, Practise!

Progress

As you practise you will first revert back to achieving **"Sit!"** at heel on just the verbal instruction, then complete the **"Down!"** at heel as described above.

Dispense with the **"Sit!"**

Everything else about the exercise remains the same, but now you are going to have your puppy perform the **"Down!"** at heel as soon as you both halt, skipping the **"Sit!"** at heel stage.

As it is a further progression, the first time you do this reintroduce the treat to your left hand and simplify temporarily by reducing the speed at which you walk your puppy at **"Heel!"**

Begin from the **"Sit!"** at heel position and move into the **"Heel!"**. Walk slowly for a short distance before coming to a gentle halt. As you do so, with your left hand attached to her nose by the imaginary thread, lure her into the **"Down!"** at heel position and **add** the verbal instruction; **"Alice...Down!"** as she touches down.

Mark and **reinforce** a successful response from your puppy.

Progress

Gradually, over a series of training sessions, bring the **"Alice! Down!"** instruction in when she is halfway down on the hand signal, then subject to the 80% success rate, give the instruction as you halt and at exactly the same time as you give the hand signal.

Progress

Practise until the "Down!" at heel can be performed on the hand signal and voice signal together at full speed to the minimum 80% success rate.

Fading the Hand Signal

Fade the hand signal gradually, in exactly the same manner as you did when training this exercise from a stationary position.

Generalise and Proof It

As ever, this exercise must be generalised in a number of locations, on different surfaces and in the presence of progressively stronger distractions. You and your puppy know the drill by now! Don't forget to train it on different surfaces.

Latent Learning

I'm sure you are getting a bit bored with me reminding you about this. But I don't care! Always allow your puppy her 5 minutes reflection after every session.

===

Teaching the "Stay!"

Many owners find the stay exercise is the one that their puppies have most trouble with. There are a few reasons for this.

The first reason is that you have invested so much time in getting your puppy to "Watch" and follow your left hand. Just as I did with baby Alice, you have put in a good deal of time and effort to convince your puppy, with a high degree of success, that you are the best, most interesting and rewarding person in the world. Nothing she can imagine is better than you are. But now, after all that, you are about to clear off and leave her on her own, albeit very briefly.

Ah, the old "Sit! Stay!" with distractions

The second thing that often leads to confusion is that your voice and the hand signal may sometimes contradict each other, unless you keep your wits about you.

At this stage of training your puppy she will have been responding to hand signals for much longer than verbal instructions, so the chances are that your puppy is going to follow the tried and trusted hand signal, which has always worked before, rather than the verbal instruction.

In order to prevent this occurring you need to ensure that the hand signal for **"Stay!"** is different from any other hand signal you use. And that the hand signal remains clear and constant throughout the early stages of training, until your puppy has fully mastered the exercise. Only then should you drop the **"Stay!"** hand signal.

A third thing that affects the success of this exercise has nothing to do with your work on the training field or at your training classes.

Owners often teach this exercise quite early, at home, by making their puppy wait or **"Stay!"** before they put her food down for her. As feeding time is an extremely important event in the life of most puppies the idea that the exercise is always connected to feeding can be difficult to break, especially as it has usually been practised frequently (4 times a day) during an extremely important period of your puppy's development. For this reason, I recommend that you do not train the stay in that way.

The final reason that you may struggle teaching your puppy to **"Stay!"** is that it is so easy for your puppy to get this exercise wrong, and still find the outcome rewarding.

This is because if you remove the lead or allow it to drop onto the floor, tell your puppy to **"Stay!"** then walk away, it is just too easy for her to think, "Stuff this for a game of soldiers, I don't want to be separated from my Mum. I'm going to join her!"

She gets up and runs to you. So what do you do now?

Well there isn't really much that you can do. Other than repeat the exercise, but as she has now discovered just how rewarding it is to ignore the new word and hand signal and run back to you, your options are limited.

You could bellow, **"No!"** at the top of your voice in order to stop her in her tracks, but that isn't going to help her to understand what is required of her. It's just going to frighten her. There is only one thing worse that a puppy who gets up and runs back to you when told to stay. That is a puppy who is afraid of the exercise because she has been shouted at and therefore decides to run away!!!

In many training articles I still see photos of owners holding a lead up high over puppy's head at arm's length giving the hand signal and presumably giving the verbal instruction to **"Stay!"**

This is a really good technique to use…but only if you don't intend teaching her to stay at a greater distance than 3 feet, or if you have a really, really long arm!

Different Positions

The **"Stay!"** may be performed in the **"Sit!"** or **"Down!"** positions. At advanced levels, it may also be performed in the **"Stand!"**

When training your puppy you should start in the **"Sit!"** position, and when this has been mastered, train the **"Stay!"** in the **"Down!"** position, following exactly the same process as explained below.

Time and Distance

When you are training your puppy to **"Stay!"** you should consider that it comprises 2 different elements.

The first of these is the **time**; the length of time that you wish to teach your puppy to **"Stay!"** You should be thinking in seconds, not minutes.

The second element is the **distance**. You should measure this in normal-length steps.

Later, after you and your puppy have mastered the basic stay at say 10 paces for 1 minute, you can consider teaching an out-of-sight **"Stay!"** or increasing the distractions on the training area, but these are things that you should only consider after you have built a solid foundation of the **"Stay!"** exercise.

As with everything else, build firm, solid and deep foundations, then you can build a bungalow, or a cathedral, according to your needs. If you don't build solid foundations they won't support a garden shed. Don't be in a hurry.

Selecting the Training Area

Before training the **"Stay!"**, as with every other exercise, you must ensure that your puppy has been exercised and toileted.

The area in which you train the first attempt is important. Make sure that the area is secure and that other dogs or people cannot disturb you whilst you are training. This exercise requires a great deal of concentration, so she needs to be able to work free of distractions.

It should be an area that you have previously trained in, so that your puppy already has the right association in her mind.

Equipment

When training this exercise your puppy should be on her usual training lead, your treat bag and some treats.

You should also use something to which you can tether your puppy whilst training the exercise. Because I train on grass most of the time I use an electric fence pole that I can stick securely into the ground. An electric fence pole will cost you about £3 from a farm supplies shop.

If you can't get hold of an electric fence pole use a solid fence or a gate, but ensure that the fence or gate haven't been piddled on by 15 passing dogs just before you start training. Distractions should be kept to a minimum.

Train It

Begin as usual with a short period to stretch her legs and have a sniff and a piddle.

Stick the fence pole securely in the ground, take your puppy a short distance away and perform your 3 sets of 5 “Warm-Up” routine.

The Method

Having pressed the fence pole into the ground take your puppy to the pole, drop the loop of your puppy’s lead over the top of the pole, and then lure her towards you, so that her lead is attached to her collar, and is running down her back.

Position her by luring her so that the lead has a bow in it. It is not so tight that she can feel it holding her back, as this will have a tendency to make her pull against it, which is the opposite effect to that which you are trying to achieve.

Having signalled her into the position of an upright **“Sit!”** you have her undivided attention.

Show her the flat of your left hand. The hand is held high, so it isn’t the same as it is during the **“Watch!”** and she can clearly see that your left hand is empty. Your hand is held up like a traffic policeman giving a stop signal.

Iona and Saskia using the pole

When she is in the **"Sit!"** and looking up at the **"Stay!"** hand signal, give her the verbal instruction to **"Stay!"** and take just 1 normal-sized step backwards, at normal pace. Remain still for just 1 second, then step back to her.

If you follow this instruction closely this will have happened so quickly she hasn't really had a chance to move and get it wrong.

When you step back to her, pause for a second, during which she remains sitting and staring at your left hand, which has not moved, nor been waved around in a manner likely to attract her to follow it.

Give the verbal **"Yes!"** marker, then with your left hand, take a treat from the treat bag and present it to her.

Don't go overboard with praise and fussing at this point. No verbal **"Good Girl"** praise at the moment, because you want to repeat this process about 5 times in quick succession, **marking** and **reinforcing** each success.

Complete 3 sets of 5 in exactly this way, with appropriate breaks.

End the Session

After the last set is completed, **marked** and **reinforced**, tell your puppy she has **"Finished!"**

Latent Learning

After the training session allow your puppy to have a few minutes to quietly reflect upon what she has just learned.

How To Progress

It is very important that you remember that the exercise comprises distance and time. You have successfully trained your puppy to **"Sit! Stay!"** for 1 second at 1 pace.

You will now build the time, and **just** the time. Remember the 80% success rate required before you can push on. This progress should take no less than a couple of days and may take longer.

1 pace for 2 seconds, practise and consolidate.

1 pace for 4 seconds, practise and consolidate.

1 pace for 6 seconds, practise and consolidate.

1 pace for 8 seconds, practise and consolidate.

1 pace for 10 seconds, practise and consolidate.

Having successfully achieved a reliable 10-second stay at 1 pace, it is time to push the distance. We are now going to increase to 2 paces, but when we push the distance, we drop the time. Like this:

2 paces for 1 second, practise and consolidate.

2 paces for 2 seconds, practise and consolidate.

2 paces for 5 seconds, practise and consolidate.

2 paces for 7 seconds, practise and consolidate.

2 paces for 10 seconds, practise and consolidate.

Having achieved a minimum 80% success rate, push the distance, drop the time, and then build:

3 paces for 1 second, practise and consolidate.

3 paces for 2 seconds, practise and consolidate.

3 paces for 5 seconds, practise and consolidate.

3 paces for 7 seconds, practise and consolidate.

3 paces for 10 seconds, practise and consolidate.

If you are working slowly and methodically it will take you about 5 days to 1 week to achieve a reliable 10-second stay at 3 paces. You have established a good foundation.

You can now build it up in bigger increments, but always dropping the time when you have pushed the distance and never pushing time and distance at the same time.

5 paces for 1 second, practise and consolidate.

5 paces for 5 seconds, practise and consolidate.

5 paces for 10 seconds, practise and consolidate.

80% success rate. Push on:

7 paces for 1 second, practise and consolidate.

7 paces for 5 seconds, practise and consolidate.

7 paces for 10 seconds, practise and consolidate.

80% success rate. Push on:

10 paces for 1 second, practise and consolidate.

10 paces for 5 seconds, practise and consolidate.

10 paces for 10 seconds, practise and consolidate.

Well done. Having reached this stage you will have now established an effective **"Sit! Stay!"** which your puppy fully understands.

It should have taken you about 2 weeks to arrive at this point. Take your time and work steadily and methodically. As with every exercise; you can have quick, or you can have good. Good is always better!

Fade the Hand Signal

The fading of the hand signal should be done gradually once your puppy is performing a reliable stay at 10 paces for 10 seconds. Don't be too keen to fade it out too soon. Reliability is more important.

To fade, just make the hand signal slightly less apparent to your puppy. Reducing its visibility in gradual stages until your puppy is listening to your verbal instructions only. But a word of caution - make sure your voice and hands are not sending contradictory messages to your puppy. Remain aware of what you are doing with your hands at all times.

Generalise It

Having established a reliable response to the **"Stay!"** you now need to generalise it. You should carry out the same exercise in a different place, but once again without too many distractions.

As you are in a different place simplify it for your puppy by reverting back to a short distance and short time. You don't need to go back to 1 pace for 1 second, but you should certainly consider dropping back to, say, 5 paces for 5 seconds, and then build it steadily up to 10 paces for 10 seconds, remembering not to increase time and distance at the same time. (You might also reintroduce the hand signal for the first couple of sessions.)

Repeat this whole process in up to 6 different locations. Having achieved reliability in 6 places you can consider the exercise has been generalised.

You can now start to build time and distance up to, say, 10 paces for 1 minute. This is the level your puppy would be required to attain to qualify for her Good Citizen Bronze award.

Proof It

Having achieved a solid generalised response to the stay it is safe to assume that providing you have been doing so in a number of different outdoor locations, you will have already achieved a degree of proofing.

But it is wise to train your puppy in the presence of distractions, which become ever more distracting as she progresses.

There is no end to distractions that you can proof against, but it makes sense to prioritise those distractions your puppy will encounter in her everyday life.

Once again, in the initial stages of proofing, drop the time and distance of the **"Stay!"** and build as your puppy becomes more experienced.

In the photo, MWD Buzz is being proofed against the presence of horses. At this point he is about 7 months old and is very experienced and steady, as he will need to be throughout his career. In the light of his future working role, the term "Bomb Proof" is quite appropriate.

Military Working Dog; Buzz. Proofing his stay in the ménage

===

Real-Life Applications

The whole point in training your puppy to perform the control exercises is not to win a big silver cup. It's so that you can use them in her real life in order to make her life fuller and more enjoyable. The more control you have over your puppy the more freedom she will enjoy and the more she will be able to share in all family adventures.

I once had a conversation with a bloke who stated that he wanted his dog to have a nice relaxed life. He didn't want his puppy to be a slave, doing all sorts of acts of obedience. No. That wasn't what having a dog was about, in his view.

I met him a few months later and he was walking with his dog on the lead on a public footpath in the middle of open farmland. I had my previous 3 dogs with me, Sophie, Hollie and Ozzie.

When I saw him approach and noticed his dog was on the lead, I called my 3 dogs back, clipped them on their leads and had a chat for a few minutes. I asked him if his dog was friendly towards other dogs, he said he was, but he kept him on lead when being walked because he wouldn't come back when he was off the lead.

He added that even if the front door was left open, his dog would escape and run off. This was a regular event, and one that often took up to an hour to resolve, following a major seek and apprehend operation.

A few weeks later I met him in the village, as I was tying my dogs up outside the Co-op. (Other food retailers are available.) He didn't have his dog with him.

I asked him why he didn't bring his dog to the shop and was told that his dog became distressed when left outside the shop and would bark incessantly if left alone.

He could not grasp the idea that by not training his puppy for life skills and control skills he had in effect condemned his dog to a life of confinement. In fact he had condemned his dog to a half-life, spent in captivity and semi-isolation.

Fortunately, I later met his wife, who obviously possessed the family brain cell allocation, and she brought the dog to classes, where he picked everything up really quickly and was soon enjoying a life of freedom, whilst being under control. (But only with his Mum!)

The control exercises that you have read about and will practise with your puppy are the building blocks for her "real" life. By using each exercise in isolation or by linking them together they will make managing your puppy in her daily life much easier, keep her out of trouble and enable her to live a full life, participating in daily activities with you and your family.

The real-life exercises that follow are not an exhaustive list of real-life activities, but illustrate how to use the core control skills in your puppy's everyday life and activities.

===

Leaving the House

Introduction

A calm, controlled departure routine is a really important exercise to teach your puppy. Setting a good departure routine will help to set the tone for the whole of the time you are outside the house.

If you leave home in a calm, controlled manner, then you are just looking to maintain that attitude throughout the expedition. If you start off with your puppy completely out of control, you spend much of the time trying to regain control. This is generally about as successful as going downhill on a bike with no brakes.

Pre-Departure Training Using Core Skills

Before you train your puppy to leave the house, you should have spent a decent amount of time training her to perform the component parts of the departure routine to a reliable standard, albeit without being able to generalise them to any great extent.

If your puppy is competent in the **Watch, Sit, Stay,** and **Heel** exercises, then departing your home will be a relatively simple routine to train.

Other Factors

Certain things will help with a good routine and certain things will hinder it. Other things have the potential to both hinder and help, depending upon other factors.

Anticipation. Good or Bad?

In some instances when you are training your puppy, anticipation can be a good thing. In some instances it can be a bad thing. It all depends upon what you are training her to do, how much control you have already established and what she is anticipating.

Anticipation at the doorway where your puppy has a little picture in her head of tearing along the canal bank for half a mile with a gang of her mates, is likely to lead to a loss on control when leaving the house.

But having seen you fill her treat bag, attach it to your belt and pick up her lead might result in her anticipating the regular training session where she sits at the door and has it marked and rewarded, before a short session of heelwork on the drive, which again results in reinforcement for the desired response. This might be topped off with a short session of training to get in and out of the car.

This sort of anticipation can be beneficial to her level of performance. It all depends what you have already begun training her for.

Controlling Anticipation

Anticipation when leaving the house for a walk nearly always starts at a much earlier point than anticipation in any other area. This may be largely due to the fact that going for a walk is one of the highlights of your puppy's life, but it is certainly helped by the amount of little clues that you give your pup in the first few weeks.

You often walk at the same time each day. You keep her lead in the same cupboard. You have a dog walking coat and in the winter a pair of wellies. (Better to be prepared and treat every month apart from July and August as winter if residing in the UK.)

After a few walks that start with this routine she certainly doesn't need to be descended from Sherlock Holmes to work out what comes next.

If you have trained your puppy well, you will find that whilst you are getting ready she is sat patiently at the door for her lead to be attached. If you have not trained her well, or haven't got round to it yet, this is probably the cue for her to commence her wall-of-death routine around your living room.

The Impact of Toilet Training

Once again, it is important that you teach your puppy that leaving the house is a routine matter, rather than something that is essential to her toilet routine. Of course, you won't have this problem because having read the section on Toilet Training, you have already successfully trained your puppy to piddle and poo before she goes for a walk.

This ensures that she is not desperate to get out of the house before she bursts. It also means that you know full well that she is not desperate to perform, because you have already taken her into her toilet area and watched her piddle and poo before you prepared to take her out.

Knowing this means you can be absolutely consistent and resolute when training her to leave the house. If you haven't trained her toilet habits in this way, go back and read the section again, then crack on with it.

Controlling Excitement

In addition to attending to your pup's toilet training, you should also have been carrying out socialisation, veterinary training and travel training.

This means that you have not limited your expeditions outside the house to things that your puppy finds extremely exciting. In fact you have already taught her that some trips out are pretty boring. In this instance boring is good.

Train It

Training a good departure routing depends upon you actually training it as an exercise, with sufficient practice and repetitions to ensure that your puppy has learned the lesson. As with everything else that you are training your puppy to do, consider how it can be broken down into individual elements, with each part practised, marked and reinforced.

Be in no doubt a good departure routine will not happen without specific training. It will not evolve by some fortuitous accident, particularly if the only time your take her through the front door is when you are actually taking her for a walk.

When to Train It?

As with all other control and life skills, the best time to teach it is when you don't need it. When you aren't actually going for a walk and don't need to succeed in carrying out the whole departure routine. This means you can be patient and break it down into individual component parts.

This breakdown into component parts will help you reduce the high levels of anticipation that will inevitably occur if you only ever go through the routine when you are actually leaving the house.

The worst time to train it is when you desperately need to get her out for a poo. I don't need to elaborate on the consequences of failure in this situation!

Top Tip: As you have probably acquired your puppy at 8 weeks, it will be at least 2 weeks, and probably longer, before she can be walked outside the house. This gives you the ideal opportunity to perfect this routine, before she has even been for her first walk, so she won't be anticipating an exciting time, nor would she ever dream of going out of that door for a poo! Don't squander this golden opportunity.

Links to Common Core Skills

Happily, when you are training your departure routine, you can call upon all the other pieces of training that you have already begun teaching, which will form a common core of most control exercises.

The routine depends upon a good **"Sit!"** and **"Stay!"** A basic response to **"Come!"** or a short distance of competent **"Heel!"**

Hopefully, you will already be training each of these control skills in your garden and if you have enrolled on your puppy-training course at the training school, then that is 2 locations where you are training the individual components that will help your puppy master a desirable departure routine. Now is the time to train them close to your front door.

Starting the Training

Begin by starting to train the **"Sit!"** and **"Stay!"** inside your front door, but don't go and put your wellies on, nor your rainproof coat. There are 2 reasons for this. The first is that you don't want to build up anticipation in your puppy's mind. The second reason is, you are not leaving the house, so you will look like a bit of a mentalist if you do! That said, later in the training, you may do exactly that, dress up and look a bit daft when proofing your puppy's response.

As with every training session, prepare your treats and treat bag and begin the session with 3 sets of 5, hand targets, sits and downs, just to get your puppy in the training mindset. Do this a short distance from the door from which all walks begin, or will begin in the future. (Note, you don't need her lead at present.)

Now move to the door and instruct, or signal your puppy into the **"Sit!"** position. **Mark** and **reinforce**. Complete 3 sets of 5 **"Sit!"** with appropriate breaks.

At the end of these 3 sets, end the session by telling your puppy **"Finished!"** Then allow her to relax and absorb what she has just learned.

You should repeat this routine on at least 2 or 3 further occasions before progressing.

Progress

The next stage is to begin your training session as described above, but during the next couple of sessions, stretch the **"Sit!"** into a **"Sit!"** and **"Stay!"**

Slowly build the length of the **"Stay!"** up to about 10 seconds before **marking** and **rewarding**.

By this stage your puppy should now be comfortable and controlled when you take her to the door and have her **"Sit!"** and **"Stay!"** for about 10 seconds, at a distance of only 1 pace.

Attaching the Lead

She will have been practising her loose-lead walking and **"Heel!"** in your garden and will already have worn her lead on a good few occasions, so attaching it should not be an issue.

It is now time to repeat the previous stages, but this time you are going to attach the lead whilst she remains in the **"Sit!"** and **"Stay!"** position. Mark and reward a desirable response.

Opening the Door

The next stage is to repeat the previous routine, but this time, during the **"Stay!"** have an assistant open the door. All your puppy has to do at this stage is remain in the **"Sit!"** and **"Stay!"** when the door is opened in order to be **marked** and **reinforced**.

Practise and consolidate, until you are ready to open the door yourself, with your puppy remaining in the "Sit!" and "Stay!" Then mark and reward.

Recap

So just to recap. You now begin your training session with a quick set of 3 of 5. Then you move to the door. Instruct your puppy to **"Sit!"** and **"Stay!"** Attach the lead and then open the door. The door can be left open for increasingly longer periods, maybe up to 15 seconds, and your puppy remains stationary. The door is then closed and your puppy's success **marked** and **reinforced**.

Progress

Well done to you both. It's now time to move on and take the first step through the door. You can do this in 2 different ways and the way you choose to do it may depend upon the layout of your house, what you have already trained your puppy to do, or perhaps just your personal preference.

Method 1

The first method is to go through the previous routine, but when you have opened the door, and your puppy is stationary, remind her of the **"Stay!"** instruction and step through the door. Show her your left hand to signal a reminder of the **"Stay"** instruction, and after a short period, step back inside.

When you are back in front of her, **mark** and **reward** the desired behaviour.

Why, I hear you ask, did you not just call her through the door? Because she isn't ready for that yet!

The first thing she must learn is that if you tell her to **"Stay!"** she should expect you to come back to her. On rare occasions you may decide to call her to **"Come!"** but her default position to the **"Stay!"** instruction is exactly that, to **"Stay!"**

This stage should be consolidated before moving on to calling her through the door to join you.

Progress

Practise the whole of the rehearsed routine up to the point where you are now outside the door holding the loose lead and she is inside in the **"Sit! Stay!"** position. She is looking at your left hand, which is raised like a traffic policeman, then you call her; **"Alice, Come!"** As you do so, move your left hand from the **"Stay!"** signal to the lower, **"Watch!"** position.

She may be a bit reluctant at first as she is expecting you to step back inside, so be prepared to encourage her verbally.

When she steps forward and makes contact with your left hand, **mark** it and **reward** her. You can then signal and verbally instruct her into the **"Sit!"** position and **mark** and **reinforce** the desired response.

The Return Journey

Of course we don't just want her to leave the house nicely. We want her to go back in nicely, as well as to go through all other doors and gates nicely. So be prepared to teach her the procedure to get her back inside.

Going through the Door at Heel

The other method of achieving a controlled departure is to teach your puppy in exactly the same way, right up to the point at which you instruct her to **"Stay!"** as you step through the door.

But in this method she accompanies you in the **"Heel!"** position. In order to use this method, you must already have begun teaching her the **"Heel!"** in your garden, or other places. This should not be her introduction to the **"Heel!"**

At your start point, you have her in the **"Sit!"** and **"Stay!"** at the door, and the door is open.

Show your left hand to your puppy and give the instruction and hand signal to **"Alice, Heel!"** and walk through the door with your puppy following your left hand.

Once outside, turn around to face the door, because you will have to close it once you start doing the leaving routine for real, and give her the hand signal and verbal instruction to **"Sit!"** **Mark** and **reward** her response.

Dress Rehearsal

If you have started training this exercise before your puppy has ever been for a walk, then there is no need for a dress rehearsal, as she doesn't know what a walk is yet, so there's no point.

If however she has regularly sampled the comradeship of the local gang of canine reprobates, and is highly excited when she thinks she is about to go for a walk, as well as practising the routine of departure you also need to desensitise her to the excitement of it.

So the final stage should be a full dress rehearsal, which involves putting on the dog-walking kit in exactly the same way as for a real walk, but simply focusing on training the **out of the door, in through the door routine**, time and time again, until it loses its allure.

Generalising It

It is quite difficult to generalise this behaviour in your own home. I suppose you could practise it by leaving and entering through a different door. And that would reduce the excitement and anticipation of departure. But the routine can and should be practised when you go in or out of any other building that you may visit, or through any gateway. It is important that your puppy learns that going through any doorway or gate must be done in a controlled manner.

Proofing

Once at a reasonable standard of proficiency, if you are a 2-dog household, you would repeat the whole process with both dogs, to ensure that her response is the same whether she is alone or accompanied by her best doggy mate.

If you are a dog and sprog household, you should proof the exercise with children departing at the same time.

End Your Training Session

Don't get all sloppy now, just because you aren't working on the training field. Remember, at the end of each training session tell your puppy she has **"Finished!"** Clear beginning, clear ending.

Latent Learning

After being told **"Finished!"** allow your puppy to have a few minutes to quietly reflect upon what she has just learned. Why not have a cup of tea and a sponge finger together?

===

Getting In and Out of the Car

Introduction

In the initial stages, the act of getting your puppy in and out of your car is a bit of a non-event. If you have taken on board the advice given earlier, your puppy will be travelling in the car from 8 weeks when you first bring her home and then regularly throughout her early weeks with you and her new family.

At this age and stage of her development you would not even consider trying to encourage your puppy to get in and out herself. But your early successful travel training will ensure that your puppy has had no bad experiences that will make her reluctant to get into the car herself.

It will be some time before your puppy is old enough to do so, which is quite an advantage, because by the time you need to teach her to get in and out under her own steam, you will have already trained her in the core skills required to make this exercise a success. Your puppy will also be confident when travelling in the car.

The method described can be adapted whether you are travelling with your puppy secured on the back seats or in the back of the vehicle. The principles remain the same, only the finer detail changes. Once again it is worth reminding you that your puppy must be securely and comfortably restrained when travelling in the car. Your child's lap is not a secure place.

When to Train It

The time to begin training the actual getting in and out will depend upon your puppy's age and size. But as with everything else, the best time to train it is when you are not going anywhere and have the time to do so.

The worst time to train it is when you actually need to make an important journey. If you try to train it then, you are doomed to failure.

Preparatory Work

Before teaching this real-life skill you will have carried out a great deal of preparation work in order to habituate her to car travel. She should be responsive to **"Heel!" "Sit!" "Stay!" "Watch!"** signals and instructions. She must be responsive to her name.

Depending upon the size of your puppy you might need to be inventive and provide some additional equipment to make it a bit easier. You can buy specially constructed ramps for dogs, and although these are large and quite heavy, if you have a large-breed puppy, one of these might be a good investment.

For most puppies a small wooden box about 8 inches high or a home-made ramp made from thick plywood should suffice. Alternately, if you position your car next to a kerb so that she is already a bit higher up in relation to her access point, this little bit of elevation often does the trick.

What Are You Training Her To Do?

Think about what the main purpose of the exercise really is. Unless you are planning to leave her in the car for the remainder of her life, you are going to teach her 2 different exercises. Get into your car. Get out of your car. You may decide to teach both exercises in the same training session, or you may decide to split them into 2 different sessions.

My own preference is to teach getting in as a separate exercise, so that if I am teaching my puppy to get into the car, once she has done so and had her correct response **marked** and **reinforced**, I then lift her out of the car.

Once she has mastered this part of the exercise, only then do I extend it to include the **getting out** phase.

Which Door?

When beginning to teach the **getting in** phase I recommend that you have an assistant to help you and you don't train it on a busy road, for reasons that will soon become clear. If you are very posh, like what I am, you may have a drive. If not, go somewhere quiet, or begin to teach it at your training school.

You are going to teach your puppy to get into the rear, nearside door of your car. Why? Because when you park your car correctly at the kerbside, with the flow of traffic, this will be the door you will use, unless you have some sort of death wish!

The First Session

Prepare your puppy by giving her a leg stretch and piddle period. Begin your session with 3 sets of 5.

Sit on the back seat with your bum on the seat, but with your legs out of the rear nearside door, and with your feet on the ground.

Have your helper hold your puppy on her lead and approach you. As she does so, call her name and present your left hand to her as a target. As this is a new exercise, you will have a treat in your hand.

Your hand should be low, so she does not need to take her front paws off the ground to make contact with it. This is very important, as we do not want her to jump or climb at this stage.

When she makes contact with your left hand, **mark** and **reinforce**. Have your assistant lure her away with a call of her name and a treat. Your puppy is only moving a pace or so back from you, before allowing you to repeat the call; **"Aaaliis!"** and present the hand target. **Mark** and **reinforce** success, as before. After the first couple of successful repetitions you may add the **"Watch!"** instruction to the hand signal.

Complete 3 sets of 5. End the session by telling her she has **"Finished!"** and allow her to reflect. Practise for a few sessions before progressing.

Progress

When moving onto the next stage, prepare your puppy and your car as before. If your puppy is so small she will not be able to clamber into the back of your car you have a decision to make. Do you delay the training until she is bigger? Or do you introduce a box or ramp to enable her to make progress? I am assuming she is big enough to get in herself, or you are going to provide some form of assistance as described.

Position yourself as before, and if using the box or ramp have this between your feet and positioned securely. You don't want anything a bit wobbly spooking her!

With your assistant, carry out 3 sets of 5 as previously described. The only difference is that this time your puppy will have to put her front paws on the box in order to make contact with the target hand. As she does so **mark** and **reinforce** as before.

If she does not, just be patient, and gently lure her into position a tiny bit at a time. **Mark** and **reward** each little bit of progress. If you need to take a couple of days of training in order to get her comfortable putting her front paws on the box...do it. This is not a race. You can have quick, or you can have good. Good is always better.

Progress

Repeat the routine until your puppy is moving forward on the lead to target your hand, either with or without the box/ramp. The next stage is to simply move slightly further back onto the back seat of your car in small stages. Not so far that in order to contact the target hand she has to take a flying leap (that is very bad!), but so she can slowly climb into the back and have her successful response marked and reinforced.

She has now successfully climbed into the back of your car with you. **Mark** and **reinforce** her success.

Now, pass her to your assistant who will lift her out of the car and take a couple of steps back, before the whole routine is repeated. Carry out 3 sets of 5. End the session in your usual way and allow her reflection time.

Practise, Practise, Practise!

Progress

The next stage is to have your puppy follow your left hand into the back of the car, but without you sitting in the back. You are standing outside the car with your puppy on your left-hand side.

She is now in effect just following your left hand as a lure, just as she would when hand targeting on the **“Watch!”** or as in the early stages of the **“Heel!”**

With regular practice your puppy will soon be walking slowly towards your car, from a couple of paces away, following your hand. If I am doing this just a couple of paces from the car, I tend to keep using the **“Watch!”** signal and instruction at this point, but as I progress to walking towards the car from a slightly greater distance I introduce the **“Heel!”** instruction, because that is what my puppy is now doing.

As I approach the back of the open car door I lure her in ahead of me. As I do so, I **add** the instruction **“Alice, Up!”** just as she **completes** the action. Having added the instruction I will, as ever, bring it further forward in the sequence over the forthcoming training sessions, until it is being given at the same time as the hand signal. Having done so successfully, I will gradually fade the hand signal.

Teaching Her to Dismount

This whole process will have taken a very short time to complete, because you are both getting pretty good at this training lark. Hopefully, you have remembered that until this point you are still **lifting your puppy out** of the car. Now is the time to start teaching her to get out under her own steam.

You can train this separately, by lifting her in and then training from scratch, and this is a good principle. But you are both at the stage of your development where you can safely add the new exercise to the end of the getting **in** routine.

The First Session

Start your training as you always do. Go through the whole **in** routine. But this time, after she has completed the in stage, **do not mark and reinforce**.

Instead place your left hand on her nose, and give a second **“Watch!”** instruction, then lure her gently back out of the car, (down the ramp) and onto the ground. Do it slowly and gently, using your imaginary thread, as opposed to allowing her to launch herself into space like a hairy version of Eddie the Eagle.

Progress

Train regularly until the routine of getting in and out is firmly established. Ensure that you **vary** the point at which you deliver the **marker** and **reinforcement**. Sometimes **mark** and **reinforce** the getting in and then **reinforce** her again for getting out. Sometimes just **reinforce** the getting out part, when she has completed the whole cycle.

Progress

Begin to add control elements into the routine. Do so slowly and introduce just one control element at a time, practising and consolidating each control element before adding another. For example: Begin to add a longer distance at **"Heel!"** before she gets in.

Once this is established, insert a **"Sit!"** before instructing her to get in.

Consider adding a **"Stay!"** to the **"Sit!"** and building up to about 10 seconds before instructing her to get in.

Add a "**Sit!** when she is in the car.

Add a short **"Stay!"** to the **"Sit!"** once she is in.

Progress

Now do all of the above as a full routine, then secure her in the car, before releasing her and performing the getting **out** routine.

Having achieved this stage, start closing the car door, between the **in** and **out** stages, before building in a short trip around the block. (Always making sure you have secured your puppy.)

You might think there is no need to do the drive stage as your puppy has been travelling in your car regularly for some time. But remember you are training her to perform a complete routine, linking a number of exercise and life skills together, so don't start cutting corners now, or we are going to have a bit of a falling out!

Train the whole exercise as it would be done for real. Don't leave it to chance and don't forget to **generalise** it and **proof** it.

Estate Car Drills

If you are training your puppy to get into the back of an estate car, begin as described above, but at the luring phase have your assistant take your puppy to the back of the car, whilst you sit in the back seats. Fold the back of one of the seats down flat. You can then put your left hand through into the back and present it as a hand target for your puppy during the luring phase.

Hatchback Drills

If you are using a hatchback, this will definitely be too high for your puppy to jump in to for quite some time. Use a ramp, or lift her in. Don't risk injuring a growing puppy.

===

Loose-Lead Walking

Charlotte and Alice, just walking in the rain

Introduction

Pulling on the lead is the most common problem people who attend my puppy classes want to prevent, or correct. Why do so many puppies pull on the lead? Well for exactly the same reason as they do most other things, because we train them to do it and make sure that pulling is rewarding. If it works…they will do it.

Training Your Puppy to Pull

So how do you teach your puppy to pull? It's easy really. You put her on the lead and take her out of your front door into a big exciting world. When she leans into the lead, even just a bit, you continue to go forward. After a short drag, you both make it to the park for a play or a much-needed toilet break… or both!

By going forward with her, she learns that pulling is the norm. In fact very soon she probably thinks you are unable to get to the park under your own steam and her efforts are the only way you are able to make it to your common destination.

Whilst pulling is hard work for her, the rewards are well worth the effort. And as an added bonus, it's almost like a body-building exercise. The more she practises, the stronger she gets.

If you have followed the frequently dispensed advice, to "stand still" when she pulls, this often provides her with a much-needed breather, enabling her to recuperate just in time for the next round of pulling as soon as you step off again.

When your puppy does something and achieves her goal, she repeats the behaviour. They all do what works, and this pulling caper works like a dream. So she does it again and again, until the behaviour becomes well and truly established and she is thoroughly proficient at dragging you up the street. The bigger and stronger she becomes, the faster and more efficiently she drags you.

She's Strangling Herself!

Why would she continue doing this? I mean it sounds as if she is strangling herself, and surely it can't be comfortable, so why would she keep doing it?

She is motivated by the consequences to work through discomfort. Because she has learned and has been allowed to learn that the goal she seeks will be attained and it is sufficiently rewarding to keep her doing it. As we all know; **Consequences Shape Behaviour!**

So what consequence could be so rewarding that she is prepared to go through this discomfort? How about a trip to the park to play with all the mates in her new found puppy gang? Or to the place where you take her to throw her favourite ball or Kong?

What if she is busting for a poo? She has to get to the park to do this and after a good night's sleep she might well have a decent load to dispose of. Being desperate to relieve herself is a really powerful motivator for a fastidiously clean little puppy. (Unless of course the advice given earlier in the book has been followed and she has been trained to toilet in the garden, thus making going for a walk dependent upon her having done her ablutions in the garden.)

Not Competition Heel Work!

Nearly all of you reading this book will want, sorry, need your puppy to grow into a dog who can be walked in a relaxed manner on a loose lead. Very few will require your puppy to carry out competition heelwork. We have already covered how to teach short periods of **"Heel!"** Now we need to pay specific attention to what most of you really want and need, so let's focus on loose-lead walking.

When I teach my puppy to walk in a relaxed manner on a loose lead, I usually use a 6-foot training lead that can be doubled over to shorten it. I usually set it to about 5 feet in length. When being walked on a lead of this length, my puppy is relatively free to sniff, move about and explore. She is not allowed to walk with the lead tight and she is definitely not allowed to lunge and pull me towards something she wants to sniff.

Communication and Co-operation not Correction

I often see problems arise in loose-lead walking when there is little or no co-operation or communication between owner and pup. In such situations there is a real tendency to over-correct the puppy and the **pull, drag back, pull, stand still** routine that follows just develops into a war of attrition, in which the combatant with the tail usually prevails.

I like to use enough verbal communication to give baby Alice a bit of direction when she is walking well and attract her attention when the leash is getting a bit tighter and I want her to slow down a bit.

Most of the time just telling Alice; **"Steady, Puppy!"** is sufficient for her to check over her shoulder and look towards me, and just that little action means she stops pressing forward and takes the pressure off the lead before it becomes tight.

On other occasions, just moving my hand towards her a little, or feeding out a few more inches of lead means she doesn't make the lead tight and we can keep walking forward. In this instance I am giving her a little leeway, but it means that we are working as a team. The lead is not tight and we are not doing a constant stop-start action that human and puppy find so frustrating.

Some might argue that I need to be stricter rather than co-operative and they might well be correct, although 30 minutes before writing this I was walking Alice, Jimmy, Daisy, Tilly and Molly the lodger down the lanes near my house, together on loose leads; a combined canine weight of about 320lb. I am a bit like a puppy really. If it works and is rewarding, I do it again.

Pace and Planning

One of the biggest problems I see with dogs that pull on the lead is the pace of the walk. Most of the time it is far too fast and it looks like dog and owner are racing each other. Start as you mean to go on. Adopt a nice, steady relaxed pace, and don't allow it to gradually get faster. Be disciplined in regard to pace.

If you control the pace of the walk, you control the walk. If you control the walk, you control your puppy. Controlling the walk with a puppy is far easier than controlling the walk with an adult dog, particularly if the adult was a puppy that you have put a great deal of time into training to pull.

When training your puppy to perform any routine or exercise you need to look at what is going to motivate her to perform it well and remove anything that might motivate her to do something you don't want her to do; in this case pull on the lead.

When training loose-lead walking always make sure that you have removed any motivation to make her pull, as in this exercise such motivators are often much stronger than what you can offer her not to pull.

When starting to train, always make sure that you have sufficient time to give to the walk. If you are in a hurry, you will not control the pace of the walk. You will be moving too fast, never mind your puppy! Allow about half an hour for a 15-minute walk.

Anticipation

Make sure your puppy is not anticipating that she is going to her favourite park for a riotous time, but rather just going for a mooch around the local roads, lanes or fields. The object of the walk is not to get to a particular place any time soon. It is just a mooching session and you are in no particular hurry.

And finally, you should certainly make sure that your puppy has already had a wee and a poo at home, and so you have removed this key motivator for lead pulling.

I wonder how many training failures in lead walking and toilet training there have been based upon this imaginary conversation between a full-to-the-brim puppy pulling desperately on the lead and her human companion:

Human: "If you don't stop pulling on the lead I won't let you walk any further!"

Puppy: "But Dad, I need to get to the park. I am absolutely bursting."

Human: "No, sorry. I have read all the books, and if you keep trying to pull I will simply stand still until you stop."

Puppy: "But Dad, I nearly always stop pulling when we aren't moving, don't I? I mean it is very difficult to pull when we are standing still. I need to get a bit of momentum going."

Human: "I hadn't thought of that one. But anyway, we aren't moving when you pull and if necessary I will take you home. That'll learn you!"

Puppy: "Oh Dad! That'll just "learn" me to poo in the house again!"

This scenario has the following alternative outcomes: a.) Dad gives in and allows puppy to pull to the park, or b.) Dad digs in and takes puppy home to piddle and poo on the carpet. (The puppy nearly always pulls all the way home, anyway!)

Starting to Train

Always start lead walking in the garden or secure area without her being on the lead. Ensure that your puppy has done her toilet routine and any other distractions are minimised. Remove from view all toys, or anything else that might distract her, including the kids.

If she is full of beans, you may play a little game with her to get rid of some of that excess energy, but not so much play as to leave her tired. A tired puppy doesn't learn well.

To begin with, unlike other training sessions, do not let her know that you have a load of really nice treats in your training bag, which should be in your pocket, rather than its usual place on your belt. When teaching other, more precise exercises, you want her to know that you have treats and you will have started the training session with 3 sets of 5, but on this occasion you do not.

Just start walking around the garden, with your hands in your pockets, let your puppy have a sniff about, but when she looks towards you, or approaches you, tell her, **"Good Girl!"** Then take a treat from your pocket and give it to her from your left hand. Then continue to amble around the garden at the same pace, and once again, when she looks towards you, or approaches you, tell her she is a **"Clever Girl!"** And reward with a treat from your left hand.

After a couple of repetitions she will probably begin walking quite loosely at your left side. This is a positive step. Continue to walk slowly and as she maintains this loose position at your left side praise her, take a treat from your pocket and give it to her from your left hand.

Stand still from time to time. On these occasions your puppy will usually stop and look up at you. Generally, don't reward this because you are training the walk, not the stand and look at you, but a nice word to her would be welcome, to let her know you appreciate her attention.

After a few seconds looking up at you, if not reinforced with a treat, she will generally go and have a little sniff. Let her do this, and then after a couple of seconds walk on slowly. When she follows you, tell her she is a **"Clever Girl!"** and reward as previously described. If she doesn't follow straight away consider a little prompt, a little whistle or tongue click, but definitely not her name.

The whole session only takes about 3 to 5 minutes. Then get down on your knees with her and tell her **"Finished!"** and give her a gentle stroke. Allow her a few minutes to quietly take in what she has just learned.

Finally, because you have been working her, and she has been preoccupied, tell her to "Wee Wee!" and let her have a piddle before you take her back inside the house.

Important Note: I haven't described using the marker word; **"Yes!"** in this training exercise because the desired behaviour is a bit vague. There is no precise position as there is when training the **"Heel!"** Your puppy can be a little bit ahead of you, a little bit behind, or a little bit wide.

The only rule is that the lead must have slack in it. That is too vague to warrant a precise marker in my opinion. In the short term, an occasional treat is the motivator to walk on a slack lead; in the long term, getting to where she is going or the journey itself becomes the motivation. (Although you will continue to reinforce with a treat, on occasion, throughout her life.)

Practise!

Repeat this training every day, usually 2 or 3 times a day. If you start training it at 8 weeks, by the time you can take your puppy out on the road she will have had lots of practice and will also have been introduced to the lead.

Introducing the Lead

I always find this is the difficult bit, mainly due to the fact that I teach my pups to pick things up and carry them, as in later life they will be trained to retrieve, track, search and bite. I want them comfortable using their mouth in an appropriate manner. This usually means that as soon as the lead goes on, after training without it for the first few days, they want to pick it up and carry it.

I don't actively discourage or correct this, simply because I don't have to. If your puppy also carries the lead don't worry; just like baby Alice, your puppy will stop doing it very quickly when she realises that she can't eat a treat whilst she has the lead in her mouth. She will make this connection very quickly and you will help her to learn it even faster, by timing your **"Good Girl!"** to coincide with when she is not carrying the lead in her mouth.

In the unlikely event the lead carrying persists, maybe because she has a natural desire to retrieve or carry, just encourage her to carry something more acceptable such as a small Kong toy, until the lead-carrying behaviour has been eliminated.

Continue in this way until you can walk your puppy around the garden, or down your path, on a 5- or 6-foot lead, nice and slowly, letting her have a sniff and take in her surroundings, for about 5 minutes.

Taking it out on the Road

I am very lucky because I have about 10 acres of land where I can walk baby Alice before she has been given clearance from the vet to go out and about after completing her inoculations. This means that by the time I take her out on the road, she is well-practised in loose-lead walking. But for most of you the first walk on the road will be a very exciting event for your puppy.

I will describe how I did it with Alice and you can mirror it, or adapt it to your own circumstances.

Rather than do the initial training with baby Alice in the big field I deliberately restricted the initial practice to my smaller garden area and a short length of the drive. I did this to deliberately replicate the amount of space I had when training all my previous pups. It worked for them, so why would I want to change anything?

Having carried out our early work in this way, the next stage is to get her out and about.

Before leaving home I make sure she has been toileted and had a little scamper and sniff about the garden. Rather than begin the walk from the house I usually take Alice for a short drive, just a few minutes away from home. I open the car door and attach a light lead, about 5 foot in length, to Alice's flat collar.

I lift her from the car, lock it and place her on the ground. I remain stationary whilst I let her sniff her immediate surroundings. I don't start her walking until she has had a good sniff. Before setting off I put my hand into my left pocket and give her a nice treat. Now she knows I have got some really good stuff with me.

I then start to walk really slowly, allowing her to sniff and slowly make progress. If she becomes too slow, I increase the pace for a few yards, giving her a little voice prompt, **"Quick, puppy!"** and then walk on. As she follows I again tell her she's a **"Good Girl,"** and then walk on at my chosen pace. I will only walk her for about 5 or 10 minutes.

After walking Alice in this manner for a couple of minutes, I change direction and turn around and come back the way I have walked for about 20 or 30 yards, before turning gain and continuing on the original route. This is a regular pattern I adopt when I am walking my dogs either on or off lead. During this initial loose-lead training I don't want baby Alice looking along a 300-yard road and wondering what is at the other end of it. Regular direction changes prevent this happening.

We practise this every day for about a week, with me taking her to a slightly different place each day. This has the effect of reducing Alice's anticipation about what is about to follow, particularly as whilst I am training her to loose-lead walk, I am also training her for car travel, with many car journeys being short, mundane and not culminating in anything very interesting.

Both these exercises have a knock-on effect, being mutually beneficial. Unless of course you do it wrong, in which case each exercise becomes mutually detrimental and serves to whip your puppy into a bigger frenzy.

Walking From Your House

As you progress, the loose-lead walk will begin after leaving home via the front door and walking along your own street. Your pre-departure preparation is exactly the same regarding toileting your puppy before departure.

Let her have a good sniff around the garden, and I would encourage 5 minutes or so of gentle play to allow her to burn off a little energy.

It is essential that before beginning your walks from home, you have trained a reliable, calm departure routine. If you have, then the walk will commence in the same calm manner. If you haven't mastered this, be prepared for your puppy to go up your drive on her hind legs, just like the Lone Ranger's horse.

When departing from the house ensure that each day you take a different direction and ensure you go to a different place or nowhere in particular. The walk serves no purpose other than just to walk, have a sniff around the local patch and see what calling cards have been left by her mates.

You are not going for a play. You are not going to meet other dogs. You are not taking her for a poo. You are just out for a casual, leisurely stroll.

Make Effective Use of Her Core Skills

As you can see, nothing is being trained in isolation, many aspects of your puppy's training for life and her control training are being linked to each other, and successful practice in one area always contributes to success in the other areas, but you need to ensure that you generalise and proof those core skills you train your puppy to perform on the training field, so they are practised and polished in as many real-life scenarios as possible.

Be imaginative and make effective use of your puppy's core skills at every opportunity. If you don't use them in real life, these core skills are merely party tricks. If you do make effective use of them, they will be the building blocks for an active life of adventure. For both of you!

===

Controlled Greetings

Introduction

An effective controlled greeting is an important life skill that should be trained as a formal exercise on the training field and in an informal manner in the home and when out walking with your puppy.

It is a relatively easy skill for her to master with a little help from you, providing you and your family are consistent and don't spend a short time training her to greet politely on the training field and the remainder of the day training her to jump all over you. Unfortunately this is exactly what most puppy owners do.

Different Types of Greeting

Encounters between your puppy and people fall into 1 of 3 categories/ scenarios.

The first type of encounter is with members of your family, and this is invariably the most problematic. The main problem in a family setting is largely due to a lack of consistency in the way you interact with your pup. Because of the length of time your puppy spends with all of you, it often proves difficult for you to be aware and consistent all the time, and as most puppies are masters of manipulation, bad habits on the part of family members slowly creep in.

There is no easy way around this. You are all different and with the best will in the world different members of your family will interact with your puppy differently. There is no way a 6-year-old lad and his 30-year-old Mum will ever be able to behave in exactly the same way towards their puppy.

As a family, you simply have to do your best. The whole family must accept the need to teach a controlled greeting, but it is up to the adults to ensure as best you can that this is put into action and a consistent approach established and maintained. Most puppy owners nearly always appreciate the need for a controlled greeting, they just never seem to get around to putting in into action.

The second scenario is with visitors to the home, which is much easier to train, because you control who comes into your home and you can brief them in advance. Visits also have a beginning and an end, so it is possible to achieve a level of consistency during most visits, because you are dealing with a defined time scale, i.e. the 2-hour visit.

The third scenario is with strangers or neighbours you meet when you are out and about, walking or exercising your puppy off lead. Your success or failure in this area largely depends upon whether your puppy is on or off the lead.

If your puppy is on her training lead, or on her long training line, then short of the stranger jumping out like some urban ninja, you should be able to prepare for the greeting.

If your puppy is off the lead, you must have a reliable recall, which has been generalised to different locations and proofed in the presence of people. If you have achieved a reliable recall, you are able to call her back to you and put her on the lead when you meet another person, rather than have her run over to them at full pelt and make her own introductions. If you don't yet have a reliable recall use the long training line. Don't leave it to chance.

Your puppy's behaviour and actions are your responsibility. She must be well mannered in relation to other people within your community. That's not me who says that. No, that's what Betty Windsor, God bless her, said. She meant it so much that she gave Royal Assent to all the current legislation governing how we all have to control our puppies and dogs!

Controlled Greetings with Family

You have already begun to train controlled greetings in her daily life training. Right from the outset you have trained your puppy, starting with her first meeting with your children.

Although training a controlled greeting is one of the first things you begin to teach your puppy, it is also one of the first things you begin to lose consistency with.

It's so nice to be greeted by a happy puppy when you come home from work, or the kids come home from school, that you forget the basics and begin to train her to jump up on you when you greet her and she greets you. Remember, self-discipline on the part of the humans is the key.

Core Skills?

As ever, an essential starting point when training any skill is to consider what other stuff you have already begun teaching her. This will help you create the right motivation for a good controlled greeting, or change her motivation if things have started to go a bit pear-shaped.

Earlier we looked at hand targeting using the verbal signal, **"Watch!"** As she is already learning this skill and is quite proficient, it makes sense to use it as part of the greeting process.

Whenever you greet your puppy why not just employ this technique? There is no point teaching a new skill when you have a good one already being learned that will serve your purpose just fine. The more she has to learn the harder it is. She only has a little head, don't fill it up with stuff she doesn't need. Simple is good!

When you meet your puppy, present her with your left hand, at nose height, as part of the greeting process and reward her for performing the desired behaviour with a treat. You should then double up on the reward, by going down to her, in order to calmly stroke her, and give her a tummy tickle. This will encourage her to remain in this position with all her 4 paws on the ground. (Unless she is on her back for a tummy tickle, but even the tummy tickling must be done calmly.)

This is a routine that you must make sure everyone adopts. No one is allowed to go into the room where little Miss Rocket is confined without first being equipped with a few treats, one of which is held in the left hand as described earlier in the book. As the incoming, fur-covered missile arrives, the left hand goes down and she is encouraged to target the left hand.

Adults and older children usually get this with little difficulty, in fact children generally get it a lot faster than adults, but young 'uns will need assistance.

Small Sprog Routine

When I trained baby Alice to do this with small children I first made sure that the youngster she was going to meet was confident and well-briefed. I also did a few run-throughs with Alice, so the nipper could watch and see how it was done. It also gave baby Alice an opportunity to practise the technique and get rid of any excitement.

The training was carried out as a proper session, with all the pre-training prep being done.

It was carried out slowly, in order to discourage Alice from reaching Mach 2. Alice was also secured on a light training line.

Alice was allowed to approach the stationary sprog at a steady pace. As Alice was already learning to **"Sit!"** this core skill was adopted and Alice was instructed to **"Sit!"** just a pace or so in front of the youngster. As soon as her bum touched down, the young apprentice puppy trainer would then throw a slightly larger treat over Alice's head, so as to make her go backwards to collect the thrown treat rather than have her target the child's hand.

Once Alice had stopped and had been thrown the first treat, the nipper was allowed to toss a few more nice treats on the ground a couple of feet away, so that Alice had no motivation to go in particularly close. Why would she? All the good stuff was a couple of feet away. And Alice is definitely not slow on the uptake where grub is concerned.

Alice soon learned that these little fellas were like walking treat dispensers and would follow them with her nose firmly on the ground. There was nothing to be gained from seeking treats from their hands. She had never been rewarded from their left hand, and as I said before, puppies do not flog a dead horse. They do what works for them. And this worked for baby Alice. It will also work for your puppy.

Having achieved a good response with a single youngster, repeat the entire process with the next, and so on, until this becomes a firmly established pattern of behaviour.

Controlled Greeting with Visitors to the Home

The routine to be adopted with visitors is almost exactly the same as it is with adult family members. But remember to **train** the exercise with visitors, not just leave it to random visits.

Arrange for daily visits by one trusted person, unknown to your puppy, but who you know and to whom you can explain the routine. Maybe you can let them watch you doing it with your puppy. If you can't do this in person, make a short recording of the routine on your phone and let them watch it. (Technology-assisted Prior Preparation.)

Place a small Tupperware container just outside the door so that visitors may arm themselves with a few treats before they ring the bell.

At this stage, you should still be using a light house line, to prevent your puppy becoming over-excited and making mistakes. When the bell rings, go to the door with your puppy on her house line and open the door.

Step back inside so the person can enter.

The lead should not be pulled tight, but there should not be enough slack to allow her to jump up. As she approaches the visitor, the visitor lowers his left hand to nose level and when puppy's nose makes contact with his left hand, he may release a treat to her.

At this point call your puppy's name and instruct her to **"Watch!"** As this is one of her core skills, she should turn and target your left hand. The correct response by targeting your hand is **marked** with a **"Yes!"** and **reinforced** with a treat.

She can then turn back to the visitor and he should ask her to **“Watch!”** When she targets his left hand he can **mark** it with a **“Yes!”** and **reinforce** with a treat.

Once again, you should call her name and repeat the process.

The whole cycle should be repeated at least 5 times targeting your hand and 5 times targeting the visitor’s hand before the visitor leaves, or until your puppy becomes dizzy and falls over.

Practise!

This process should be repeated daily over the next few days, with the same visitor. When your puppy has become proficient at it, you may wish to add a little more control by introducing a **“Sit!”** then rewarding her response to this instruction instead of the hand target.

Having achieved this result with the first visitor, repeat the whole process with a second and then third visitor, each time going through the same routine.

Once the routine at the front door is established, move it into different parts of the house, working through the same process.

In a relatively short time she will learn that visitors are not to be leapt upon, but if hand targeted, or sat in front of, they are always likely to give her a treat. If this works, she will do it.

Important Note

If the visitor is a child, prepare for it well and consider the method previously outlined for use when introducing your pup to youngsters. If you have any doubts about the confidence of the youngster, put your puppy away. Don’t risk a bad experience for either your puppy or the youngster concerned.

Out and About

This routine for meeting and greeting adult visitors to your home is easily adapted to adults you meet outside the home. The only thing missing in terms of practical stuff is your front door. Don't be tempted to carry one with you on walks, as they are very heavy.

When walking on the lead, go through the same process. Brief and arrange to meet up with a trusted friend and train the exercise in the way that you have planned.

Unfortunately you cannot enforce an exclusion zone in the streets around your home, so you are always likely to encounter people you don't know and who wish to fuss your puppy. In the early stages, do your best to minimise the occasions when such people are likely to set your training schedule back. Lay your plans well, but accept that on occasions real life will conspire to muck up your training plans.

Alice and her gang performing a pre-arranged controlled greeting

Outside and Off Lead

Until you have established and proofed a reliable recall, you must ensure that your puppy is on a long training line whenever there is a risk that she will do a runner and go and make her own introductions to strangers.

She can then be called back when a stranger appears, placed back on her lead and the greeting can take place in a controlled manner as outlined.

Once the Controlled Greeting has been mastered outside the home, the next thing to teach your puppy is not to greet them, but to return to you and walk past strangers in the **"Heel!"** position rather than greet them, because let's face it, not everyone is a fan of dogs.

=========

EPIDOGUE

I hope that you have found this book useful. Writing it has certainly been useful to me. It has enabled me look at my training methods in greater detail, breaking things down in my own mind and writing down detailed methods for you to follow with your puppy. Following the methods will help you train your puppy quickly and more efficiently.

But remember, it isn't a race. You can have good, or you can have quick. Good is always better.

I hope that writing the book will also enable me to improve the way in which I deliver instruction to people who attend my training classes for many years to come. As I said in the introduction, I am a dog trainer, not a writer.

Regardless of how well (or badly) this book sells I won't be breaking out the cigars and Jack Daniels and knocking the training classes on the head. I would just get bored.

Use this book wisely, but seek out and engage a good trainer, they are worth their weight in dog treats. For further practical assistance with the exercises explained in **Part 4 Training for Control**, visit the **Educating Alice** and **Cosford Dog Training Channels** on **YouTube**.

Never forget that you and your puppy are ambassadors for the dog-owning community. Just because people who dislike dogs are not really "the full shilling", they still have a right to have their feelings respected.

An encounter with an unruly puppy may frighten them, and at the very least it will reinforce their dislike of dogs. Whereas an encounter with a well-trained, well-mannered puppy and a respectful owner just might change their opinion.

Your relationship with your puppy over the next 10 to 15 years should be a great experience for you both. Make it so. Nurture that relationship and cherish it. Treat your puppy with love and respect. He or she is going to make you proud.

Best wishes,

Fitz and Alice.

Made in the USA
Columbia, SC
29 November 2018